MORMON
GARMENTS

MORMON GARMENTS

Sacred and Secret

NANCY ROSS, JESSICA FINNIGAN,
AND LARISSA KANNO KINDRED

UNIVERSITY OF
ILLINOIS PRESS
Urbana, Chicago, and Springfield

Manufactured in the United States of America
1 2 3 4 5 C P 5 4 3 2 1
♾ This book is printed on acid-free paper.

Cataloging data available from the Library of Congress

ISBN 978-0-252-04954-5 (hardcover)
ISBN 978-0-252-08919-0 (paperback)
ISBN 978-0-252-04869-2 (ebook)

The manufacturer's authorized representative in
the EU for product safety is Mare Nostrum Group
B.V., Mauritskade 21D, 1091 GC Amsterdam, The
Netherlands. Email: gpsr@mare-nostrum.co.uk

To the Mormon feminists who helped us understand

CONTENTS

ACKNOWLEDGMENTS

First, we want to thank all the church members who participated in our survey and bravely told their stories. Their willingness to be open about a taboo topic has added so much richness to our understanding of the lived experience of Mormonism and has pushed us to become better scholars.

Many people have offered feedback and given us support through the evolution of this project. Gary Shepherd and Gordon Shepherd invited us to present our work at Mormon Social Science Association conferences, encouraged us, and gave us feedback on the early attempts at making sense of our data. Likewise, Michael Nielsen also provided feedback and pointed us toward his own work on men's agency in religion. Liberty Barnes read and commented on the first draft of the book manuscript and provided us with solid writing and organizational advice that paved a way to completing this project. Completing this project would have been impossible without her valuable feedback.

A number of friends and colleagues have been listening and conversational partners in the developmental process—namely, Heather Sinclair, Chelsea McCracken, Lauren DiSalvo, Jana Riess, Beverly Wallace, and the informal writing group at Utah Tech University. Cyrus Simper pointed us to documents for garment history and gave insights on the material culture of garments as lived in different Mormon denominations.

A grant from the Utah Tech Research Office helped us complete the first draft of the manuscript. We used the money to hire Virginia Batty and Stephen Gubler, two undergraduate research assistants, who helped us reach that important milestone.

We have a stack of journal editor desk rejections and peer review reports that ultimately encouraged us to continue to think through our data in more complex ways. We want to thank our editor, Alison Syring, who has been positive about this project from our first conversation, Leigh Ann Cowan, who coordinated production, and our anonymous book reviewers who gave generous and positive feedback.

Many thanks to our spouses and children who have spent considerable time listening to us and supporting us through this work over the last twelve years.

ARTIST'S STATEMENT

Savannah Liddicoat

In my experience as a member of the Church of Jesus Christ of Latter-day Saints, I have witnessed many occasions of judgment directed at those who live differently, especially in regard to how individuals choose to wear the garment. It has troubled me to see self-proclaimed "holy men or women" looking down on others and assuming superiority. In truth, it is often those being judged who embody greater humility and kindness, qualities I associate with Christlike behavior.

My inspiration for this piece comes from a talk given by President Nelson, whose words urged me to reflect on compassion and respect in matters of personal faith and how individuals show that outwardly. The title, *They Do Not Need Your Judgment*, speaks both to his counsel and to the broader call to let individuals worship in the way they feel is right.

INTRODUCTION

THE MORMON MOMENT

On the evening of September 26, 2012, Ann Romney, wife of Republican presidential nominee Mitt Romney, appeared on the *Tonight Show with Jay Leno*. She asked the American public to set aside prejudice and elect the first Mormon president. By the next day, Mormon social media spaces were full of chatter—not about what she said but about her underwear.

During the interview, Ann Romney wore a skirt that nearly reached her knees. This sparked online commentary among some members of the Church of Jesus Christ of Latter-day Saints (often referred to as Mormons or LDS), who noted the absence of her white religious underclothing or *garments* peeking beneath the hem. Garments, consisting of a T-shirt top and knee-length bottoms, are worn night and day by adult church members as a religious practice. Whereas these visual cues might not resonate with those outside of Mormonism, within the community, wearing garments is an essential practice that signifies good standing in the community and strong adherence to church teachings. The telltale signs of garment lines, seen at the neck, arms, and thighs, make garments visible to those in the community, signifying that the wearer is a *good* Mormon. Ann Romney's appearance on national television aimed to affirm her husband's, Mitt's, Mormon identity to a broad American audience. However, some Mormon commentors on social media noted her missing garments and cast doubt on the sincerity of that identity. If Ann wasn't wearing her garments, they argued, she was not upholding her religious commitments. Conversely, other Mormon voices online criticized the public discussion of garments, highlighting the secrecy around this practice.

Jezebel posted an article about the social media chatter the next day, prompting Mormon feminist blogger Lisa Butterworth to ask Mormon women to stop policing each other's underwear choices. Butterworth charged that these judgmental comments made Mormon women "look ugly, petty and small."[1] Outside journalists were bringing the internal dynamics of the Mormon community into public view. As Butterworth observed, the look was not a flattering one.

All of this took place during the *Mormon moment*, a period that began during the run-up to the Salt Lake City 2002 Winter Olympics, encompassed events like the *Book of Mormon* musical, both Romney presidential campaigns, and ended with the public excommunication of Kate Kelly, who advocated for the ordination of women, in 2014.[2] Mormons were regularly in the public eye, and the LDS Church tried to capitalize on that with a marketing and outreach campaign in 2010, where online videos, photos, and articles showed ordinary church members declaring "I'm a Mormon." While Ann Romney was persuading American voters to view her Mormon husband as a potential U.S. president, this was also a moment when the LDS Church was using its limelight to press the social image of Mormons as upstanding, family-loving, community-contributing, tax-paying neighbors into the minds of the American people. The Mormon community's response to Ann Romney challenged the what-you-see-is-what-you-get messaging of the "I'm a Mormon" campaign, revealing something strange and hidden to the outside world.

UNDERSTANDING GARMENTS

Garments are officially known as the *Garment of the Holy Priesthood* and are also referred to as the *temple garment*.[3] Today, adult church members receive garments in an initiation ceremony, which is one of several sacred ceremonies that take place in the closed spaces of LDS temples. This ceremony is known as the *initiatory*, or the Washing and Anointing. After participating in the initiatory ceremony, LDS Church leaders expect that church members will wear garments day and night throughout their lives.[4] Church members who have been through the initiatory ceremony and wear garments must later answer questions about garment wearing as part of the interview that is needed to reenter the temple and maintain good standing in the community.[5]

LDS temple rituals prompt Mormons to envision the afterlife as real and tangible. Garments and the symbols embroidered on them are meant to connect the wearer to this divine reality, to God, and to the creation story, biblical figures, and angels.[6] While most Mormons participate in temple rituals occasionally, garments are the daily reminder that church members are part of these larger sacred stories. Wearing garments is a central religious practice for Mormon adults. However, church teaching and culture discourage discussion of this central practice with both outsiders and with other church members, with the justification that the sacredness of such things warrants silence.[7]

Nancy's Story

I received my own garments in the initiatory ceremony in the LDS London Temple in 2004. My graduate student peers at the University of Cambridge were mostly atheist or agnostic-leaning and their coming-of-age rituals included being able to drink alcohol at the pub and moving out of their parents' homes. Wearing garments was my proud moment of becoming an adult in my faith community. This was a step I was taking at the age of twenty-three, but many of my friends from my home ward (congregation) had made this step at the ages of nineteen or twenty. I was taking out my endowments, the LDS way of saying that I was going to go through the initiatory and endowment ceremonies for the first time, making significant commitments, or covenants, in the process. These ceremonies, together with the requirement that I now wear garments night and day, marked my full embrace of adult Mormon responsibilities. These rituals prefaced young adult Mormons serving an LDS mission or getting married in a sealing ceremony in an LDS temple. I was looking forward to my temple wedding just six weeks later.

The first rule of wearing garments is that you are not supposed to talk about them. I knew that if I discussed such things with my graduate student friends, there would have been never-ending jokes about my new underwear. The taboo on speaking about garments made it easier not to share this change in my life with those outside of my faith community. After all, I still wanted to belong in my graduate program and with the friends I had made there. The required secrecy around the issue made it easier for me to balance fitting into the secular world of my university while holding tightly to my faith community. At that time in my life, this required secrecy felt convenient as I tried to navigate belonging in multiple spaces. Secrecy helped me compartmentalize the more awkward parts of my religious experience.

I encountered references to Mormon garments in pop culture that made fun of magic underwear, but that did not put me off. In describing garments at a storytelling event, journalist and former Mormon storyteller Karen Duffin explained that "the reason why your Mormon friends don't think it's funny when you make fun of their underwear is because it's actually the most sacred symbol of their faith."[8] I wanted to belong in my Mormon congregation and in the broader Mormon world. My engagement to my fiancé hid my quiet bisexuality and my whiteness and religious commitments hid my Jewish heritage. I did not have Mormons in my extended family like other Mormons I knew. But my beliefs were important to me and I felt like I could claim Mormon belief in a way that was both authentic and orthodox. I knew that wearing garments was an integral part of belonging to God and belonging in community, even if we did not discuss them.

I sat in the instructional room on a cushioned chair with another woman my age and her mother. My own mother had died years before, and for some reason my friend and designated escort had not been ushered into this meeting. The other young woman and I were both about to go through the initiatory ceremony for the first time, where we would both receive our garments. Prior to this initiation, we were meeting with the temple matron to discuss the wearing of garments and how to keep them spotless.[9] I was only to take them off for the three S's: swimming, showering, and sex. The matron warned me that my bishop would now ask me questions about my garment-wearing habits in regular interviews.[10] There was a brief pause for questions. I was ready for this moment. Garments were not a topic for open discussion and were rarely discussed in private. This was a rare opportunity to break that taboo.

Inherited wisdom said I must wear my garment top under my bra, as my mother wore them. Rumors from younger women indicated that it was now OK to wear the garment under or over a bra. Wearing garments over my bra seemed like the more comfortable option. Ever the rule follower, I wanted clarification and confirmation on this controversial issue. My bishop had not mentioned bras during his instructions for wearing garments, and my dad had insisted that I must wear the garment next to my skin, meaning under my bra. Of course, neither my bishop nor my dad wore bras or could speak to the experience of wearing garments as a woman.

In asking my question, I was hoping for a bit of flexibility in the answer but had every intent of abiding by whatever answer I received. I felt that I did not have the power to make such decisions for myself but that God expected me to follow official teaching and instruction. It seemed to me that to take on the practice of wearing garments, I had to give control over to the church to set the rules about wearing them. In my understanding at that time, giving over this control to the church was an act of faith that God would reward with eventual blessings.

And so I asked the temple matron the question I'd had for some time, waiting for this big day and this singular moment to get authoritative information from a woman: Could I legitimately wear my garments over my bra and/or under my bra? Was that kind of flexibility allowed?

"What a rude question," said the temple matron without further comment or answer.

My question came from a desire to make correct choices, but her answer filled me with hot shame. I never asked anyone that question ever again but remained confused as to why my desire for clarification was met with such hostility. I wore my garments under my bra for years out of a fear of doing it wrong, of going against instructions I'd been given from the male authorities in my life, and offending God. These experiences of secrecy, shame, and control coexisted with my understanding of wearing garments, formed from Mormon teaching, as sacred, representative of temple covenants and my own worthiness, and an act of obedience that returned God's blessings. It was my job, my body's job, to hold this tension between official teaching and the complexity of lived experience in silence.

The temple matron's response continued to confuse me, though it would be many years before I shared the story of what happened. My initial question, never answered, grew into further questions. A decade later, my friend Jessica Finnigan and I decided that we were going to find answers and conducted the survey that informs this book. As our personal questions transformed into research questions, we realized that our project was about more than our underwear. Instead, garments were a window into the internal power dynamics of Mormon communities, where social power is available to men and women through their belief but in complex ways. This book explores the meanings, group behaviors, and challenges that describe and engage this religious practice.

Jessica's Story

I joined the LDS Church in 1999 while I was still in high school and started wearing garments in November 2001 in preparation for my marriage. My parents did not wear them, and I never heard about them during my extensive conversion process. I first learned about garments when someone made fun of them. I was shocked and did not know how to handle this information, especially since I had significant texture issues with clothing, particularly underwear and socks. I tried not to worry about it at the time since it wasn't an immediate concern.

After a few years at Brigham Young University (BYU), I heard a lot of hushed mentions of garments, but the information was inconsistent. I remained in the dark but became adept at spotting garment lines on fellow students, which answered fundamental questions like who had been on a mission or was married. The most detailed advice I received about garment wearing came from a wedding dress shop attendant, who told me I could wear larger garments to show more cleavage while still technically following the rules. I was scandalized.

When it was time to buy my first garments, there was no process to try them on to see which fabrics or styles I preferred. Rough measurements were taken over my clothes, and the employee made an educated guess about what I should get. Garments were not cheap and the process was stressful. Tops and bottoms were in separate sealed bags and they couldn't be returned if I found I'd purchased the wrong size or style. I bought a selection of fabrics and hoped for the best.

For the most part, I adjusted to wearing garments. I think I was lucky that garments were largely designed to fit my petite white body. However, one day at BYU, I tried on a new style and quickly realized on the way to class that I had made a horrible mistake. I became very uncomfortable and physically unwell.

I was fortunate to start wearing garments a few months before getting married, allowing me to adjust before also dealing with living with another person. After marriage, my husband thought I wasn't wearing my garments correctly because I believed I was supposed to wear my bra directly against my skin. Where was I supposed to go for help? When I received my endowments, I didn't get any detailed instructions from the temple matron. My practice of wearing garments was based on the most obedient interpretation I could manage. As a convert, wearing garments was one way I could achieve legitimacy in my church community. I wore them while working out at the gym for decades and felt guilty when I was not wearing them in the hospital during childbirth. The intense pressure around wearing garments, without any discussion about necessary modifications, shaped many aspects of my life.

Larissa's Story

I was twenty-one years old when I put on garments for the first time. It was 2002 and I was in the Mount Timpanogos Temple, just blocks away from my childhood home. The temple matron gave me instructions on the proper way to wear garments. I should not find excuses to take them off, never manipulate the garments to fit clothing styles, wear my bra over the garment top so that the fabric was always next to my skin, and not let them touch the ground. My devout mother had followed these instructions fastidiously, so none of this was a surprise.

When I first put the bottoms on, they fell well past my knees. I felt sick with dread. Baggy and long, I did not like the thought of wearing these under my clothes for the rest of my life. They were not made for my body. Worried about sounding vain, I didn't say anything at that moment. I later figured out better sizing, and so my garments hit my leg just above the knee. Relieved with this improvement, I fell in line and followed the matron's instructions.

Going to the temple for the first time and starting to wear garments were key for me to accomplish two significant goals. First, I was engaged to my college boyfriend and had to wear garments to get married and sealed to him in an LDS temple. I had been taught from a young age that I would not be able to be with my family in the afterlife if I didn't get married in the temple. Second, participating in temple endowment and wearing garments would signify that I finally belonged in my church—an acceptance I had been chasing for a long time.

I grew up in Utah County, an area with one of the highest percentages of Mormons in the world. Almost all of the students at my high school were middle-class, white Mormons from two-parent homes. My mother is a traditional white Mormon multigenerational woman whose ancestors joined the church in England in the 1800s and came to the United States to join their fellow "saints." My father, on the other hand, is Japanese. His parents were Buddhist but baptized their children into Mormonism. They wanted their children to assimilate into American society after they experienced extreme racism in the aftermath of the bombing of Pearl Harbor.

Many people with a mixed-race identity feel that they are a child of two worlds, without being fully accepted by either. This was my experience. Messages about race are integral to Mormon theology with the Book of Mormon, the foundational scripture of the faith, describing dark skin as a curse from God—a method used to mark those who were not obedient. While the church has tried to separate from this narrative in recent years, it was commonly taught in the 1980s and 1990s when I was in my formative years. As I struggled to make sense of my own racial identity, I asked a close family member where the Asian slanted eyes came from. This family member confidently explained to me that they likely came about in the same way as dark skin did, as a curse from God. Much of my childhood was spent trying to hide my Asian identity in favor of a more mainstream Mormon identity.

My desire to wear garments was consciously tied to my desire to feel validated and accepted by my community. Being biracial, low-income, and having divorced parents put me on the margins of Mormonism. Despite embracing Christian messages of caring for the needy, having a low socioeconomic status is highly stigmatized in church culture, specifically in areas of the United States with a high concentration of members like Utah, Idaho, and Arizona. Sermons given in local congregations, as well as in larger general meetings, commonly tell stories of receiving financial blessings as a reward for faith and obedience. Promotions, new jobs, and better pay were often cited as symbols of God's favor.

When my parents divorced when I was ten years old, I felt very palpably that we were now second-class citizens in our church community. We were referred to as a broken home. Local church leaders spoke with concern about our family because there were no male priesthood holders in the home. My experience in the church was that my family was a project that needed to be helped by those that were stronger and more righteous.

For me, these issues are inextricably tied to my relationship with the church and therefore my relationship to garments. Being endowed in the temple, which is marked by the wearing of garments, was an important step for me to feel validity and acceptance as a real member of the church. Throughout my adult life, I used garment wearing as a way to show that I was fully obedient in all the things that were asked of me. Because my garments were serving this validating function in my life, I did not question my experiences with them.

I became interested in studying garments in 2022 when I was working on a Women's and Gender Studies degree at the University of Massachusetts Dartmouth. That fall, protests had broken out in Iran with the death of Mahsa Amini, a Muslim woman, at the hands of police when she was detained for not wearing hijab in the way prescribed by lawmakers. Just a year earlier, the New York Times had published an article detailing how LDS women were struggling with their garments. I knew that the conversation about women's experience with religious clothing was just as relevant now as ever and that LDS women needed to be part of that conversation. If I had to choose one practice from Mormonism to portray what Mormonism is all about, it would be the wearing of garments. Garments will tell you one of the more expansive stories about Mormonism. They are crucial to the ways in which people relate to their faith. This story tells the history and sociology of Mormonism far better than any institutional study. These pieces of underwear hold so much meaning, produce so many feelings, and have generated so many community behaviors. In that sense, they really are "magic" underwear because they preserve this hidden story of my community.

Nancy and Jessica's Story of This Book

Jessica and I met in the social media spaces of Mormon feminism in 2013. In these forums, we witnessed and participated in many discussions of women's experiences in the church. Some of the longest discussion threads in those spaces were about women's challenges with wearing garments. These conversations were not limited to teachings on covenants, protection, and modesty. Away from prying eyes, women broke the taboo on discussing garments and shared their questions, suggestions, and experiences openly. Many women reported yeast infections and urinary tract infections from wearing garments and poor relationships with their bodies, among other bodily challenges. They commiserated over the judgment they felt when they made their own choices about how and when to wear garments or when they stopped wearing garments. Jessica and I had never encountered so much frank conversation around this daily religious practice. More than discomfort, we both felt some dread around garments that was difficult for us to describe or understand at that time. We started to wonder if Mormons' experiences with their garments broadly lined up with official church discourse or if they looked more like the discussions in these forums or something else entirely.

We started to consider the many meanings of garments. In popular culture, they were laughable magic underwear. In some corners of the internet, they were part of a subgenre of pornography (we do not recommend searching for this). In LDS Church discourse, they were the armor of God. In internet forums of Mormon feminists, garments took on many more meanings that emerged from lived experiences. We wanted to know what other people experienced with their garments and what those experiences meant in the lives of ordinary Mormons. We believed that answers to these questions would provide context for understanding our own experiences as either typical or unusual.

CHURCH TEACHING ON GARMENTS

"We are at war!" general authority Carlos Asay declared in a 1997 article on garments for the *Ensign*, the official church magazine for adults. There is very little theological writing on garments, and this lone article does a lot of heavy lifting for church members in search of meaning. Asay continued,

> Our enemy is not an invading army from a bordering nation or a navy of some overseas power. Bullets are not whizzing above our heads, nor are bombs exploding in and around our homes. Nevertheless, we are engaged in a life-and-death struggle with forces capable of thrashing us inside out and sending us down into the depths of spiritual defeat if we are not vigilant.[11]

In the minds of Asay and other church leaders, Latter-day Saints are soldiers in an apocalyptic battle between good and evil. Garments, described Asay, are the battle armor God provided for this apocalyptic fight. Asay compared garments to the allegorical armor described in Paul's letter to the Ephesians. He described three ways that garments serve as this battle armor. First, they are a reminder of temple covenants, or promises, made to God. Second, Asay taught that garments will serve as a "protective covering for the body" and a "protection from temptation and evil.[12] Third, he described garments as "a symbol of the modesty of dress and living that should characterize the lives of all the humble followers of Christ."[13] Because of the way in which they covered the body from shoulders to knees, garments encouraged the wearing of clothing that covered these same body parts. Authors of the 2004 manual *True to the Faith: A Gospel Reference* repeated Asay's understanding of garments as a reminder of temple covenants, protection, and modesty.[14] This one article, which is the lengthiest church publication addressing garments, influenced all later church teaching on the issue.

While these three meanings are an important part of understanding the limited discourse on garments, garments also take on a social value, around which group behaviors have formed. In a letter dated October 10, 1988, the First Presidency, the highest governing body in the church, articulated this social value of garments. In it, the First Presidency stated that "wearing the garment is an outward expression of an inward commitment to follow the Savior." This same statement is repeated in Asay's 1997 article and again in *True to the Faith.*[15] The letter describes the garment as an *outward* symbol, not as a *private* one. Other outward symbols of religious identity include the wearing of crosses, stars of David, or hijab, but the outward symbol referenced here is hidden under outer layers of clothing. It is a marker, hidden to some but visible to others, of the wearer's commitment and worthiness within the church community. These church statements not only speak to an individual's choice to wear or not wear garments but also to the ways in which the community should understand and interpret the choices of others in wearing or not wearing the garment. In this way, garments become a discreet symbol of religious belonging.

These limited official pronouncements on garments also outline the ways in which church leaders expect church members to go about the "sacred privilege" of wearing garments.[16] The October 1988 letter reads,

> The fundamental principle ought to be to wear the garment and not to find occasions to remove it. Thus, members should not remove either all or part of the garment to work in the yard or to lounge around the home in swimwear or immodest clothing. Nor should they remove it to participate in

recreational activities that can reasonably be done with the garment worn
properly beneath regular clothing. When the garment must be removed,
such as for swimming, it should be restored as soon as possible.[17]

Local church leaders and family members typically instruct soon-to-be garment wearers that garments should only be removed for sex, swimming,
and showering. Some believe that exercise in general is also part of the
exception, while others wear their garments while exercising. Whereas
Jana Riess's recent work suggests that younger generations of Mormons
hold these rules in a more flexible way than their parents and grandparents
do, many church members understand that they should be wearing their
garments continually.[18]

The letter goes on to explain that "you should not expose [garments]
to the view of those who do not understand its significance," encouraging
church members to keep garments hidden from those outside the church
community.[19] Church members covenant to keep parts of temple ceremonies secret, but church members often interpret this covenant to include
most elements of temple ceremony and the garments that are the everyday
reminder of these ceremonies and covenants. Some Mormons and former
Mormons who are involved with social media spaces have both called for
more openness and transparency, but the taboo remains.

The First Presidency letter, the Asay article, and the *True to the Faith* entry
all give official instructions on how to practice garment wearing and what
that practice is supposed to mean in the lives of ordinary church members.
The statements of priesthood leaders in official publications and venues
carry significant weight in the LDS community. In a tradition that defines
priesthood as "the eternal power and authority of God," the pronouncements of priesthood leaders are an extension of that divine power.[20] Still,
church members who wear garments have their own lived experiences with
their sacred underwear. These experiences both resemble the themes of
church teaching and diverge from that teaching. Some members have determined a different meaning for their garments as a result of challenging
or positive experiences with them. For many, their relationship with their
garments is a complicated one and this book explores that complexity.

Above all, garments reflect the power that the LDS Church has over
Mormon bodies, with a formal system of accountability through temple
recommend interviews. The visibility of garments to LDS members creates an informal accountability system, where friends, family, and com-

munity members might offer comments or judgment if they notice that garment lines are missing.[21] Ordinary church members of any gender can claim religious power and authority for themselves by commenting about someone's garment-wearing habits, which reinforces this practice for the whole community.

GARMENTS ON YOUTUBE

Soon after Jessica and Nancy began researching this topic, the church's Newsroom released a YouTube video on garments for a broad public audience. The video compared garments to the ritual clothing and vestments worn by clergy or monks in different religious traditions from around the world.[22] As Mormon women who were active participants in our local congregations, we had never participated in a discussion or had read church materials that described us as being vested as clergy through the wearing of garments. Our church did not ordain women and considered asking questions about women's ordination in public spaces to be in violation of community norms and worthy of excommunication.[23] The video did not mention garments as reminders of covenants or sources of protection. In our minds, there was a significant disconnect between the LDS Church's public discussion of a taboo topic and official church teaching, not to mention our own experiences with garments.

THE SURVEY

Previous studies of garments interviewed relatively small groups of participants. Colleen McDannell's study interviewed thirty-seven Mormons in the Salt Lake City area of Utah.[24] Nazneen Kane interviewed eighteen Mormon women, and Alexandria Griffin interviewed fourteen Mormon women.[25] Jean Hamilton and Jana Hawley conducted formal and informal interviews with about twenty-four Mormons.[26] Jana Riess used data from her survey (1,500+ respondents) and interviews (63 interviewees), though her focus was not on garments but on religious practice more broadly.[27] We wanted to hear from a much larger group to determine a fuller range of garment experiences.

Given the taboo topic, we imagined that a survey, rather than interviews, would help church members feel more comfortable sharing about their experiences with garments and give us the ability to capture a much larger sample. We were aiming for five hundred respondents and for this dataset to become the basis of a journal article. Ultimately, participants from many different political and social orientations within the LDS Church took and shared the survey with their social networks. We received more than 4,500 responses. Mormons answered questions about their identities, beliefs, and practices surrounding garments. The data gathered in this survey are not statistically representative of all Mormons, but they do represent a wide range of Mormon views and experiences with their garments. This study focuses on the 4,529 survey respondents who answered questions about gender and belief.

It is challenging to tell a story based on anonymous survey data. To flesh out the lived experiences of garments, we've included some of our own personal experiences with garments throughout the book, labeled with our names. All three of us have been *conforming* and *nonconforming* believers in the Church of Jesus Christ of Latter-day Saints, meaning that we have all experienced faith without doubt and, later, with doubt. At this point in our lives, we have also all left the church but hold different relationships to Mormonism. Our stories are situated within these two different frameworks of believing, together with our other identities. This autoethnographic approach gives further insight into garment experiences and the ways in which garments function in community. We tell this larger story through the lens of intersectional feminism and with the assistance of Michel Foucault's panopticon.

In beginning this research, our initial hypothesis was simple: We thought that men and women would describe very different meanings and experiences with their garments, with women having far more physical problems with garments than men, who probably did not think about them much. Men's garments looked a lot like a regular men's undershirt and boxer briefs, while women's garments did not resemble or function in the same way as contemporary secular women's underwear. In our inexperience, we thought that gender alone would explain all of the data, which would be straightforward and uncomplicated. We did not anticipate that both men and women would report a huge range of experiences with their garments and that other kinds of identities would be essential to understanding the full range of Mormons' lived experiences with garments. We were naive but had the good sense to include many demographic questions on the survey that would allow us to explore different issues of identity at a later time.

Many researchers find that few participants want to write open-ended responses in surveys, but we were lucky. Our survey participants were eager to discuss their experiences with garments in an anonymous survey. One of the biggest surprises of this project was that many respondents wrote lengthy answers to our open-ended questions. After the survey closed, we were quickly overwhelmed by the quantity of data we had collected and by the amount of text that had been written in response to open-ended questions like "What do your garments mean to you?" and "Why do you wear your garments?" Mormons shared answers that we did expect and many more that we did not anticipate. We had hoped for simple answers to our questions but received a giant, tangled mess of stories, experiences, and meanings for garments that was not easy to explain. Gender alone did not explain the huge range of survey responses. Other variables like race, socioeconomic status, education, and age could not, on their own, explain our data. Combinations of these variables did not explain the data. We were overwhelmed by what our respondents had told us and were not yet experienced enough in the sociology of religion to know how to parse it. This was in 2014.

THE SOCIAL STORY OF GARMENTS

Garments serve as a window into Mormon history and culture. Joseph Smith, founder and proclaimed prophet of the Latter Day Saint movement, instituted the practice of wearing garments before his death in 1844.[28] Garments were part of the temple rituals that served to legitimize the practice of polygamy in Mormon communities. In the twentieth century, the Church of Jesus Christ of Latter-day Saints, the largest of the Latter Day Saint churches, stopped practicing polygamy and sought instead to find acceptance in mainstream American society and especially with white Evangelical Protestants. As it made these changes, garments took on new meanings related to sexual purity. In the twentieth century, garments became an extension of sexual purity teaching and helped to regulate the sexual behavior of adults by absorbing modesty rhetoric and transferring church messaging onto Mormon bodies. Individual church members, then, are caught in the middle of the larger religious, political, and social aspirations of the LDS Church.

This sociological study of garments examines the responses of a large sampling of members of the Church of Jesus Christ of Latter-day Saints. The study is not statistically significant, but it does capture a wide range of lived experiences. Intersectional theory drove the analysis of survey responses, with a focus on the categories of gender and belief, to reveal the internal power dynamics of Mormon communities. Michel Foucault's panopticon illuminates the ways in which garments shape individual and group behaviors within these communities through the mechanism of surveillance. Wearing garments produces meanings, feelings, and behaviors in the bodies of those who wear them *and* garments are a reflection of institutional power over those bodies and the church's desire to assimilate into the American religious landscape. The analysis of the survey data focuses on themes of belief, secrecy, shame, and control and argues that garments are a religious technology that restrains the sexual behavior of Mormon adults.

In very recent years, church leadership has made efforts to distance the church from its familiar *Mormon* moniker.[29] However, the nickname Mormon has been embraced by members and leaders of the church for over a hundred years, with the church spending millions of dollars on a national "I'm a Mormon" ad campaign between 2010 and 2018. This book uses the term *Mormon* because it is the most recognizable and commonly used name by those who are not members of the faith. When we did the survey in 2014, the participants of the survey identified as *Mormon*, though it is also important to note that not all those who identify as Mormons are members of the Church of Jesus Christ of Latter-day Saints (LDS Church). *Mormons*, as used in this book, references specifically LDS Mormons.

OVERVIEW OF CHAPTERS

Chapter 1 examines the history of garments in the LDS Church, arguing that they function as a religious technology to restrain sexual behavior. Garment history is situated within and builds on related histories of Mormon polygamy, race, and assimilation. Joseph Smith's first garments are situated within the context of underwear history and religious material culture. The chapter argues that garments serve a dual purpose, both as a unique Mormon practice and as a tool for conforming to broader societal expectations, with their hidden nature allowing for the coexistence of these competing goals. While garments were a holdover from polygamy, associated with promiscuity and a lack of sexual restraint in American media, they came to mean something very different in the twentieth century. Garments became a religious technology that helped Mormons embody a restrained sexuality, one of the defining ideals of white Evangelical Protestants. This exploration of garment history reveals shifting meaning over time and conflicts about the role of women in the church.

Chapter 2 explores the relationship between belief and gender that emerged from the survey. Believing is an essential part of Mormon practice and is tested in regular temple recommend interviews that begin in the teenage years and continue through adulthood. Mormon belief has three identifiable parts: intellectual content, expected emotions, and embodied practices. The LDS Church instructs members in *doing* belief in these three ways throughout the lifespan. Mormon garments absorb the content of all of this belief and are heavy with meaning, and these meanings are transferred onto Mormon bodies. As an extension of temple ceremonies, garments remind Mormons of religious obligations, discussed as *covenants*. The lived experience of garments speaks to the way in which these items of everyday sacred clothing break through the boundaries of the symbolic meaning and take on more literal meanings. Conforming believers, those who did not experience doubt, were more likely to see their decision to wear garments as one that had a positive impact on their lives, regardless of the personal cost. Conforming believers discuss the ways in which garments prevent sin and specifically sexual sin. Nonconforming believers, who did experience doubt, were more likely to understand the requirement to wear garments as a system of surveillance and control. Once nonconforming believers were aware of this system of control, they lost trust in the church and reported feeling a loss of agency in their personal choices.

Chapter 3 discusses the tension between the sacred nature of garments and the secrecy surrounding them and how this can impact those who wear them. Church teaching frames secrecy in terms of *sacredness*. Many women struggled with wearing garments through medical problems, menstruation, pregnancy, and lactation, and the silence around garments left them to navigate these challenges in isolation. Respondents commented on why they wore garments, and their answers revealed that social reasons were important to most of the gender and belief groups. Nonconforming respondents indicated that they wore garments to hide their nonconforming belief from family members. Many respondents judged others for breaking the silence around garments by complaining about garments and experienced shame around a loss of control with their underwear choices.

Chapter 4 examines garment wearing through the theme of shame, which is framed as *worthiness* and *unworthiness* in Mormon teaching. Secrecy and surveillance around garments generate feelings of shame in many garment wearers, regardless of belief type. Understanding shame and worthiness with garment wearing relates to church teaching about sexuality and modesty. Teachings around purity culture begin in childhood, escalate through the teenage years, and are then maintained and made tangible in adulthood through garments. Purity culture can lead to negative body image and self-objectification, particularly for women. The chapter concludes by highlighting the disconnect between church teachings on modesty and the lived experiences of Mormons, with many reporting that modesty practices and garment wearing lead to feelings of shame and anxiety rather than spiritual uplift.

Chapter 5 investigates the complex interplay between garments, sexuality, and control, which is understood through the language of *obedience* in church teaching and as *agency* within the discipline of sociology. Building on themes of belief, secrecy, and shame, this chapter argues that garments function as a religious technology to control or restrain the sexual behavior of Mormon adults. It delves into the experiences of Mormon women and men, with both conforming and nonconforming belief, and how garments impact their sense of self, bodily autonomy, and sexual relationships. The chapter highlights the ways in which the church's teachings on modesty and purity become absorbed by garments and then work to harm body image, reduce sexual desire, and limit sexual behavior in single people but also in heterosexual married couples. Church teaching and culture couch garments as a control mechanism in religiously beneficial terms. Ultimately, the chapter raises important questions about the role of agency and the costs individuals pay to conform to or resist religious norms within the LDS Church.

The concluding chapter explores the concept of agency within the sociology of religion and also within a Mormon context, expanding existing ideas about agency by examining the *costs* of agency. Garments are a symbol of conformity and control, embedding deep feelings of shame and obedience in its members. Garments serve as a religious technology that manipulates sexual behavior under the guise of sacredness (secrecy), worthiness (shame), and obedience (control). This system of control impacts individual autonomy, leading to a significant internal conflict among members who must navigate these imposed meanings with their personal experiences.

1
A SHORT HISTORY OF GARMENTS

Nancy's Story

Before my temple sealing to my fiancé in 2004, my bishop expected me to attend private meetings with him in the months and weeks prior to our ceremony. This was, and remains, standard practice in the LDS Church. The bishop asked me if my fiancé and I were abstaining from sex and instructed me on how to navigate garments and sex once we were married. He said that we should be careful and intentional about taking them off and putting them back on. We should not take them off too early in the process of having sex, and when it was done, which I understood to be at the point of ejaculation, we should put them back on promptly.

I did not think much about these directions at the time. Once I was married, though, my rule-observing self started to feel considerable anxiety about the appropriate times to take garments off and to put them back on again. Garments created boundaries around my married sexual behavior that I had not anticipated. A few times we accidentally fell asleep naked, only to wake up in the middle of the night ashamed that we had not yet put our garments back on. These unintentional transgressions felt like serious moral failings and encouraged us to prioritize putting garments back on quickly, often at the expense of pleasure. Our concern around the timing of putting garments back on intruded into our most private moments and disrupted our physical and emotional connection. Our garments created religious boundaries, governed by church teaching, and surveilled in bishop's interviews, around our married sexual behavior and pleasure.

Even though this is an awkward story to share, I have come to understand that this is a common one among those who wear garments. Many Mormons have heard church members describe the mood-killing, purity-reinforcing nature of garments in stories of men taking off their clothes to have sex outside of marriage but being stopped by the power of their garments in reminding them of their commitment to chastity (see chapters 4 and 5). What is less discussed are the ways in which garments hinder sexual encounters within marriage, reducing sexual behavior, and changing the relationship between individuals and their bodies in ways that further inhibit sexual expression, connection, and pleasure. For a long time, I thought it was just me, but I now understand that the particular concerns I developed around garment boundaries and sexuality were part of a larger system.

The central argument of this book is that garments are a religious technology for restraining the sexual behavior of LDS adults. This story is just one example of this kind of restraint. The sexual behavior of Mormon adults takes shape through mechanisms of belief, which employ concepts of secrecy, shame, and control. Early in my marriage, I could not see this clearly because I understood these themes as they were presented in church teaching, which framed them as sacredness, worthiness, and obedience. Late in our decade-long garment research, we began exploring the history of garments within underwear and fashion history and religious material culture. This shift in focus clarified clothing's long-recognized power to shape identity and behavior.

INTRODUCTION

Garments serve as a window into Mormon history and culture because they are an item of clothing that ties contemporary religious practices, including temple rituals, covenants, and interviews, with the historical practice of polygamy. Understanding how garments came to restrain Mormon sexual behavior through practices of secrecy, shame, and control requires an examination of their complex history. This narrative includes the development of garments over time but also the ways in which underwear practices and meaning shifted in the late nineteenth and early twentieth centuries. In the nineteenth century, garments were associated with polygamy and aligned with health reform movements. By the mid-twentieth century, garments were used by church leaders to enforce Evangelical sexual norms in an effort to recast Mormons as sexually restrained white Christians. The evolving meanings and uses of garments follow broader patterns of Mormon assimilation into the American religious landscape and an institutional desire to control the bodies of church members to achieve this. As the meaning of garments evolved, though, the wearing of garments remained a marker of status within the community, always signaling an individual's allegiance to church leaders and their teachings.

FIRST GARMENTS

Mormonism emerged from the American Restorationist movement, an outgrowth of the Second Great Awakening (1790–1840). Restorationist churches were founded on the belief that the full truth of Jesus Christ's teachings had been lost over time and that God's church must be restored in its pure, New Testament form.[1] Today, Mormonism is known for its peculiarity, or its unique features, but at its inception, it shared many beliefs, biblical interpretations, and teachings with their white Evangelical contemporaries.[2]

Joseph Smith, founder and proclaimed prophet of the Latter Day Saint movement, instituted the practice of wearing garments before his death in 1844.[3] Church members received garments in temple ceremonies that Smith created for his fledgling religious movement. Smith drew inspiration for garments from Freemasonry, the esoteric fraternal movement that was popular in nineteenth-century America, and from his visions of heavenly beings.[4] It is hard to underestimate the near-divine status of Joseph Smith in Mormonism. In many Latter Day Saint denominations, Mormon history and particularly the actions and words of its early leaders, hold a canonical status. The things Joseph Smith said and did serve as a foundation of belief for many today.

During his lifetime, Joseph Smith (1805–44) instituted the practice of plural marriage. Within the belief framework he created, polygamy was a requirement for the best outcomes in the afterlife.[5] Plural marriages were legitimized and sanctified by a series of three newly created temple rituals.[6] The Washing and Anointing ceremony, also known as the *initiatory*, bestowed garments upon the participant and included divine blessings of protection in return for wearing them night and day. The *endowment* focused on the dramatic reenactment of the creation story and commitment making. Garments featured in the story and were identified as symbols of a commitment to obey God.[7] The *sealing* ceremony married committed LDS couples, who had completed the initiatory and endowment ceremonies, and bonded any children to them for eternity, as long as partners were faithful to covenants made in all three ceremonies. While there was some initial variation, a man could be sealed to multiple women, but women could be sealed to only one man.

Early in the twentieth century, LDS Church leaders discovered that Joseph Smith did not leave an official description of garments or instructions about their making.[8] The husband of seamstress Elizabeth Warren Allred recorded the story of the making of the first garments in Nauvoo, Illinois. This story, told in a letter dated July 10, 1844, was recorded about two weeks after Joseph's murder by a mob.[9] It is unclear exactly when Joseph Smith instituted garments, but they are probably the marked "Knights shirt" referenced in an 1842 exposé of Mormonism.[10]

According to the letter, Joseph Smith told Elizabeth Warren Allred that he saw the Angel Moroni wearing garments and that he wanted her to make some from unbleached muslin, a mass-produced, inexpensive, and transparent fabric in the early nineteenth century.[11] Elizabeth cut the pieces out three times before Joseph was happy with them. He "told her he wanted as few seams as possible and that there would be sufficient whole cloth to cut the sleeve without piecing."[12] Perhaps Smith wanted to echo the supposed seamless robe worn by Jesus, as described in the Gospel of John (19:23), but a common complaint by later garment wearers was that "the one who designed . . . garments had no conceptions of comfort for the human body."[13] These first garments reached just above the ankle and just above the wrist. Elizabeth used Turkey red thread to stitch the seams. Later versions encased the edges of the fabric in ribbon and used white thread.

Joseph Smith adopted the compass and set square from Freemasonry, incorporating them as cut marks on garments worn over each breast.[14] Additional marks were cut into the navel and over the right knee. Despite his induction as a Master Mason in March 1842 in Nauvoo, Illinois, Smith considered the Masonic ceremonies a corrupted form of worship, leading him to establish temple ceremonies to correct them.[15] Sources diverge on the consistency of garment markings in the church's early years.[16] These cut marks would later become embroidered marks.

Initially, the garments lacked collars. Emma Smith, the first wife of Joseph Smith, later attached small white collars to make the garment appear more finished. These collars remained concealed under outer clothing. Eliza R. Snow, a polygamous wife of Joseph and a prominent leader of the Relief Society, the LDS Church's organization for women, had a different approach. Snow fashioned large white collars that were "worn on the outside of the dress."[17] This early tension between concealed and visible garment features would continue to shape Mormon identity and culture.

PROGRESSIVE UNDERWEAR

Joseph Smith created and instituted garments within a pivotal moment in underwear fashion history, a time when nineteenth-century social reformers increasingly understood clothing's capacity to create both liberation and oppression.[18] Contemporary women's underwear included many layers of structured and unstructured undergarments that limited women's movement and placed a physical strain on women's bodies.[19] Women's fashion was a particular target for social reformers, beginning in the 1830s and leading to the founding of the National Dress Reform Association in 1856.[20] Members of the organization, borrowing abolitionist and women's rights rhetoric, campaigned against women's contemporary fashion as a form of slavery that was unhealthy for women's bodies.[21] Mormon garments, at their inception, represented Joseph Smith's strategic alignment progressive ideas mixed with symbols that recalled, in his view, an ancient and corrupted priesthood. This approach was on brand with Smith's Restorationism, which reached into an imagined ancient past to engage with contemporary problems and issues.

Early Mormon garments resembled a new form of underwear that emerged in the 1840s. In August 1843, English writer Thomas Carlyle described a new "uniondress" that was a single piece undergarment for women.[22] This item, and others like it, was supposed to replace the petticoats, chemises, corsets, and other shaping underlayers that served as underwear with a single practical layer. Such simple styles were on the cutting edge of fashion and health trends. The uniondress was a forerunner of the 1868 "emancipation union under flannel," later known as the *union suit* or *combination*.[23] Dress reform groups championed such innovations in underwear for the purposes of supporting women's health, but it would be decades before such items were in general use.

In developing specialized clothing with religious significance, Joseph Smith followed the lead of Freemasons and other religious groups. Freemasons in particular understood the power of ritual combined with ritualistic clothing to create a shared identity that promoted civic behavior and group norms.[24] Masonic ceremonies typically involved ritual clothing. Smith may have been inspired by the separate pair of underwear, or *drawers*, for special use during the Entered Apprentice degree.[25] Many of Joseph Smith's contemporaries shared a broad understanding that attaching particular values to clothing would have an impact on behavior.

Mormons were not the only nineteenth-century religious group that was interested in prescribing dress. Ellen Gould Harmon White, who founded the Seventh-Day Adventist tradition, was concerned that women's fashion was having a negative impact on "health, behavior, culture, and even spiritual salvation."[26] She insisted that women should wear plain, loose, frugal clothing with hems that were shorter than the norm so as to not drag on the ground.[27] Quaker women resisted contemporary fashions in favor of plain dress that did not include ribbons and other decorative elements.[28] Abolitionists Sara and Angelina Grimke converted to Quakerism and adopted plain dress, which Angelina's husband did not approve of.[29] He worried that associating particular elements of dress with religious ideas and values "could render women slaves" to these restrictions.[30] This wariness of assigning too much meaning to clothing reflected an understanding of its power to shape behavior.[31] Embedding religious ideas into items of clothing would give religious groups an easy way to monitor and control bodies.

To understand the social dynamics of garments, the concept of the panopticon, as described by French philosopher Michel Foucault, offers a useful framework. Borrowed from Jeremy Bentham, the panopticon is an idea of a prison with a central tower allowing guards to observe a ring of isolated and always-visible cells.[32] Foucault explained that the main impact of such a system is "to induce in the inmate a state of conscious and permanent visibility that assures the automatic functioning of power."[33] Scholars of Evangelicalism have applied the panopticon to purity culture to study issues of control.[34] Similarly, garments serve as the panopticon through which the LDS Church exerts power over Mormon bodies, particularly to control their behavior and sexual conduct.

Feminist historian Gerda Lerner observed that throughout history, groups have used clothing to enforce social norms and hierarchies and other scholars have expanded on this idea.[35] Linda Arthur, who studied clothing and textiles, asserted that "strict dress codes are enforced" in conservative religious groups "because dress is considered symbolic of religiosity" and that "dress becomes a symbol of social control as it controls the external body."[36] Fashion historians have long made the point that religious clothing had the power to discipline the body.[37] In describing how this process works, religious studies and material culture professor David Morgan has observed that "clothing is an agent, a device that works *on* our bodies to change how we experience ourselves and *with* our bodies to affect those around us because we live in webs of relationships."[38] Garments, then, are an item of clothing that shapes behavior and embodied experience in Mormonism and impacts the social and structural relationships of Mormon communities.

Joseph Smith modeled garments on the clothing worn by an angel during his religious visions. Later, church leaders described other heavenly visitors as also wearing garments. The *Journal of Discourses* recorded church leader Heber C. Kimball (1801–68) as teaching that when the New Testament figures of Jesus, John the Baptist, Peter, James, and John appeared to Joseph Smith in various visions and visitations, these figures were wearing "the garments of the Holy Priesthood."[39] In a separate event, Frederick G. Williams (1787–1842) told George A. Smith (1817–75) that he saw Jesus appear at the dedication of the Kirtland temple, which took place on March 27, 1836. Williams described Jesus's garments in great detail.[40] Garments, then, connected wearers to divine messengers and even to the person of Jesus.

Mormon temple rituals give further meaning to garments. A dramatization of the creation story is a central feature in the endowment ceremony. The character of God gives Adam and Eve garments as a sign of their commitment (covenant) to obey God. The narrative then pauses as the endowment narrator draws the connection between the characters of Adam and Eve and the participants in the audience, who are separated by gender. All of the women in the room become Eve, just as all of the men become Adam. They then echo this same commitment to obedience, signified in the wearing of garments.

Primary sources indicate that the connection between garments and the creation story originated with Joseph Smith. Benjamin F. Johnson, an early Latter Day Saint in Nauvoo, Illinois, recounted in his diary a story of Joseph Smith showing his garments to Benjamin in April 1842.[41] Smith described garments as the same item of clothing from the creation story "as the Lord made for Adam from skins."[42] God gave Adam and Eve "garments of skins" before casting them out of the Garden of Eden (Genesis 3:21 NRSV).

While temple ritual connected garments to the creation story and a particular covenant to obey God, the endowment also included more sinister meanings for garments. The language of the ritual included threats of violence on the bodies of garment wearers, known as the "penalties" for breaking an oath of secrecy around temple covenants. The text of the ceremony and the ritual gestures indicated that those who broke this oath would be killed by having their throat slit, their heart torn out, and by being disemboweled.[43] The language of the penalties was removed from the endowment ceremony in 1990, but the secrecy around temple covenants did not disappear.[44]

At the same time that garments promised violent retribution for breaking covenants of secrecy, garments also symbolized bodily protection. The earliest reference to garments in the historical record is in an exposé of the Mormon temple ceremony published in 1842 by Dr. John C. Bennett.[45] This book referenced sacred marks made on a shirt that took on a protective function.

The story of Joseph Smith's death has been used to emphasize the protective meaning of garments in Mormon communities. Smith and other church leaders were imprisoned and attacked by a mob in Carthage, Illinois in June 1844.[46] John Taylor, who would later become the third president of the LDS Church, was present and wearing his garments on that day and survived.[47] Joseph Smith was famously not wearing garments when he was murdered, and many Mormons later attributed his death to a lack of garment protection. One story indicated that Joseph had talked with his first wife, Emma, before his death and had indicated that the protective function of garments was so strong that he could not be killed while wearing them, and so he would take them off so that he could become a martyr for the Latter Day Saint cause.[48] In July 1846, newly appointed church president Brigham Young declared, "Let no man be without his Temple undergarment."[49] Such comments from Young changed the practice of wearing temple garments from an occasional practice to an ongoing night-and-day requirement. From that time forward, Mormons have told stories about the ways in which their garments have saved them from physical harm.[50]

When Brigham Young left Nauvoo in February 1846 with a large group of followers to settle in the West, Emma Smith and others stayed behind. She taught her children that their father, Joseph Smith, had not practiced polygamy. Her son, Joseph Smith III, became the first president of the Reorganized Church of Jesus Christ of Latter Day Saints (RLDS Church, now Community of Christ). The RLDS Church refuted plural marriage, believing that their founder had not practiced it. It did not adopt esoteric temple ceremonies or the practice of wearing garments, as RLDS leaders associated both with polygamy and the Mormons who had followed Young.[51]

In a meeting for the training of church leaders in 1883, John Taylor, then president of the LDS Church, gave a lengthy explanation of garments. He referenced the story of church leaders' vision of Jesus at the 1836 Kirtland temple dedication, where Jesus was wearing garments. Taylor was not present at the 1836 Kirtland temple dedication, but the minutes of this meeting recorded a description of Jesus's garments as

> the patter of the garment given to Adam and Eve in the Garden of Eden, and it all had a sacred meaning. The collar: My yoke is easy and my burden is light. [Crown of the Priesthood] the strings on each side have a double meaning, the strings being long enough to tie in a neat double bow knot, representing the Trinity; the double bow knots the marriage covenant between man and wife. The Compass: a guide to the wearer as the North Star is a guide in the night to those who do not know the way they should go. The Square: representing the justice and fairness of our Heavenly Father, that we will receive all the good that is coming to us or all that we earn, on a square deal; the navel mark: meaning strength in the navel and marrow in the bones. The Knee Mark: representing that every knee shall bow and every tongue confess that Jesus is the Christ. The whole garment to be a covering and a protection from the enemy. The sleeves reaching to the wrists, and the legs to the ankles. This was the pattern given to Joseph Smith by two heavenly beings.[52]

By the early 1880s, then, garments had collected many meanings. Taylor affirmed the creation story origin for garments and further connected the pattern used by his fellow church members to the divinely inspired pattern given by God in the Garden of Eden. Emma Smith's collars were referenced as the "Crown of the Priesthood" and given a meaning from scripture (Matthew 11:30). Each part of the garment takes on its own meaning, from the nature of God to marriage. Whereas the navel and knee marks were borrowed from Freemasonry, the meanings of the navel and knee marks were borrowed from scripture (Proverbs 3:8 and Isaiah 45:23). This assortment of scriptural references lent garments, which were a nineteenth-century invention, the feeling of an ancient and biblical past.

The accumulating stories and meanings associated with garments shaped the lives of Mormon individuals. Garments rapidly became central to the daily religious practice and permeated life, shaping behavior on personal and collective levels. Wearing garments came with expectations of obedience to church leaders, narratives of divine visitors, and threats of violence. Moreover, English-speaking church leaders and members have long understood references to "garment" or "garments" in the Bible as referencing Mormon temple garments, constructing ancient Jewish and Christian histories for a modern practice and normalizing both garment wearing and temple ceremonies.

PERCEPTIONS OF MORMON POLYGAMY IN AMERICA

When Brigham Young and his followers settled Utah in 1847, polygamy was already a defining element of Mormon society and a main point of tension with the U.S. government.[53] This practice became the source of significant conflict with outside groups. Anti-Mormon speakers described polygamy as "monstrous."[54] Historian Christine Talbot argued that many Americans were deeply disturbed by different family structures and sexual practices, but most groups that practiced outside of sexual and familial norms were small groups set within existing communities in the eastern United States.[55] As settlers of Utah territory, Mormons represented a different kind of threat to Americanism.

Historian Paul Reeve observed that from the earliest days of the church, outsiders saw Mormons as racial others because of their nontraditional, polygamous families.[56] Reeve argued that "despite being overwhelmingly white, Mormons were imagined as a racial deterioration from the advances of Western civilization."[57] Historian Amanda Hendrix-Komoto asserted that "to abandon monogamy as the Latter-day Saints had done, then, was to abandon whiteness."[58] Popular media viewed polygamy as both extreme sexual deviance and deception and linked representations of Mormons to anti-Muslim images and ideas.[59] Political and religious opponents used this racialized image of Mormons to marginalize, discriminate, and enact legislation against them.[60]

Mormon sociologist Armand Mauss argued that the main project of the LDS Church in the nineteenth century was determining its distinctive beliefs and practices, including things like polygamy, temple ceremonies, the Book of Mormon, and garments.[61] In the twentieth century, that central project changed to one of achieving legitimacy and assimilating into mainstream American culture.[62] In doing so, the LDS Church followed a trajectory well known to sociologists of religion. He later observed that "Mormons' continuing concern about their public image" is one of the driving forces of Mormon assimilation.[63]

Mauss identified an LDS movement toward "moderate Protestants" in the 1960s, though today, scholars describe Southern Baptists, unspecified Presbyterians, and Missouri Synod Lutherans as white Evangelical Protestants whose religious and political stance tends toward fundamentalism and conservatism.[64] LDS Church leaders wanted to overcome the racialized and sexualized stigma of polygamy and find acceptance within the American religious landscape. Mauss concluded that the success of Mormonism was in its holding of an "optimum tension" between maintaining distinctive Mormon teachings and practices and assimilating to Protestant Christianity, as represented by the groups he included in his study.[65]

Mauss saw these efforts at assimilation as taking place on a number of different fronts. He identified a shift in church teaching and an interest in improving the church's public image. These changes resulted in the church distancing itself from its polygamous past. It officially gave up polygamy in 1890, but plural marriage continued. In the 1930s, the LDS Church excommunicated church members who self-identified as Fundamentalist Mormons by continuing to practice polygamy.[66] Church members in the twentieth century increasingly sought out higher education and engagement with professional bodies that helped bring many Mormons into the middle class. Political participation and particularly the political careers of George Romney (1907–95), who served as the governor of Michigan and the U.S. secretary of housing and urban development, created a sense that it was possible for Mormons to be trusted by Americans and to serve in public office. Together with an investment in public relations and humanitarian service, the LDS Church worked hard at normalizing Mormonism in American society. But moving the public image of Mormonism away from its polygamous past required more than a bit of distance from Fundamentalists. To reform its image in the American mind, Mormons needed to learn from their past and embrace a view of sexuality that more closely aligned with white Evangelical norms. Garments were a unique feature of Mormonism that was new enough and flexible enough to accumulate meanings. As garments took on meaning, they could be used to shape group behavior, identity, and the perceptions of outsiders.

The church began to distance itself from polygamy in 1890, and at the same time there were growing tensions around garments and contemporary underwear trends around sexuality. Where garments started off as a fashion-forward design with health benefits, the belief that the sewing pattern was divinely inspired meant that some church leaders and members would struggle with allowing the pattern to evolve. Underwear designs and fabrics went through significant changes in the latter half of the nineteenth century. Relief Society general president Zina Diantha Huntington Young, who had been a plural wife to Joseph Smith and later to Brigham Young, approached church leaders in 1890 to ask if knitted garments would be allowed. Earlier documents indicated that some women in the 1880s wore knitted union suits as garments, and it appears that Zina was seeking institutional approval for the practice.[67] Her request specifically referenced knitted underwear like those made "in the East" to which she could add marks and a collar. The First Presidency denied her request.[68]

Advertisements for knitted underwear survive in magazines from the period. Often full color and with erotic undertones, these illustrations recall the staging and iconography of Victorian erotic photographs. Knitted union suits hugged the body, unlike earlier woven fabrics that did not. The illustrations for such advertisements showed women in union suits standing in front of full-length mirrors, highlighting the curves of their bodies, and lounging seductively on couches. One fashion historian commented that the purpose of this style of underwear was "no longer to conceal, but to display the female form divine."[69] This was the Eastern knitted underwear Zina was referencing. She wanted Mormon women to be able to wear this new, fashionable, and sexy underwear and at the same time meet their religious obligations. Knitted garments were later permitted by church leaders but not while they were in stylistic alignment with contemporary sexy underwear. Likely, some women chose to wear the knitted style anyway.

The turn of the century brought about significant shifts in society including expanded roles for women, the creation of dating culture, and a rise in premarital sex. Garments were later connected with adulthood, but in the early twentieth century they were associated with puberty and sexual development, perhaps as a way to curb sexual behavior. In 1902, LDS Church leaders issued a set of guidelines for temple attendance, indicating that children "of a naturally ripe and early development, of mind and body . . . may receive endowments at the age of twelve years; but as a rule, fifteen years old is sufficiently early."[70] Receiving garments in the initiatory ceremony was a necessary precursor to the endowment. In 1906, LDS Church president Joseph F. Smith, nephew of founder Joseph Smith, declared that the sewing pattern for garments was divinely inspired and should not change. He understood garments as something that set the wearer against the "foolish, vain, and . . . indecent practices of the world."[71] If the world, as Joseph F. Smith saw it, was becoming less traditional and more promiscuous, garments would fix that problem. To address some of the fear around deviation from approved patterns, Beehive Clothing Mills incorporated in 1910 and mainly produced garments.[72] It would later become the sole manufacturer of garments, giving church leaders significant control over design and fabric choices.[73]

After World War I, women's fashion changed in significant ways, making skirts and sleeves shorter and reducing the number of layers of undergarments women were expected to wear.[74] The death of Joseph F. Smith in 1918 opened the door for new thinking on garments. LDS Church leaders responded by creating a new garment pattern in June 1923.[75] The changes included removing the collar, replacing the strings with buttons, closing the crotch, shortening the sleeves to elbow length, and shortening the legs to end just below the knee.[76] Knitted fabrics were now acceptable. In the nineteenth century, open-crotch underwear was the norm, but early twentieth-century underwear design favored closed crotches, which became associated with modesty.[77] At this time, buttons were widely available due to the manufacturing advances of the Industrial Revolution, an obvious choice for replacing the older ties.[78] These changes came with the affirmation that it was religiously acceptable for members to wear the older style or the newer style, as both styles were to be considered orthodox.[79]

A *Salt Lake Tribune* article from June 1923 highlighted this new change. Under a headline declaring "OLD STYLE UNCOMFORTABLE," the author of the article describes the older style of garments as "uncomfortably large and baggy."[80] The article gives insight into the intergenerational tensions and experiences of Mormons in Utah at that time:

> the old-style garment is faithfully adhered to by many of the older and sincerely devout members of the church. These regard the [garment] as a safeguard against disease and bodily harm, and they believe that to alter the texture of cloth or style, or to abandon the garment altogether would bring evil upon them.[81]

The article went on to give context for the new style. Young women wanted to wear shorter skirts, which were seen as more sanitary. They also wanted to wear newer styles of hosiery, which had a "knotty appearance" with ankle-length garments underneath.[82] Young men preferred the shorter garments for exercise. The author praised the inclusion of "finer knitted goods" as opposed to the "coarse, unbleached, irritating material" of the older muslin, linen, and wool fabrics. These knitted fabrics were more form-fitting and the newer garments resembled the garment design that Zina Diantha Huntington Young had wanted church leaders to adopt decades before. "Altogether, and except in a few instances, the permissive modification is welcomed as a sanitary move and a change looking to the comfort and health of those who wear temple garments." Anecdotal evidence suggests that the new garments were a hit. A laundry worker in Salt Lake City claimed that 95 percent of his clients used the newer style of garments.[83] The complaints of older generations remained but did not prevent the community from using the new style.

Historian Juanita Brooks, in a 1934 article for *Harper's* monthly magazine, discussed this intergenerational tension over the 1923 changes.[84] She wrote,

> I shall never forget how wrought up [Grandpa Leavitt, a polygamous man] became when knitted "garments" were introduced into our town. He threatened those who wore them with dire evils because, he said, these articles were a deviation from the true form. Gentiles [non-Mormons] had probably had a hand in making them and they were desecrated and defiled. The "garment" should be made and marked in the home by the Latter Day Saint wife, according to the revealed pattern and design. It was secret and sacred and not to be traded in or flaunted in public.[85]

This anecdote highlights the weight that an older generation gave to the belief that the pattern of the garment was divinely inspired and the source of garments' protective powers. While the American media vilified Mormons who practiced polygamy and described them as having an unrestrained sexuality, Brooks wrote this picture of her polygamous grandfather against those stereotypes. Brooks also described garments as both sacred and secret, a theme that will be discussed further in chapter 3.

As the LDS Church made changes to the garment pattern, Fundamentalist Mormons continued to use the older wrist-to-ankle style with ties instead of buttons. For these Mormons, polygamy was foundational to their faith and necessary for achieving the highest degree of heaven. The fathers of the Fundamentalist Mormon movement, like Lorin Woolley and Joseph Musser, rejected the 1923 garment changes, blaming them on Mormon women's vain desires to be fashionable.[86] They viewed the sanctity of garments in the preservation of the original pattern and style. Fundamentalist belief emphasized the connection between garments, divine authority, and polygamy. While the earliest story on the origins of garments indicates that Joseph Smith got the idea for garments from a visionary experience with the Angel Moroni, where Moroni was wearing garments, later versions of this story indicated an unnamed heavenly visitor. Iterations of this story by Lorin Woolley and Joseph Musser came to include not one heavenly visitor but two, who were later identified in fundamentalist circles as Jesus and one of Jesus's wives.[87] The story of the original garments also later includes Emma Smith handing the original pair to one of the wives of Martin Harris to take west to Utah.[88] Once copies had been made, the story relayed, an angel took that original set of garments back to heaven. This tale echoes the story of the golden plates, from which Joseph Smith supposedly translated the Book of Mormon, being taken back to heaven by an angel once Joseph was done with them.

The *Relief Society Magazine*, published from 1915 to 1970, included advertisements for garments from a number of companies from the beginning of the magazine through to the 1937 issues. The ads indicated that Mormons could choose to buy garments from Zion's Garment Company, Salt Lake Knitting Store, Barton and Company, Model Knitting Works, Utah Woolen Mills, Cutler's Utah Made Goods, Utahweare Knitting Factory, the Reliable, Mose Lewis, Billings Mercantile Association, and Wasatch Woolen Mills. Unlike the magazine ads in Eastern publications, garments in the *Relief Society Magazine* did not include illustrations of products.

In 1938, the First Presidency sent a letter to local church leaders expressing concern that some people were wearing garments that did not conform to church standards and others had stopped wearing garments altogether.[89] The letter indicated that a new tag would appear on garments to indicated that they were approved by the church. The First Presidency warned that not wearing the garment appropriately was a serious violation of temple covenants and that people who state that they do not intend to wear garments after being endowed "should not be given temple recommends."[90] Church leaders were eager to take measures to ensure compliance. To achieve this, they built up the capacity of Beehive Clothing Mills, which would later become the sole distributor of approved temple garments.[91]

In the 1930s, a committee recommended to top LDS Church leaders that sleeveless garments be approved because of the tendency for garments to peek out of women's clothing and a desire to preserve the hidden nature of garments.[92] This recommendation was not accepted. The same committee suggested that an explanation of the meaning of markings on garments be included in the temple ceremonies, which they hoped would bring about "more reverence for the garment itself."[93] The suggested text came from LDS Church president David Kay and included an explanation of the square as representative of "honor, integrity, loyalty, trustworthiness"; the compass as "an undeviating course in relation to truth. Desires should be kept within proper bounds"; the navel mark indicated "that the spiritual life needs constant sustenance," and the knee mark meant "reverence for God, the source of divine inspiration" and "that every knee shall bow and every tongue confess that Jesus is the Christ."[94] This was a change in teaching that emphasized the sacredness of garments as stemming from the marks, instead of the original pattern. This new idea differentiated LDS teaching and practice from that of Mormon Fundamentalists and created flexibility for future design changes.

The committee went on to recommend that if garment wearers were going to need to expose the garment to "the curious, the unbeliever or the scoffer," it was best to not wear the garment. They made the suggestion that companies that made and sold LDS garments should refrain from advertising them or adding the sacred marks to garments because "no underwear becomes a temple garment until after it has been properly marked by those having authority to do the marking," including those who had been endowed, members of the Relief Society, or other authorized individuals.[95] By 1938, there were no garment ads in the *Relief Society Magazine*.

This period of garment history reveals a dual narrative. First, LDS Church leaders, and also Fundamentalist Mormon leaders, position garments in opposition to threats of promiscuity and sexual deviance, reflecting broader cultural anxiety about these issues. The second is the increasing control that the LDS Church exerted over time in all facets of garment production. From their initial creation and prescription through to the late 1930s, the church steadily consolidated its authority over production, distribution, and meaning of garments, making them a powerful symbol of institutional control and religious authority. These episodes in garment history highlight the tension between the religious requirement to wear garments and a belief in their divine origin with shifting ideas about health, fashion, comfort, and consumer choice.

SEXUAL PURITY, RACIAL PURITY

A new wave of church teaching identified premarital sex as having similar moral weight as murder and of the importance of young Mormon adults marrying other Mormons. In 1942, the First Presidency issued a message "that sexual sin—the illicit sexual relations of men and women—stands, in its enormity, next to murder."[96] In 1943, J. Reuben Clark spoke in a church-wide conference about the importance of young Mormons marrying within the faith. Clark was the U.S. ambassador to Mexico, a lawyer, and a professor of law. He later became an apostle and a member of the First Presidency, the church's highest governing body. In his 1943 talk, he declared that "we stand for a single standard of chastity for boys and the girls. We look upon unchastity as a sin next to murder."[97] This description of sexual behavior outside of marriage as a "sin next to murder" was repeated throughout church curricula and has not, as of writing this book, been removed. This change in church messaging emphasized sexual purity as a top priority for church leaders in shaping the behavior of church members.

Whereas garments started as progressive and innovative underwear in the nineteenth century, garments took on a different meaning in the twentieth century. Early church leaders like Brigham Young and Joseph F. Smith preached against following women's fashion trends, but Mormon women did not take much notice of these messages.[98] This changed in 1951 when Apostle Spencer W. Kimball, who would later become the church president, initiated a new wave of church teaching on modesty. In a devotional presentation at BYU, he told young adult Mormons that women needed to abide by a specific set of dress guidelines and tied his guidelines to church teachings about womanhood.[99] Kimball connected women's modesty to sexual purity and promiscuity in women to the destruction of the church and society.[100] Crucially, this new emphasis on modesty was not abstract but made concrete through the wearing of garments, which dictated the specific coverage of women's bodies. The length of garment sleeves, necklines, and legs ensured that Mormons, and especially Mormon women, conformed to these standards.[101]

Religious studies scholar Sara Moslener observed that Christians in the nineteenth century embraced sexual purity.[102] Continuing that project, twentieth-century Evangelical Protestants emphasized men's sexual restraint and promoted the ideal woman as one who did not experience sexual desire.[103] Groups that were able to successfully represent their women as sexless were able "to secure their religious and cultural superiority."[104] Renewed interest in modesty teaching aimed at women, the wearing of garments to police those boundaries, and the naming of premarital sex as a serious sin with significant moral weight were important steps for Mormon assimilation. They aligned church teaching with Evangelical teaching, but garments were a further tool that helped church leaders enforce specific standards of modesty and sexual behavior.

Ideas about race also shaped religious and cultural understandings of sexuality. Stereotypes about racialized groups often propagated myths regarding their supposed unrestrained sexual behavior.[105] In contrast, to be white and to be a white Evangelical was to embrace a restrained sexuality. The LDS Church actively sought to distance itself from the racializing impact of polygamy, evident in American media. Scholar Taylor Petrey has documented that church leadership consistently linked sexual purity to racial purity in their teachings.[106] After polygamy became an excommunicable offense in the 1930s, the LDS Church's messaging on appropriate marriage centered on racial purity and controlled monogamous heterosexuality.[107] Utah's legislators followed federal policy and outlawed interracial marriage and sexual relations in 1888, a ban that was not lifted until 1963.[108]

The LDS Church's difficult relationship with sexuality and race manifest in other practices. Black Mormon men were forbidden from receiving the priesthood between 1852 and 1978.[109] Black women and men were not allowed to participate in temple ceremonies until 1978, meaning that Black Mormons were systematically excluded from garment wearing during this time frame. With garments as a key marker of adult Mormon identity, this was something that Black Mormons named as a significant loss.[110] Garments absorbed all of these messages about sexuality, modesty, and race. The whiteness of garments, then, was associated with white racial identities, sexual purity, and marking women as uninterested in sex. Garments served as a tool of assimilation, controlling Mormon bodies to legitimize the church within the American religious landscape.

Where Joseph F. Smith had resisted changes to garment design and American cultural trends in the early twentieth century, church leaders had changed their priorities by the 1950s and embraced assimilation. Early twentieth-century underwear designs covered less of the body and took on more obviously sexual meaning.[111] In 1953, LDS Church president David O. McKay asked the famous Mormon swimsuit designer Rose Marie Reid for suggestions on garment design, stating, "I want the members of the Church to love wearing them."[112] Such statements indicate McKay's awareness of many members' dislike of garments. Reid promised that she could make garments "like beautiful lingerie" and recommended lace edges for women's garments, nursing and maternity garments, and a form-fitting pattern that accommodated breasts, which McKay approved.[113] Reid was keenly aware of the power of clothing to discipline women's sexuality, aiming to make garments more palatable to wearers while retaining messages about sexual purity.[114]

Prior to this, men's and women's garments were the same but came in different size ranges. Reid's changes gendered garments in ways that they had not been before, reflecting the postwar gender-binary messaging in American society and echoed in LDS Church teaching. This gendering of garments allowed church leaders to control women's bodies in different ways than it controlled men's bodies, assigning each gender different necklines and sleeve and leg lengths.

Reid also recommended a two-piece garment, with a separate top and bottoms. The single piece garment that had been in use during that time used a split crotch design, which had replaced the pre-1923 open crotch. The two-piece garments she recommended had a completely closed crotch. The church did not implement the two-piece garment until 1979, after Reid's death.[115] At that same time, the church also discontinued the pre-1923-style garment in an effort to distance itself and the garment from their polygamous associations.[116]

Just as Reid was finding ways to give garments more sex appeal, church leaders started emphasizing the destructiveness of unrestrained sexual behavior in their sermons. The sexual revolution of the 1960s and 1970s created an anti-sex backlash among conservative religious traditions. In the 1970s and 1980s, Evangelicals responded by emphasizing the importance of saving sex for marriage and satisfying sex within marriage. Evangelicals produced numerous sex manuals to answer Christians' questions about sex and guide inexperienced newlyweds through this transition in their lives.[117] Mormon leaders went in a different direction. Church leaders emphasized the destructiveness of unrestrained sexual behavior in their sermons. An oft-repeated comment about the dangers of sex in church teaching was from non-Mormon authors Will and Ariel Durrant in their book *The Lessons of History* (1968), which read,

> A youth boiling with hormones will wonder why he should not give full freedom to his sexual desires; and if he is unchecked by custom, morals, or laws, he may ruin his life before he matures sufficiently to understand that sex is a river of fire that must be banked and cooled by a hundred restraints if it is not to consume both the individual and the group.[118]

This comment urged listeners to think about sex as something that must be restrained in a variety of ways because it was an overwhelming and irresistible force of harm.[119] Mormon leaders used this quote in church-wide conferences in 1970, 1987, 1993, and 1998.[120] The authors were speaking about young, unmarried people, and the church used this quote in a manual for young adults, married and unmarried.[121] The statement was repeated in many public sermons not limited to that group, and these messages were not balanced with positive messages about sex within marriage. The understanding of sex as dangerous was, then, the dominant message from church leaders.

Beginning in the 1960s, the LDS Church produced and distributed a pamphlet called *For the Strength of the Youth* which detailed the church's guidelines for behavior and dress among its teenage and young adult members. Earlier editions addressed issues like wearing curlers out in public, dancing with dignity, and the appropriate places for women to wear pants. The 1990 edition was a significant update, influencing later editions, and it was the first version of this publication to address the topic of sexual purity.[122] It stated, "The Lord specifically forbids certain behaviors, including all sexual relations before marriage, petting, sex perversion (such as homosexuality, rape and incest), masturbation, or preoccupation with sex in thought, speech or action."[123] Where previous guidelines about sexual behavior had been conservative, this pamphlet attempted to make sexual boundaries clear.

The LDS Church achieved a milestone of assimilation in the 1980s when it joined the Moral Majority, an Evangelically centered conservative political movement that sought to grow the political power of its affiliated churches.[124] Scholars and observers named this as a significant marker of Mormon assimilation. As this was in progress, an alternative student newspaper at BYU published an article in 1981 with insight into the garment development process.[125] The article commented on the new two-piece garment, emphasizing that the church did not cave to pressure rooted in fashion trends but made the change "due to considerations of modesty and taste."[126] The author described the garment design process as one of continuous refinement because, in the words of one Beehive Clothing representative, "we are always looking for new and better ways to make garments more comfortable."[127] The article outlined the way in which new garment fabrics and designs are adopted. Beehive Clothing sent proposed new items to the Presiding Bishop's Office and then on to the First Presidency, who personally tried on items before approving or rejecting them. All of the decision-makers were men. The author noted that a bigger committee used to do this work, including committee members like the Relief Society general president, but this was no longer the case.

With the success of the Moral Majority membership and the disbanding of the garment committee, the LDS Church turned its attention toward internal dissenters and critics. In November 1991, the LDS Church published a statement in the *Ensign*, *Church News*, and *Deseret News*, signed by the First Presidency and Twelve Apostles, that church members should avoid such conferences where sacred things are discussed in the open.[128] These comments, published in church-owned outlets, were aimed at speakers and participants of the Sunstone Symposium, a conference for church heretics. Sunstone gathered historians, social scientists, and those on the fringes of the LDS Church to discuss Mormon history and culture.[129] A follow-up article named Colleen McDannell's academic presentation on her oral history work on garments as one of the offending items.[130] Such a strong institutional reaction prompted her to reflect on her work with the Mormon sacred as an outsider to Mormonism and in the relationship between things that are held as both sacred and secret. The LDS Church wished to

keep these details of garment history and experience hidden from the view
of its members.

While trying to discourage the breaking of sacred taboos, some in the
LDS Church recognized an opportunity to better control church messaging
about garments. In 1997, Carlos Asay gave a General Conference talk on garments, which became the main source for contemporary church teaching
about garments, discussed further in chapter 2.[131] General Conference talks
hold a great deal of weight in LDS discourse and are viewed as part of the
ongoing revelatory process of church leaders to learn the will of God for
church members. This is one of the few public expositions on garments. Asay
added to the official discourse by describing the garments as "the armor of
God" that offered wearers *spiritual* protection rather than physical protection.[132] This spiritual protection is emphasized eleven times in the short
talk. In line with earlier teaching, modesty is emphasized seven times as an
important meaning for garments. Although sexuality is not named specifically, the combined themes of spiritual protection and modesty within the
context of church teaching emphasize garments as a tool that protects the
wearer from sexual sin.

LDS Church teachings on sexuality and modesty intensified in the middle
of the twentieth century, intertwined with concerns about racial purity
and exclusion. While early calls against worldly fashion held little sway,
the 1940s witnessed a stark condemnation of premarital sex as a severe
sin and emphasized in-group marriage. This focus on marital purity, then
converged in the 1950s with Spencer W. Kimball's directives on modest
dress, enforced through the wearing of garments. This emphasis on the
outward appearance as a marker of morality occurred within a broader
context where the church had actively sought to distance itself from the
racialization of polygamy and where societal norms, as reflected in Utah's
marriage laws, underscored the importance placed on racial endogamy and
the exclusion of interracial unions.

GARMENTS IN THE TWENTY-FIRST CENTURY

Nothing broke the secrecy and silence that had long surrounded garments
like the widespread use of the internet and social media in the first decade
of the twenty-first century. Online forums, blogs, Facebook groups, and
podcasts all provided a platform for people, often using pseudonyms, to

chat about their experiences wearing garments. These spaces facilitated open and critical discussion about garment history, culture, and practice in ways that had not been possible previously. Prior to the creation of these social media spaces, the LDS Church took charge of its own narrative and the curation of its public image and sacred story. Social media discussion challenged the church's truth claims and institutional narratives about its history. Mormon feminist bloggers at Feminist Mormon Housewives and Exponent II shared personal experiences with garments and hosted comment-based discussions with thousands of practicing and former church members joining the conversation. These online discussions gave ordinary Mormons the power to voice critique about the rules and social expectations around their underwear. Some took that critique in a different direction. Multiple companies have created and distributed Mormon-themed films, including pornographic films, featuring performers wearing and removing garments in an effort to reframe desexualizing garments (see chapter 5) as inherently sexual.

Just as Jessica and Nancy were beginning their research in late 2013, the LDS Church Newsroom released a video discussing and showing garments.[133] Although there are many photos of garments online, this was the first time that the church released a photo of garments as part of their official media. The video compared garments to the ritual clothing and vestments worn by clergy or monks in religious traditions around the world, but we, the authors, had not heard garments discussed in this way before. Official church teachings did not describe women and their garments as being vested clergy. The LDS Church did not ordain women and considered asking questions about women's ordination in public spaces to be in violation of community norms and worthy of excommunication.[134] Nor did the video reference garments as the *armor of God*, described by Asay in 1997.[135] There was a significant disconnect between the LDS Church's public discussion of this taboo topic and the internal church teaching and messaging.

Mormon-themed films have also became a place for producers, writers, and performers to break the silence and secrecy around garments while offering keen insights into the garment-wearing experience for a broader public. John-Charles Duffy's and Dai Newman's commentaries on these films offer significant insights into the lived experience of garments. Duffy observed that many of these films represent Mormon missionaries whose bodies are disciplined by the rigid dress and grooming expectations set by the church.[136] Some films represent the experiences of gay Mormons, where the removal of garments prior to sexual activity signals a change in a character's thinking and a shift in identity.[137] Newman observed, "The garment stands between the world and the wearer, constraining body, controlling emotion, and structuring needs yet doing so without being seen by others."[138]

A series of online news articles chronicled the development of the subgenre of Mormon garment porn. Vice published an article in 2014 on LeGrand Wolf (not his real name), who founded MormonBoyz.com, and Brooke Hunter (not her real name), who founded MormonGirlz.com.[139] Both founders were former Mormons who had served missions and discovered that they were gay during that time in their lives. Garments often featured in video content, identifying the characters as Mormon. The narratives of the videos played on the nineteenth-century myth of Mormons as possessing an unrestrained sexuality.[140] In interviewing Mormon porn performer Maxine Holloway, journalist Isha Aran commented that Holloway had spent her career "eroticizing the religious to undermine the moral power of guilt and shame."[141] Journalist Stephen Dark commented on this further when he wrote that such content served as

> an exploration of the world of sexual fantasy within a LDS culture context— everything from temple garments to characters with various church callings—that can prove liberating, particularly for people who are struggling with what some deem the sexually repressive nature of a faith that, for example, while permitting gay and lesbian members, insists they be celibate.[142]

For some, then, Mormon pornography offers a potent critique, a liberating subversion of the ways in which garments restrain the sexual behavior of LDS adults in real life.

In July 2021, Ruth Graham wrote an article for the *New York Times* that discussed Mormon women's specific experiences wearing garments.[143] She interviewed Mormon Instagram influencer Sasha Piton, who had posted to social media about her issues with garments and received thousands of comments and many private messages where women expressed their medical issues and physical discomfort with garments. Graham's article described another Mormon woman who was able to meet with a garment designer and gave him a PowerPoint presentation with many slides that outlined the problems she and others had identified. "You're talking about pads and gore," he told her, dismissing her feedback, as though pads and menstrual blood were not a legitimate part of women's sacred garment—wearing experiences. Natalie Brown, in a guest post for By Common Consent, reacted to this article and explained why Mormon women felt they had to reach out to the press.

> This is a post on why I believe we have seen, and will continue to see, many LDS women turn to the media or to outside organizations in order to voice their complaints, despite the fact that the Church (and I suspect most members) would prefer to resolve concerns internally rather than through a mainstream media that has often sensationalized the Church, its members, and its underwear. The short answer, of course, is that there is no effective channel for most members' voices to be heard when working within the Church.[144]

When left with no recourse, Mormon women broke the silence and secrecy around garments in a public way. This marked a significant shift in the power dynamic, but it was unclear how the church would respond.

About a week later, Nancy received an email from someone at the LDS Church's Correlation Research Division asking if she could present some of her research findings on women's experiences with garments to them. She agreed and asked for their specific research questions. Jessica and Nancy presented to the group of researchers, who were receptive and asked many good questions. They promised that they would write up some recommendations and send them up the administrative chain, but they could not guarantee any particular outcome. Jessica and Nancy understood that but hoped that someone with some power would take notice and hear our concerns and recommendations.

There were no apparent changes until recently. In an April 2024 churchwide conference, Annette Dennis, a member of the Relief Society General Presidency, spoke about church members' sacred duty to wear garments. She reiterated the covenant-reminding, protection, and creation story meanings of garments while also introducing new, additional meanings for garments. She indicated that they were symbolic of Jesus's atoning sacrifice and that church members covered themselves with the power of that sacrifice in the act of wearing garments.[145] She justified these interpretations by connecting these new meanings for garments to Hebrew words, giving listeners the sense that wearing garments was part of an ancient Jewish or early Christian practice discussed in scripture. It was unusual for a woman to be speaking about such an important issue usually reserved for male leaders. It does seem as though this particular move was meant to entice women to wear garments, regardless of the issues they experience with them. This talk came with new rules for wearing garments, which asserted that there was no flexibility or personal interpretation allowed when answering temple recommend questions about garments.[146] Predictably, bloggers, TikTokers, podcasters, and social media users took to their platforms to address this latest attempt at control. In 2024, the LDS Church's official *Handbook of Instruction*, for the first time, was updated to allow exceptions for members who have certain medical issues that were exacerbated by garments.[147]

In late 2024, the LDS Church announced new styles of garments, including sleeveless tops, a full slip, and half-slip styles.[148] First considered by church leaders in the 1930s, it took nearly one hundred years for the church to make this design change. These styles were available in some Asian countries right away but not yet available in the United States until later in 2025. Mormon women influencers in the United States found ways to acquire the new garments from other countries and immediately demonstrated the freedom of the new sleeveless styles in TikTok videos.[149] In these videos, the influencers show off sleeveless tops with garments hidden underneath, encouraging women who no longer wear garments to return to the practice.

In the decade since the 2014 survey, the LDS Church has made incremental changes to garment designs and fabrics. New styles have been introduced, including ones meant to be more breathable and comfortable in warm climates. The church has also modified some garment lengths and added more size options. Even with a sleeveless option, these changes have been relatively minor. Such changes may allow garment wearers to have more clothing options, and some will be happy with this. These changes, however, have not fundamentally altered the core requirements of wearing garments day and night or the medical concerns of survey participants, described in chapters 2–5. The basic expectations around when and how to wear garments remain largely unchanged from when this survey was conducted. Although the church has become more willing to publicly acknowledge garments, as evidenced by the 2014 video and Dennis's 2024 conference talk, the practice continues to be surrounded by secrecy, surveillance, and strict behavioral expectations. The survey data from 2014, described in chapters 2–5, remain relevant for understanding the lived experiences of garments and the ways in which this practice shapes belief and behavior in Mormon communities.

One of the challenges of discussing the history and meaning of garments is that this one item of underwear takes on a multitude of meanings. Garments borrowed Masonic symbols. Garments are referenced in two of the main temple ceremonies, the initiatory and the endowment, where they are symbolic of covenants to obey God. Through the endowment ceremony, garments take on a particular role in the creation story, where participants are instructed to think of themselves as Adam or Eve. Garments are a prerequisite for getting married in Mormon temples and going on Mormon missions. Garments have a connection to Mormonism's polygamous past and the Mormon Fundamentalists who still wear garments today. Wearing garments and keeping covenants are a requirement for the best spaces of heaven within Mormon teachings about salvation.[150] Garments are priestly vestments, but women should not ask questions about that. As of April 2024, garments are also a symbol of Jesus's atonement for sin. Worn daily by church members, the interplay between story, meaning, ritual, and bodies remains complicated and multilayered.

CONCLUSION

The history of Mormon garments is complex and multifaceted, shaped by factors such as evolving fashion trends, religious beliefs, and the church's efforts to assimilate into American society. Garments, initially a progressive form of underwear, transformed into a symbol of religious devotion and obedience, carrying multiple meanings related to covenants, protection, modesty, and identity. The tension between adhering to a divinely inspired pattern and adapting to changing societal norms led to modifications in garment design and materials. Ultimately, garments became a tool for the LDS Church to exert control over Mormon bodies and sexual behavior, reflecting a broader effort to align with white Evangelical values to shed the stigma of polygamy.

2
GARMENTS, BELIEF, AND GENDER

Nancy's Story

I was six weeks away from my temple wedding when I started wearing garments. I was glad, at the age of twenty-three, to finally become a full adult in my church community. I believed the things that my church taught, ranging from the more traditional Christian elements to the Mormon particulars. I saw Jesus as my savior from sin, paid for by his blood at his death. I was an obsessive reader of the Book of Mormon and believed that Joseph Smith was ordained by God to restore God's one true church to the world. I could affirm these beliefs and other central tenets of LDS faith during temple recommend interviews that my bishop gave me semiannually as a teenager and annually as an adult. I had to regularly affirm that my faith and practice conformed to institutional norms in order to fully participate in the life of my church.

These beliefs, and the meaning and connections I drew between my beliefs, God, and the afterlife brought tremendous comfort to me. My mother died when I was a teenager, but maintaining a strong faith meant that I could see her in the Celestial Kingdom when I eventually passed away, the part of heaven reserved for the most faithful. I knew that if my faith weakened or changed, I would put that reunion in jeopardy and was determined to be worthy of that privilege.

Believing and practicing Mormonism in the way that I was taught brought me a strong sense of order and safety in a chaotic world. I understood my garments as the tangible evidence of an immanent God in my daily life. My family of origin was fraught, but the strength of my belief would permit God to fix that in the afterlife. After I participated in the initiatory ceremony for the first time, my garments became the constant evidence of that commitment and the strength of my belief. In the language that I use to describe belief in this book, I was a conforming believer because I did not experience doubt.

The challenges of adult life began to change my conforming belief in small ways. I did not like some of the ways in which women were treated in my church. For a long time, I saw these problems as individual ones. Some local leaders misinterpreted church policy and doctrine, corrupting purer teachings handed down by the leaders of the church. I didn't like the overly literal interpretations of scripture that Sunday school teachers presented in the adult class, but I figured that this was down to a lack of education on the part of the teacher and not a larger or more systemic problem in my tradition. In my mind, I understood church teaching as pure but taught in a deeply corrupted way. For a long time, I held such opinions to myself, knowing that others would not share my views.

Eventually, I found others with similar understandings in online communities. We saw church teaching as divinely inspired, but there were so many problems with church culture. This mental separation of divine perfection and church fallibility allowed me and others to hold on to my conforming belief for a while. My knowledge of church history expanded beyond sanitized church narratives and I began to reflect on the ways in which I had experienced harm through teachings I had thought of as godly. As I heard other women in my congregation describe their understanding of heaven and the Celestial Kingdom as one where polygamy was a central practice, I began to wonder if that was a heaven I wanted. My belief shifted as I realized that I was working hard to earn a distant reward I did not desire. The practices that were the evidence of my strong belief no longer felt divinely required. The comfort I felt in my religious certainty diminished. I had experienced some physical discomfort and problems with my garments, but they began to feel spiritually uncomfortable as well. I still participated in and contributed to my local congregation. I taught adult Sunday school classes and tried to make space for differences of opinion. I had become a nonconforming believer even as I continued to live my life and practice my faith in the ways that I always had.

I have been a conforming believer and a nonconforming believer. These two different belief types shaped my worldview in different ways. Conforming belief offered existential comfort in a chaotic world and the reward of feeling closeness to God. I was invested in making choices that aligned with the values my church taught, which I believed would obligate God to smooth the path ahead and reserve a space for me in the best places of the afterlife. My garments represented that covenant, that contract with God. Nonconforming belief brought me a different view. Where conforming belief helped me to feel safety and security in my choices, nonconforming belief revealed to me all of the social and existential pressures I experienced in making those conforming choices. Nonconforming belief did not bring with it the same feelings of safety but instead brought clarity of the church as a system, a new freedom of choice, and an invitation to hold the complexity of other people's choices in a different way. These contrasting lenses of belief have brought me to a deeper awareness of the forces that shape not only faith but also identity.

INTRODUCTION

Belief and gender shape how Mormons understand and experience their garments. The term *belief* describes both the different meanings that church members hold about their garments and the meaning-making frameworks that surround the social experience of garment wearing. On the one hand, belief is a kind of intellectual assent that describes the way in which garments recall narratives about the creation of the world and the afterlife. These narratives *enchant* believers by connecting them to stories that are epic in proportion to ordinary life and lend significant meaning to the mundane.[1] In this way, belief can become an important part of self-conception, "charming us with a reinvigorated sense of ourselves."[2] Garments enchant garment wearers through the promise of divine connection and presence that is achieved in the wearing of sacred underwear.

Belief is also more than intellectual assent to a set of ideas. It is a system that captivates believers, who lose some control over their lives but gain social capital and a shared identity with other believers.[3] Mormons who wear garments give up control of their underwear choices in exchange for status as a community insider, upgraded afterlife experience, and confidence in the eternal nature of their family relationships.

Belief is also about the bodies and embodied experiences of believers. While the church teaches that garments hold a specific meaning, the reality is that garments interface with bodies that produce their own meaning. Gender is an important identity in Mormon teaching, communities, and temple rituals. In the endowment ceremony, all men become Adam and all women become Eve. Garments transfer these gendered stories onto gendered Mormon bodies in a religious context where power is gendered. Belief type and gender are identities that create different kinds of experiences in the bodies of those who wear garments. Conforming believers—those who fully accept church teachings—often find deep spiritual meaning and divine protection in their garments, though women in this group frequently struggle to reconcile doctrinal ideals with physical discomfort. Nonconforming believers—those who question aspects of church teaching—tend to view garments more critically as instruments of institutional control, even as they continue wearing them to maintain family and community relationships. Local church leaders, who are always men, regularly test the belief of members in temple recommend interviews. These interviews examine the intellectual content of beliefs, the expected emotions associated with belief, and the embodied practices that indicate an authentic belief and disciplined life. Church leaders instruct members in *doing* belief in these three ways throughout the lifespan. Within Mormon communities, conforming belief is an identity that carries significant social power, whereas nonconforming belief comes with marginalization. Wearing garments symbolizes that the wearer has the correct kind of belief and can be understood as a loyal community insider. Not wearing garments points to an outsider status. The experiences of garment wearing, then, point to the ways in which social power works within Mormon communities.

INTERSECTIONALITY: BELIEF AND GENDER

Intersectionality is a useful concept in thinking about how identities within the categories of belief and gender relate to social power within Mormon communities. First coined by legal scholar Kimberlé Crenshaw to explain how Black women face both racism *and* sexism in employment, it is a tool for analyzing social inequality that examines the interconnectedness of social categories like race, gender, and sexuality.[4] People with different identities (e.g., race, class, gender, sexual orientation) have different kinds of experi-

ences in society because of the way in which each identity is or is not tied
to power. Sociologist Patricia Hill Collins observed that intersectionality
challenges traditional thinking on inequality, which emphasizes single-
issue analysis, in favor of understanding the complex way in which power
operates in society.[5] Scholar Susan Shaw put it more simply: "Our identities
exist within systems of power."[6]

Scholars Chiung Hwang Chen and Ethan Yorgason observed that scholars of Mormonism rarely make use of intersectionality as a framework for
analysis and offer some ways that it might be useful.[7] The authors made
a number of observations about the internal social hierarchy of Mormon
communities:

> Mormonism is complex and powerful enough to create its own hegemonic
> values, structures of power, and sense of centrality and marginality. Thus,
> in addition to Mormon identity's combining with other social identities,
> intersectionality exists within Mormonism itself. Social centrality and mar-
> ginality within Mormonism share similarities with the American culture
> from which it stems. Whiteness, maleness, Americanness, and married het-
> erosexuality hold particularly privileged positions within its structures of
> culture and authority. Middle-class values, political and social conservatism,
> able-bodiedness, and certain age characteristics at times also position indi-
> viduals more toward the center of Mormon ideology and activity. Latter-day
> Saints who differ from these characteristics can still achieve great meaning,
> value, and social solidarity from their church experiences, but the deviations
> are typically obstacles that must be overcome or barriers preventing full
> participation within social-cultural and authority structures. Strength of
> belief itself—or "testimony" in LDS terminology—can also be regarded as
> an axis of hierarchy centrality.[8]

Using Chen and Yorgason as a starting point, this study adopts the language
of *belief type* to understand different types of belief as granting different
kinds of power in Mormon communities. Belief type, combined with gender,
explains Mormons' experiences with garment wearing.

The LDS Church is a gender-traditional religion that ordains nearly all
men and boys age eleven and older to the priesthood but does not ordain
women. According to sociologist Kelsy Burke, gender-traditional religions

> promote strict gender relationships based on male headship and women's
> submission. These religions tend to emphasize ontological differences be-

tween men and women, noting that men are predisposed to leadership, activity, and a strong work ethic, while women are naturally nurturing, passive, and receptive. Gender-traditional religions promote the belief that men and women were created to fulfill different and complementary roles that tend to privilege the status of men.[9]

The structure of the church is patriarchal, and women's participation in the governing bodies of the church is limited to the *auxiliary* organizations that oversee women, teenage girls, and children. The LDS Church teaches that gender is eternal and that men occupy a divinely appointed role as *presiders*, where women occupy a divinely appointed role as nurturers of children.[10] In this framework, there are only two genders, gender aligns with sex assigned at birth, and only monogamous heterosexual couples can form legitimate families and be sealed for eternity in LDS temples.

In this study, belief type (conforming or nonconforming) and gender (man or woman) determine the range of experiences and interpretations of those experiences that Mormons have with their garments. Gender and belief type, as applied to the garment survey data, reveal the internal power dynamics of Mormon communities and offer insight into lived experience. While the LDS Church attempts to define appropriate Mormon belief and to test it, the experience of belief is more complicated than a set of propositions offered by the LDS Church or any religious organization. When it comes to individual belief or individual theology, scholars Grace Ji-Sun Kim and Susan Shaw note that "we cannot really do theology for others, we can only do theology alongside others."[11] This is because no institution can fully control the whole process of creating and maintaining belief.

The survey only offered the gender options of "man," "woman," and "other." Few survey participants selected "other." This was a limited list that missed an opportunity to understand the experiences of transgender and nonbinary participants. A better list of gender options would have made our dataset richer by highlighting the lived experiences of transgender and nonbinary Mormons. This is an important area for further study.

THE PARTS AND TYPES OF BELIEF

Analysis of the survey data pointed to a model for understanding Mormon belief, though this model may have application with other traditions.

This book uses the language of *parts of belief* and *belief types*. This work describes two different belief types—conforming believers and nonconforming believers—together with three parts of belief—*intellectual content*, *emotions*, and *embodied experiences*.

In the LDS Church, the intellectual belief content of the tradition consists of a set of doctrinal propositions that members assent to. For example, "Joseph Smith was a prophet of God" or "The Book of Mormon is the word of God." To understand the intellectual content of survey responses, the question "What does the church teach about garments?" guided the analysis of open-ended survey responses.

Emotions are an important component of Mormon belief. Church manuals and classes train members to seek divine confirmation of doctrinal propositions through prayer. These confirmations are received as feelings and then interpreted. They are taught that good feelings, or the *burning in the bosom* described in the Doctrine and Covenants (9:8), while praying indicates the truthfulness of the proposition. Likewise, Mormons may interpret bad feelings as evidence of the presence of evil or a lack of truth. Feelings, then, are interpreted as evidence of truth. Once a member of the church has experienced warm feelings about a particular doctrinal proposition, they have a *testimony*, in church parlance, of that proposition. To understand the emotions of survey responses, the question "How do participants feel about that teaching?" directed the analysis of survey responses.

The third part of belief is not dictated or instructed by church teaching, as is the case with the intellectual and emotional parts of belief, but has to do with the embodied experiences of church practice. While these can be an extension of the language of testimony, they can also deviate from that language. Survey respondents described their experiences of wearing garments, together with other embodied experiences in the church community. The question "What do participants' bodies experience with garments?" assisted with the analysis.

BELIEF AND THE TEMPLE RECOMMEND INTERVIEW

The study of belief has a controversial history. Émile Durkheim's research, foundational to the field of sociology, focused on the idea that belief was regulated by religious institutions, while Max Weber's work, also foundational, focused on the meaning making of the individual religious person.[12] These two approaches became two different schools of thought in later generations of researchers, who have not been able to find agreement.[13] Still, religious studies scholar Robert Orsi approached belief from a different viewpoint and reminded his readers that the very idea of religion as belief has long been politically charged.[14] He observed that this Protestant idea was framed against Catholic understandings of the presence of God and the saints held in material objects and used by colonizers to invalidate the religious activities of Indigenous peoples.[15] All three concepts of belief have relevance to this study, with their different focal points on institution, lived experience, and materiality. Church leaders believe that they have the authority to define the meaning of garments and dictate appropriate practices in the wearing of garments. At the same time, individual church members have their own experiences wearing garments and accepting and challenging the church's rules around the practice. Some of those meanings and experiences will align with church messaging, but some will not. The ways in which different kinds of bodies experience garments is a kind of wild card that is not easily controlled by the church. Still, many church members view God as being present with them through their garments, making the wearing or not wearing of garments a significant issue in the community.

The LDS Church presents a unique opportunity to study belief as an intersection of identity and its impact on lived experience. While mainline Protestant churches use early Christian creeds as statements of belief, the Church of Jesus Christ of Latter-day Saints is unusual in that it has its own embedded belief test known as the temple recommend interview.[16] Sunday services and weekly activities are open to all in regular church buildings, but access to temples and temple rituals require special documentation, known as a temple recommend, in order to participate.[17] Many volunteer jobs in local congregations require a temple recommend. Receiving a temple recommend requires passing two interviews with local leaders, who use a standardized list of questions and expect particular answers. In some areas, local church leaders reach out to church members to schedule temple recommend interviews, and in other areas, church members contact church leaders when they wish to renew their temple recommends. While such interviews are not required for participation in Sunday services, they are required for participating in the full life of the church.

Baptism by immersion and confirmation bestows church membership on children and converted adults. A temple recommend allows a church member to participate in temple ceremonies that connect the believer to their living and deceased family members in the afterlife for eternity. Temple ceremonies provide a guarantee, contingent on doing belief in the correct way, of a good place within a stratified afterlife. Like baptism, temple ceremonies are physically active and require participants to use their bodies to navigate activities including sitting, standing, kneeling, engaging in symbolic washing, being anointed with oil, making ritual-particular gestures with hands and arms at prescribed times, veiling and unveiling faces (for women), and speaking. To participate in these ceremonies is to be a fully fledged adult and insider in Mormon congregations.

Temple recommend questions ask about the three parts of belief (intellectual content, expected emotions, embodied practices) by inquiring if the interviewee has a *testimony* of a church tenet and if the interviewee keeps their behavior within the bounds that the church dictates. Having a testimony of a church doctrine has two pieces: agreeing to the religious idea and having positive feelings about that idea. These interviews, then, inquire about all three parts of belief. Temple recommends can be revoked if local leaders become aware of a change in behavior or belief. They used to be valid for one year, but in the 2010s, that was extended to two years.[18]

It is also important to point out that in the LDS Church, the term *testimony* refers not just to a general sense of agreement but also to individuals expressing that they have received a divine witness of the truth of church teachings. A testimony is generally acquired through religious feelings, which are an important way of generating belief. As a Second Great Awakening tradition, religious feelings are important in LDS discourse.[19] Mormons are supposed to acquire a testimony of different beliefs by praying to know that they are true and then experiencing the Holy Ghost's affirmation of those truths through sensations in the body. A member of the LDS Church acquires a testimony of a church teaching by praying and experiencing good feelings, which point to truth, where bad feelings point to untruth. An assumption in this belief process is that a particular action, like praying to know the Book of Mormon is true, will always create the same positive feelings, confirming truth.

Church manuals reference several different scriptures to explain the process of receiving these feelings, including Luke 24:32 and especially Doctrine and Covenants 9:8–9. The latter describes Latter Day Saint movement founder Joseph Smith receiving divine instructions for interpreting feelings to determine religious truth.[20] Joseph, speaking for God, wrote, you must study [the issue] out in your mind; then you must ask [God] if it be right, and if it is right [God] will cause that your bosom shall burn within you; therefore, you shall feel that it is right. But if it be not right you shall have no such feelings, but you shall have a stupor of thought that shall cause you to forget the thing which is wrong. (Doctrine and Covenants 9:8–9)

These verses are foundational to church teaching on understanding and interpreting religious feelings as evidence of divine affirmation. Church members are encouraged to see Joseph Smith's experiences here as a model for their own behavior and interpretation of religious feelings.

The temple recommend questions are standardized by the church handbook and change periodically, but they point to the institutional requirement for LDS people to believe in several different ways, including intellectual agreement, emotional affirmation, and embodied assent. LDS Church president Russell M. Nelson recently gave the updated list of questions in the October 2019 General Conference, the semiannual general meeting of the church.[21] Of the fifteen questions, the first three ask Mormons to affirm a testimony of the Godhead, or a belief in God the Father, Jesus, and the Holy Ghost as three separate entities, Jesus's atonement, and the particulars of Mormon belief summarized in the phrase "restoration of the gospel." People participating in these interviews are expected to give answers of "yes" or "no."

The remaining temple recommend questions ask about expected behaviors, including sexual behavior, the paying of tithing, and the wearing of garments, abstaining from coffee and alcohol, among other things. There is an expectation that conforming to these behaviors and agreeing to church doctrines will *produce* positive feelings of affirmation about these embodied religious practices. These emotional confirmations, understood as divine confirmation of truth, are essential experiences in Mormonism. To pass a temple recommend interview, Mormons must give the correct answer and affirm that they are in agreement on particular doctrinal propositions, experience emotional affirmations of church teachings through embodied experiences, and that their bodies engaged in or abstain from particular behaviors as prescribed by the temple recommend questions.

LDS Church members who can affirm that they hold the right kinds of intellectual, emotional, and embodied belief then possess a temple recommend and are authorized to attend temple ceremonies, including temple sealings (weddings), and hold higher-status *callings*, or volunteer jobs, in their local congregations. Those who do not possess a temple recommend do not have access to these same opportunities. In this way, conforming Mormon belief carries religious and social benefits. Nonconforming belief carries social consequences and costs. These costs can prevent those who do not hold the correct belief from attending family weddings, a father from baptizing his child, and friction in marriages and families. In more extreme cases, those who do not hold the correct belief are treated as if they are no longer part of the eternal family unit.

While this practice of interviewing is one that demands a great deal from members of the church, it also serves as a vehicle for scholarly understanding of the complex nature of belief. It is also important to note that Mormon feminists and other activists have spent considerable time critiquing the practice of interviewing teenagers and adults about their beliefs and behavior, including sexual behavior, which they view as harmful and out of sync with other religious traditions.[22]

MEASURING BELIEF

The survey asked participants questions that were similar to the LDS temple recommend interview questions at the time of taking the survey, which we borrowed from a different study on Mormons.[23] The survey participants responded to belief statements by indicating the degree to which they believed or did not believe the statement on a five-point scale ranging from "I do not believe this" to "I believe this very strongly." In an ordinary temple interview, yes/no answers are expected, but we were interested in degrees of belief.

After receiving the survey responses, Jessica created a belief index for each participant by adding the scores of each of the belief questions.[24] Two relevant categories emerged from these data: those who do not experience doubt and those who do. Scholar Jana Riess also described two broad categories of Mormons with regard to belief—*believers* and *doubters*—though Riess also noted that this language is loaded in a community that prizes a high degree of belief.[25] In our study, *conforming believers* are those who expressed a firm belief in all of the main teachings of the LDS Church. Those who expressed any degree of doubt are *nonconforming believers*. We wanted our language to emphasize that the presence of some doubt did not invalidate all belief. Ultimately, it is the presence of doubt that made the difference in the responses to survey questions. When combined with gender, then, the data divide into four main groups: conforming women, nonconforming women, conforming men, and nonconforming men. An analysis of the garment experiences of each of these four groups reveals the ways in which conforming belief in Mormon communities is understood as a form of social power. While belief is a hidden identity, the practice of garment wearing attempts to make that hidden identity visible to those within the community. Each of these groups understands the meaning of their garments in different ways.

The church's complex history and narrative regarding race highlight the significance of considering the impact of intersectional identities as a variable in personal belief. The majority of the survey respondents identified as white (see the appendix), consistent with Mormon racial demographic statistics in the United States. However, the survey also included smaller samples from various minority groups, including participants who identified as American Indian/Alaska Natives, Asian, Black/African American, Hispanic/Latino, Native Hawaiian/Pacific Islander, and Middle Eastern. As described in chapter 1, the act of wearing garments constitutes an embodied practice that is inextricably linked to church and broader societal narratives about racialized bodies. When exploring the experiences of Mormon men and women, there is a tendency to oversimplify or homogenize the survey population. This "whitewashing" can obscure the diverse experiences of members whose identity includes overlapping social categories like race, gender, class, sexual orientation, or disability. It can also leave whiteness unnamed and uninterrogated. The discussion that follows names the racial identities of survey participants to illustrate the distinct lived experiences and perspectives that arise from varying social locations. This approach underscores the importance of understanding how such social contexts shape individual viewpoints and interactions within Mormonism.

MAKING MEANING OF GARMENTS

The following sections introduce each of the four gender-belief groups, giving some general demographic data and discussion about each group. These sections also highlight the reasons why participants started wearing garments. Following this introductory information, each section will investigate the group responses to the question "What do your garments mean to you?" This question was included in the survey in an attempt to understand the different meanings that Mormons lived with. Conforming women, nonconforming women, conforming men, and nonconforming men all repeated church teaching about garments in their answers, but there were significant differences between each group's responses. Conforming men were the most likely to answer the question "What do your garments mean to you?" by *only* giving institutional answers, and so the discussion will begin with them. For the data analysis section in each chapter, the order of gender-belief groups will be different in order to highlight the range of responses between the four groups and foster comparison. Further demographic information about each gender-belief group is in the appendix.

Conforming Men

Our survey included 481 conforming men. LDS Church leadership, at both the local and international levels, is an extension of this group of conforming men. Only men hold the priesthood, and the church ordains most men and boys from the age of eleven. Church teaching emphasizes that men are made in the image of a male God and given priesthood power because of their masculinity. Scholar Sara Patterson described the church as being particularly concerned, then, with the holders of this priesthood power and the purity of their bodies.[26]

Conforming men relied on LDS Church teachings to supply the content of their beliefs about garments and had positive feelings about those teachings. The survey asked, "What do your garments mean to you?" and conforming men gave a variety of answers, many just a single word. Some of the most common short answers included "sacred," "covenants," "protection," "safety," "promises," and "reminder." All of these words, except for "safety," appear multiple times in the article by Carlos Asay titled "The Temple Garment: 'An Outward Expression of an Inward Commitment,'" which appeared in the *Ensign*, a monthly magazine for LDS adults.[27] Since its publication in 1997, this article has served as the main source for church teaching about garments.

A brief summary of the Asay article appears on the first page and reads, "Through *sacred covenants* with the Lord, we receive *promises* of blessings and *protection*. He has given us a tangible *reminder* of our *covenants*" (emphases ours).[28] This summary gives context to those short survey responses. Of all of our four gender-belief groups, conforming men were the most likely to repeat the language of official church teachings in their answers and to have their understanding and experiences with garments represented in the limited church discourse on garments.

The lengthier responses from conforming men identify the intellectual and emotional parts of belief, which restate church teachings. Conforming men also expand on them in ways that address garments as a multifaceted symbol that references the temple experience and religious identity. One White conforming man wrote,

> [Garments] are a symbol both of the promises I made in the temple and of my membership generally in the Church. I know they are weird to a lot of the outside world, but I take satisfaction in knowing that they are one way God has set us apart from the world. He is making us a kingdom of priests and priestesses in his kingdom, as the scriptures say—they are a symbol and remnant of priestly clothing (of having a special authority and relationship with Him), but they are worn underneath where for the most part only we know we are wearing them.

This respondent identifies his garments as symbols of temple covenants, his religious identity, his specialness to God, and connection to an ancient tradition of priests, all hidden from the rest of the world. While this respondent also referenced garment-wearing Mormon women as "priestesses," only two women participants made similar connections. This respondent acknowledges the *weirdness* of garments but seems to take great pride in viewing his garments as something that makes him feel divinely *chosen*.

For this respondent and for many others, garments hold a layered symbolism that point to multiple meanings. One white conforming man wrote that, to him, garments were "a symbol of the priesthood and covenant I have made." Another Native Hawaiian/Pacific Islander man responded, "They are a symbol of my commitment to follow Jesus Christ." A third white man wrote, "They are a private symbol of who I am and who I want to be."

The Asay article also discussed garments as a symbol. Asay noted that garments were a symbol of the "armor of righteousness" metaphor referenced in the Book of Mormon (2 Nephi 1:23) and by Paul in the New Testament (Ephesians 6:13). Asay also explained that scripture uses the word *garment* to symbolically describe people's moral state of being, where garments are also associated with language such as *white, clean, pure, righteous, modesty, covering holy, priesthood, beautiful, perfection, salvation, undefiled, worthy, white raiment, shield, protection, spotless, blameless, armor, covenants, promises, blessings, respect,* and *eternal life* (emphasis in the article). In his understanding of the garment symbolism, garments take on many meanings having to do with whiteness, purity, and safety.

Asay also indicated that garments were a metaphor for the purity of the human soul. He warned his readers to "remember always that our very salvation depends, symbolically, upon the condition of our garments." In emphasizing the eternal significance of garments as symbol, metaphor, and article of clothing, the distinction between those different kinds of meaning breaks down. The weight of all of these meanings collapses into something quite literal for conforming men. One conforming man wrote, "I take the commandment and the blessings associated with the garment very literally. The garment is a symbol and reminder of sacred covenants I have made with the Lord." The use of literalness and symbolism together reflect the conflation and confusion of the two in the Asay article. Garments become less of a symbol of the idea of holiness and instead transform into an article of clothing that sanctifies the body that wears them. Many survey participants from all four gender-belief groups talk about the symbolism of garments in a way that evokes literalism.

Several conforming men also identified a further layer of meaning by referencing the story of Adam and Eve in the Garden of Eden from Genesis. The LDS temple endowment narrative holds Adam and Eve as central characters in the larger drama of salvation and the language of the endowment encourages all of the male participants to see themselves as Adam and all of the women participants to see themselves as Eve.[29] In explicit language, all participants are encouraged to understand garments as representing the clothing God gave to Adam and Eve after they ate the forbidden fruit. Finding them in a state of naked shame, God gave the couple garments to cover themselves. One white conforming man wrote, "Animal(s) had to be sacrificed for the original garment given to Adam and Eve just as Christ would be sacrificed for each of us." Garments connect wearers to this story, not only during the endowment ceremony but also as part of everyday life.

Conforming men described garments as a marker of their identity. An earlier comment indicated that one conforming man saw his garments as "a symbol . . . of my membership generally in the Church." Later in his explanation, he indicated that his garments were a divine gift that creates a privileged separation from the rest of the world. Another white conforming man wrote, "It is a sacred honor and privilege to wear the holy garment.

The garment constantly reminds me of who I truly am, and what special commitments I have made with my God!" A different white respondent put it more succinctly, noting that that garments are "like choir robes. They remind me that I am on God's team." Asay does not mention the garment as an element of privileged religious identity, but this is how conforming men described their garments.

Conforming men viewed garments as a source of protection. One white conforming man explained, "I believe that they provide spiritual and physical protection. That testimony comes from personal experiences." When Colleen McDannell interviewed thirty Mormons in the Salt Lake City area, she also identified protection as a common theme, though her interviewees mainly described the physical protection of garments.[30] This theme of protection suggests that conforming men live in an environment of fear, even if they were not able to name that. Some conforming men, however, did describe their need for spiritual protection from "temptation," "sin," and "the Adversary," meaning Satan. Other conforming men explained that the spiritual protection of garments manifest as protection specifically from sexual sin. One of the most common feelings associated with wearing garments was that of *safety*. For these garment wearers, the teaching of garments as protection manifests in corresponding feelings of safety while wearing them.

Conforming men have almost uniformly positive feelings about their garments. One white conforming man wrote, "I love what the garment represents, and the sacred symbology it carries. . . . I am absolutely proud of my religion, even if some of its aspects may seem odd to the outside world. It is a sacred honor and privilege to wear the holy garment." In this response, the words *love*, *proud*, *honor*, *privilege*, and *holy* indicate his positive feelings about the garment. In responses identified earlier, other conforming men use terms like *satisfaction*, *honor*, and *privilege* in describing their feelings.

Conforming men wrote about the spiritual element of garments, where their garment wearing informed their understanding of and relationship to God. One white man wrote,

> My garments represent a commitment to charity and Zion, to living according to Christ's standards, and to pursuing God in faith even when I don't understand His purposes or means. Wearing my garments reminds me of God's presence and makes me think of Him as a person (there's no reason clothing should do that, but that's what it means to me!) Even if I do not

understand how the Church sometimes operates- and in particular, how the leaders can be so callous, or why God doesn't cajole them to think about things the way I do (pride!)- my garments speak to a more personal (and now unmediated) relationship with God.

This experience of the garment as a reminder of God's presence, or even as the very presence of God, was a common theme throughout all four gender-belief groups.

Many conforming men connected the wearing of garments with securing a good place in the afterlife. One white conforming man wrote, "They mean I can try again tomorrow, I can be forgiven of my mistakes, I can remember Christ, and my family is eternal." Another white man wrote, "I have made temple covenants and am on the path for exaltation," which references the best kind of afterlife in the highest degree of heaven. A third white man wrote, "Garments remind me that I have made promises to God that both he and I hold sacred. They remind me that the world around me is not all that God has for me." For conforming men, garments referenced promised blessings stemming from temple covenants. In these covenants, faithfulness in life is rewarded with God's promise of a desirable afterlife with their families. Conforming men were able to hold those promises as real through the materiality of their garments.

Occasionally, conforming men offered other kinds of meanings for their garments. For one white conforming man, garments point to a sacred esotericism within the temple ceremonies:

> I am in my 30's, but also my 10th year as an ordinance worker. I work with the live endowments. I teach temple prep, among other callings. I can see immediately who has been prepared- who is familiar with the scriptures and hungers for more- and who isn't. If they haven't paid the price to gather many pieces, the puzzle- which is put together at the Temple- will be hard to discern. The more pieces they have, the more they begin to see the mosaic. I usually can see a pattern in those who complain about garments with other attributes: lack of general gospel knowledge, lack of testimony, lack of Christ-like service, lack of diligence. Often, there is usually a huge dearth in scriptural knowledge. If they knew the scriptures, they would recognize the pattern has existed since the beginning and would be receiving personal revelation on the matter. It usually leaves me heavy-hearted.

This respondent saw his garments as part of a puzzle of meaning that was not easy to construct and only available to the ultra-devout. This answer was the only one of its kind, but it does point to the ways in which secrecy around garments and temple ritual contribute to a sense of mystery and hidden knowledge around these practices. It is only through correct belief and practice that these secrets are revealed to individual conforming believers.

In describing their beliefs about garments, conforming men emphasized the intellectual and emotional parts of belief but generally did not describe embodied experiences of belief. When they did reference embodied experiences with their garments, conforming men described positive experiences. Some conforming men were unsure of what they meant after years of wearing them. Conforming men of color gave answers to this question that are indistinguishable from white men. Conforming men with lower household incomes gave similar answers to those with higher incomes. This group holds significant power in Mormon communities, which prioritize conforming belief and cisgender male bodies. They can be local leaders and international leaders of the church, conducting temple recommend interviews and setting rules around garments and garment teaching. The physical needs and religious preferences of this group become the norms for the whole church. This is consistent with a long history of Christian men belonging to dominant social groups defining God, belief, and religious practice for others with less power.

Conforming Women

Conforming women were the largest group (n = 2,387) in this study. Conforming women constructed their meaning of garments from church teachings (intellectual belief), feelings about those teachings (emotions), and lived experiences of wearing garments (embodied experiences). Conforming women often expressed different feelings and experiences with church teaching and their embodied experiences with garments, making their beliefs about the meaning of garments similar to and different from conforming men.

Conforming women had more complex answers to the question about what their garments meant to them. Common one-word answers from this group included some of the same words that conforming men used, including *sacred, covenants, protection, safety,* and *reminder*. Still, conforming women gave a greater variety of one-word responses, echoed in the Asay article, that also included *shield, temple, sacrifice, symbol, obedience, commitment, expression, willingness, belief, personal, meaning, sign, gospel, representation, respect, devotion,* and *privilege*. Some conforming woman wrote "a lot" in acknowledgment that garments carried *a lot* of meaning. Many of these words connect around themes of safety and obligation.

Conforming women expanded on church teaching by including *safety*, *love*, *tradition*, *willingness*, and *privilege*. The responses from conforming women expand beyond the vocabulary used in the limited church discourse on garments. The words *safety*, *love*, and *willingness* all speak to the feelings that garments generate in some conforming women. These words are significant, as they connect back to a framework of fear (*safety*), connection to God (*love*), and the freedom or agency to choose to wear garments (*willingness*). Like conforming men, some conforming women experience the wearing of garments as a privilege, or a sacred separation from the world.

Conforming women's longer answers suggested that they were doing more to negotiate the meaning of their garments on their own terms, impacted by the experience of wearing garments. For many conforming women, there were two different but simultaneous meanings for garments: one that stemmed from church teaching and the other from the embodied experiences of wearing garments. One white conforming woman wrote,

> [Garments] are sacred to me. I wish I felt comfortable wearing them all the time. I feel that they are a symbol of my commitment to the gospel. I feel that my devotion is something inside of me that God knows even if I'm not wearing them. I hate to see women wearing them with tight revealing clothing, I think that they do not appreciate what they symbolize, yet I envy them for wearing them all the time.

This respondent highlighted the complexity of wearing garments for many women. She began by naming their sacredness but then acknowledged that physical discomfort prevents her from wearing them all of the time, though she wished she could do that and envied women who could. This was a common theme for conforming and nonconforming women. This participant knew that God understood her situation. She also expressed concern over other women wearing garments with tight clothing and judged that this behavior revealed a misunderstanding of the meaning of garments, which she viewed as deeply connected to modesty.

Sacredness, physical discomfort, judgment of others, and modesty are all significant themes, revealing that conforming women's experience with garments is both similar to and different from that of conforming men. For the conforming woman above, her lived experience with the discomfort of garments meant that she adapted the practice to her needs and did not wear them night and day, as instructed. Another white conforming woman discussed her physical discomfort further:

> It felt very right and beautiful to have [garments] given to me in the context of the temple. However, often in real life they are just annoying. There are moments when I think about what they represent that I remember why I wear them and I resign myself to it, haha, but overall because of the way they are made and the materials I often find myself wishing there were a different and better, convenient, or more individualized way [of showing my devotion].

This second respondent affirmed the intellectual and emotional components of belief, as described by the church, but indicated physical discomfort with garments as underwear. This conforming woman also privileged the intellectual content and associated emotions above her embodied experience of garments, which she feels annoyed by. She accepts as necessary the requirement to show her commitment to God in a tangible, physical way.

Other conforming women expressed less physical discomfort and more psychological discomfort with garments. When asked about meaning, one white conforming woman responded, "Mixed feelings. I think it's weird to have marked underwear as a show of devotion. . . . I would rather show my devotion in another way, but I deal with it." Another white woman emphasized the personal cost of wearing garments when she wrote, "I do believe they provide a protection, but at a frustrating cost. I can't remember the exact covenants that the markings mean, so that doesn't seem to be an effective reminder of the temple endowment for me." These two respondents understood garments as an important part of their belief and of demonstrating their belief to others but did not express the good feelings that affirmed the need for garments. This second respondent noted the way in which the specific meaning of her garments and the details of the related covenants were lost in the process of wearing them. While some conforming women understood physical discomfort in terms of a sacrifice to demonstrate devotion to God, others saw garments as a sacrifice where they traded comfort for spiritual benefits like protection.

While the above comments are more mild, some conforming women expressed similar desires and frustrations using stronger language. One white conforming woman wrote, "I want them to mean respect and spiritual reminder of covenants but truthfully, I hate wearing them all the time. They make me hate getting dressed in the morning and hate how I look in the mirror." While using the familiar official language of respect, spirituality, reminder, and covenants, those meanings are aspirational for this conforming woman. Her embodied experiences with garments have meant that she can no longer hold to church teaching in describing her beliefs about garments. Instead, her garments inspire hatred of herself and a hatred of wearing them. Even with such a negative experience, she still expressed a desire to hold a more positive view of garments. Another white conforming woman made a similar comment: "I wish I could wear them comfortably because I love the symbols and reminders of my covenants. I wish I could enjoy wearing them instead of being in a constant battle with sliding, lumpy, hot, uncomfortable ill fitting underwear." Some conforming women wanted their embodied experiences of garments to align with the positive messaging of church teaching but could not make that happen and chose to wear their garments anyway. They sacrificed their body image and comfort to maintain their commitment to wearing them, while holding on to a hope that their lived experience would become something better than it was.

Another white conforming woman expressed a commitment to wearing them, even if she was unsure that God actually required them as a marker of devotion. "[Garments mean] that I am keeping my covenants, on the off chance that it's an essential part of getting to live with my Heavenly Parents. It's almost a 'go wash in the river' scenario. Little, kinda annoying, but not big enough to worry about too much. That said, I'd love a redesign for women!" The respondent references 2 Kings 5:10 and the story of the prophet Elisha telling Naaman to wash in the river to cure Naaman's leprosy. Elisha's advice heals Naaman, but the story is one of a miracle. In referencing this story, this respondent viewed wearing her garments as a sign of *obedience* to God but was also unsure if God really required the wearing of garments. Like others, this respondent felt that garments do not fit her body well. Her response does not exactly reproduce the content of church teaching or a positive emotional experience with garments, but she still continued to wear them.

While drawing on Mormon teachings, other conforming women found more personal meaning in their garments, interpreting their experience through the lens of gender equality. One white conforming woman wrote,

My garments are a reminder to me that even though there is sexism in the church and a huge backlash against women's ordination, God has promised me ordination, and God keeps His promises. It's the garment of the holy priesthood. I was clothed in it as part of the initiatory, where I was anointed to be a priestess. The marks in the garment are a reminder of the endowment, where I wear the robes of the priesthood and am told that I am prepared to officiate in the ordinances of the priesthood.

For this respondent, her embodied experience of garments spoke to an understanding of God and the afterlife from which she drew strength and hope for gender equality in the future. Just two women in the survey understood their garments in this way. But like other survey participants in other groups, this conforming woman saw that wearing garments compelled God to reward her.

A different white conforming woman separated God from the religious identity of garments. She wrote that garments

symbolize a commitment I have made, although right now, I don't necessarily see them as being part of a commitment to God, but perhaps more part of my commitment to being a practicing Mormon. I think they are an important part of how I would like to practice my faith (or at least, I think I would like them to be an important part of my religious practice), but I also recognize that personal meaning can only come from me—and therefore I think wearing garments should be (and would benefit from being) a personal decision between me and God, and less of a cultural expectation.

This participant wished that she saw garments as an important spiritual practice but experienced them as a culturally constructed expectation. For this conforming woman and for others, garments were an identity marker, with some uncertain about whether garments were a divine expectation or a human one. Where conforming men expressed satisfaction with such identity markers and saw them as divinely required and a privilege to wear, conforming women were much less likely to express these things. The cost of wearing garments, particularly in relation to physical and emotional discomfort, was much higher for conforming women than it was for conforming men.

Nonconforming Men

Nonconforming men were the smallest group in this study (n = 436), and many respondents in this group indicated that they were wearing garments as a sacrifice for their beliefs and marital stability. They often identified the value of this sacrifice as securing them a better place in the afterlife. Nonconforming men understood that their garments were a symbol to their wives of their commitment to their marriages, much like a wedding ring, and their church. They were more likely than conforming men to describe the wearing of garments as a sacrifice and express negative feelings about wearing garments and the LDS Church.

Nonconforming men used many of the same words that conforming men and women used to describe the meaning of garments. Some of these words come from the Asay article, including *covenant, protection, reminder, safety, shield,* and *commitment.* A few nonconforming men elaborated on the spiritual protection or spiritual shielding that garments offer them. One mixed-race Black and white man pointed to the positive influence of his garments on his choices when he wrote that they were "a reminder to be good, they've probably saved me from bad things a time or two, just because having them on made me feel guilty about the thought of doing something bad." Another respondent wrote that garments were a "reminder of current weak faith and they remind me to not have an extramarital sexual affair." This idea that garments help to prevent sexual behavior outside of marriage was a theme with nonconforming men and other groups.

While these expected answers appeared in the survey responses, so did many unexpected answers. Nonconforming men also gave one-word or short responses like *oppression, promise, pressured, clothing, ideas, important, control, discomfort, being weird, power,* and *tradition.* Where conforming women identified garments as carrying a lot of meaning, one common response among nonconforming men was *nothing.* Many conforming women experienced a gap between church teaching and their own embodied experience and held different emotions for each of those, but nonconforming men expressed a lot of dissatisfaction with church teaching around garments. Words like *oppression, pressured, control, discomfort, being weird, power,* and *nothing* all point to negative emotions around both church teaching and the experience of wearing garments. Where conforming men expressed that the weirdness of garments helped them to feel that they had been chosen by God, nonconforming men described the weirdness of garments in ways that spoke to an unwanted and awkward obligation. These negative emotions signaled that many nonconforming men experienced a loss of agency with regard to their garments. They feel that they *had* to wear them and that it was not a choice they would make freely.

While many nonconforming men expressed negative emotions and experiences around garments, there were also those whose responses ranged from indifference to holding positive feelings. One white man discussed the meaning of his garments as "not much. They're a nice reminder of certain important ideas in the temple. I appreciate the temple and the symbolism within it." Like this respondent, many nonconforming men began their responses to the question of meaning with words like *nothing* or *not much*. For them, garments do not hold the many symbolic, literal, metaphorical, or storied meanings that they do for conforming men. In the words of one white nonconforming man, garments are "literally just another piece of clothing."

Still, nonconforming men talked about the ways in which garments reminded them of their questions around God's existence. One white man wrote that garments were "a reminder of a power greater than me. While I have my doubts of there even being a God I see the value of believing in a greater power. It helps me to stay humble and encourages belief in a value system that comes from a wiser source." Another white man wrote that garments

> are not magical, they won't protect me from anything. They are a symbol of a choice I've made in my life. While I'm mostly agnostic in my belief in God, I enjoy the Mormon community and social structure (most days), and the garment for me is a symbol of Christ's teachings that I do find good.

Another white man wrote, "I don't know if God is terribly concerned with us wearing them 24/7, but since that's what I covenanted to do, I don't mind." Whereas some nonconforming men hold a lot of resentment about wearing garments, others were able to hold this practice more lightly and with less meaning.

Some nonconforming men indicated that they were once conforming believers. One nonconforming man, who did not indicate his racial identity, wrote that garments were "*an outward manifestation of an inner commitment or a commitment I once made without really knowing everything, but now question*" (emphasis ours). He began his answer by quoting the Asay article but then went on to reframe his decision to get endowed as one that was made without enough information. Another respondent wrote that his garments meant "nothing in particular, I feel that the Church has recently denied most of what I was originally taught about garments (shield and protection is now symbolic rather than real). They are another means of controlling and shaming people." This respondent's sense of shift in meaning is well founded. Colleen McDannell's research on the meaning of garments, published in 1995, suggested that garment wearers saw garments as offering physical protection.[31] This respondent experienced that shift in church messaging as a collapse of meaning.

A common theme in the responses of nonconforming men was *control*, where nonconforming men felt that their church was controlling them by requiring them to wear garments. One man wrote, "The institution of the Church is controlling every aspect of my life that they can, and that they will do everything in their power to maintain that control. Including making my wife and I wear an ugly 18th century underwear in our most intimate times." For this respondent, his garments were a symbol of the ways in which the church controlled so many elements of his life. Garments are the "visible to insiders yet hidden to outsiders" test of belonging. This respondent, and others who commented on control, saw a connection between garments and the many daily expectations of being a believing Mormon and expressed resentment about that control. They understood that the cost of not wearing garments would be ostracism from church and family. These high costs meant that they continued to wear garments even when they did not want to.

The way in which nonconforming men described garments by using the language of control echoed the ways in which French philosopher Michel Foucault described the panopticon, the circular prison described in chapter 1.[32] Some nonconforming men were unhappy with outsourcing underwear decisions to their church and the normalization of this system of social control. As men, they expected to be able to have agency in their lives, and the church intruding in their private lives in this way was upsetting. Foucault describes the main impact a panopticon-like system is "to induce in the inmate a state of conscious and permanent visibility that assures the automatic functioning of power."[33] For many nonconforming men, they were not willing to lose the social capital inherent in being seen without telltale garment lines and they resented this necessity. Some nonconforming men felt imprisoned in this system of control.

Nonconforming Women

Nonconforming women (n = 1,225) had the largest range of responses of any of the four gender-belief groups for all of the open-ended survey questions. Like the respondents in all other groups, nonconforming women described the meaning of garments by invoking the language of *commitment, protection, promise*, and *symbol*. Like nonconforming men, nonconforming women also gave one-word answers that included *control* and *nothing*. Nonconforming women also gave a number of answers that were unique to their group, like *following, community, expression, enforcement, hideous, ugly, secret, ties, membership, underwear, repressive*, and *habit*.

Some responses resisted the multitude of meanings given by conforming men and women, including *underwear, habit*, and *following*. One of the common answers for conforming women was *obedience*, which points to God and the LDS Church as sources of authority to which conforming women defer. Instead, nonconforming women used the word *following*, which suggests a different relationship, pointing to the role of church community norms in their decision to wear garments. Other common answers like *community, enforcement, membership*, and *ties* speak to garments not as a private spiritual practice but rather a group practice that is shared and valued by the community. A number of these words signal strong negative experiences with garments, like *enforcement, hideous, ugly, secret*, and *repressive*. Like conforming men, there was an acknowledgment of the esoteric nature of garments in the word *secret* but without the sacred secrecy that some conforming men indicated.

Whereas conforming men and women saw their garments as part of their religious identity in a pluralistic society, nonconforming women, like nonconforming men, expressed an awareness of the ways in which garments function as an important marker of worthiness within the community. Many nonconforming women understood garments as an outward symbol of conforming to Mormon norms and not reflective of one's relationship to God. One nonconforming woman (race unidentified) wrote, "To me, I guess they are a way to show that I am living the principles of the gospel, but not really as a reminder to myself, but as an outward symbol to others (you can totally see a G[arment] line through most any clothes)." Another white nonconforming woman offered further comments on the dynamics of Mormon communities with the following: "They represent that the church is a patriarchy and that obviously it is men who are making the decisions regarding our underwear because no woman in her right mind would design such ill fitting clothing so unsuitable to the female form." Responses like these, together with responses that used the language of *control*, *enforcement*, and *repression* all point to some nonconforming women understanding garments as representing the power that the LDS Church has over Mormon bodies, an extension of Foucault's panopticon.

Still, not all nonconforming women agreed with this. Some nonconforming women claimed meanings for their garments that more closely align with conforming men and women. One nonconforming woman, who did not identify her race, wrote,

> I find the garments to be an extremely meaningful symbol of my temple experience. They mark me as someone who has had the privilege of receiving an endowment, and as such are a powerful reminder of God's grace in my life and the commitments to which I wish to be faithful. I also find gorgeous spiritual power in the idea of passing through the veil and then going forth into the world wrapped in that same cloth, bearing the same symbols.

This nonconforming woman indicated that garments serve as a positive reminder of her temple experiences, the veil in the temple endowment, signifying the doorway to heaven, and divine grace. She had solidly positive feelings about the role that garments played in her life, consistent with the experiences of conforming women.

Both conforming and nonconforming women held multiple, sometimes conflicting, meanings and feelings about their garments. One nonconforming woman indicated that garments reminded her of the temple, a positive association, but also served as a form of control, a negative association. This nonconforming women (race unidentified) wrote that garments were

> a reminder of the temple that I have with me always. A way to remind me that my body is also a temple. They also feel like a form of control at times (eg. I don't understand why they must have sleeves . . . plenty of modest clothing is sleeveless). I wish I could choose my own underwear very much, though.

Here, she invoked the problem of feeling controlled and unable to make her own choices about her underwear, common in nonconforming men's responses. This points to the ways in which nonconforming men and women sometimes experience garments as Foucault's panopticon, where their garment-wearing status is continually on display to others. They would like to make different choices, but they cannot.

Nonconforming women were the group most likely to identify negative embodied experiences with their garments. One nonconforming woman, who did not identify her race, wrote that her garments meant "negativity. At this point I only have negative associations with garments. They mean being uncomfortable in clothes and with my own skin." A white woman in her fifties wrote that garments "used to make me feel protected. Now, I can't believe I wore such hideous, uncomfortable crap under my clothes for so many years. They are simply an outward sign of the church's duplicity." For this respondent and many others in this group, the meaning of garments has changed throughout their lives, and one of the meanings they signify is a loss of trust in the LDS Church. For these nonconforming women, part of the cost of wearing garments has been a loss of belief.

For nonconforming women discussing the meaning of garments, the loss of trust that they described is often directed at the LDS Church instead of at God. This separation of God and church is common among nonconforming men and women. One white nonconforming woman discussed her loss of trust in detail and the extreme feelings she had about garments, even as she continued to wear them. She wrote,

They used to mean everything to me. They meant I was worthy and righteous and doing what I should. Despite my physical discomfort, I convinced myself that they were comfortable and made up a portion of my identity. Now, they symbolize a prison to me. I hate wearing them. I hate that the culture [of the church] is so attached to them and places so much value on them. I hate that they cost so much, even for people who can't afford them. I hate that the church has a monopoly on producing them. I hate that they are not suitable for warm weather, even if the people making decisions about them think they are. I hate that they make me afraid to be authentic because I know some people will notice if I don't wear them and think poorly of me because that is what I used to do. I hate how they affect my health. I hate that the church thinks it needs to control people's underwear and feels okay asking questions in interviews about how people wear their underwear. I hate that they have Masonic symbols in them. Literally the only thing I like about them is they protect my inner thighs from chafing while wearing a skirt. Other than that, I hate them.

This respondent described the fluidity of her belief, having been a conforming believer and becoming a nonconforming believer, and describing her garments with those attendant meanings. In her embodied experience with garments and in the church, her belief type changed from conforming to nonconforming. For this respondent, garments were Foucault's panopticon, and she engaged imagery of a prison directly: garments were a prison that incarcerated her body. They were a prison that held her in her place in the church community. She hated them and did not feel empowered to take them off because of the high social cost. She described a loss of personal agency in making her own choices about her clothing.

CONCLUSION

For conforming men, the meaning of garments was straightforward. Garments were a reminder of sacred commitments made to God in a holy space, a source of divine protection, a symbol of identity and relationships, a reminder of the promise of a good afterlife. They framed their garments as good and as an extension of positive feelings and experiences about their connection to God and the institution of the church. They did not generally reference specific experiences with their garments or reflect on how specific experiences helped to shape their belief. Their belief framework brought meaning to their garments and a powerful sense of being special or chosen by God. This gave conforming men a strong sense of their power or agency to make good choices, and their bodies did not get in the way of these meaning-making processes. As high-status individuals in their church community, due to gender and belief type, conforming men did not see themselves as paying a personal cost to wear garments but typically expressed a number of benefits to doing so.

Conforming women identified a greater range of answers on the meaning of garments. These responses ranged from neutral restatements of church teaching to the expression of positive emotions like *love*. This group also had challenging embodied experiences with their garments stemming from different kinds of discomfort. Many conforming women expressed some degree of frustration for the gap between meaning, as determined by the church, and personal experience of wearing garments. Whether naming *sacrifice* directly or indirectly, many conforming women viewed the wearing of garments through this lens. Conforming women wanted to have good feelings about garments but often struggled to align intellectual, emotional, and embodied beliefs in this way.

Nonconforming men were more likely to describe their garments as underwear, to express doubt about garments as a divine requirement, and to express negative feelings about their garments. For many in this group, garments are part of the cost of remaining in their marriages, family, and in their church community. Some believed that their church was trying to control their bodies and behavior and that garments were a symbol of that control. Still, some nonconforming men understood their garments as a source of spiritual protection and inspiration for making good choices.

Some nonconforming women, like nonconforming men, indicated that their belief used to be of a more conforming type. Nonconforming women identified a range of meanings for their garments and sometimes conflicting meanings, like conforming women. They described physical and emotional discomforts, and the social cost of not wearing garments. Nonconforming women lamented the loss of their agency and the ways in which garments served as a mechanism of surveillance and social control in their communities.

Conforming believers were more likely to see their decision to wear garments as one that had a positive impact on their lives, regardless of the personal cost. Conforming believers discussed the ways in which garments prevent sin and specifically sexual sin. Nonconforming believers were more likely to understand the requirement to wear garments as a system of surveillance and control, similar to Foucault's panopticon, that kept them part of their communities and families but contributed to a lack of trust in the church and left them feeling a loss of agency in their personal choices.

3
SECRECY AND SACREDNESS

Jessica's Story

I was a nineteen-year-old student at LDS Church-owned BYU when I married my husband, who was also a BYU student. After our wedding, we lived in student housing designated for married couples, and I soon became pregnant. I was new to wearing garments, but my changing body made it more challenging. My garment bottoms were high waisted, and I struggled to keep the itchy elastic up over my growing belly. My new underwear covered so much more of my body and made me overheat regularly, further compounded by the additional body heat I experienced during pregnancy. I struggled to wear garments and feel comfortable during pregnancy.

Once she was born, nursing my baby was even harder. I was frustrated that my daughter struggled to latch on to my breast, and the extra layers were difficult to keep out of the way during feedings. My nipples began to bleed from poor latching and I had to hold a plastic nipple shield in place in order to feed my baby and for the skin to heal. On top of that, the sensation of breastfeeding was painful to me. I experienced overwhelming frustration with every feeding, which happened about every two hours for the first four months. My frustration soon turned into feelings of being defeated. The requirement to wear garments day and night felt like an additional burden to address during each stressful feeding.

*My church community expected and celebrated my marriage, the preg-
nancy that followed, and the maternal act of nursing my baby, but garments
added difficulty to all of these life events. It was a challenge that I had not
heard discussed before and I felt isolated, thinking that I must be the problem.
I did not feel like I had the power to modify my garment-wearing practice in
any way. I was obligated to wear them even when they caused me physical
irritation almost constantly.*

*My apartment building at that time was full of women who were at a
similar stage of life. We watched our children play on the local playground
and talked about motherhood. Occasionally, someone would complain about
their garments. The most common complaints were about the difficulty of
breastfeeding while wearing garments or managing menstruation. It was
the first time I heard someone name my challenges. I felt tremendous relief. We
all agreed that the additional layer on top made breastfeeding more difficult
and that contemporary sanitary pads were designed to work with brief-style
underwear, where the gusset hugged the body. The lack of structure around
the garment crotch and the long legs of garments made it difficult to keep
menstrual and postpartum products in place, resulting in leaks that stained
my garments red with blood. Official church messaging emphasized keeping
garments clean, white, and free of bodily fluids. The difficulty in doing this
while menstruating and dealing with bleeding after birth often made me
feel like I was failing morally.*

*In these rare playground conversations about garments, someone typically
suggested an adaptation where the woman experiencing the problem might
wear regular underwear under garments to provide better support for pads
or wear a bra under garments, instead of over them, for ease of access or to
hold breastfeeding pads in place. Without exception, another friend would
chime in to note that such adaptations were morally unacceptable and that
the discussion was an inappropriate one, ending the conversation. This final declaration always seemed to be the correct answer, even as most of the
participants in these conversations wanted a different answer. I felt like it
was never acceptable to make a change in the way I wore garments, that I
would be committing a serious sin if I did. I knew that to answer the temple
recommend questions about wearing garments, I had to be rigid and set my
anxieties and physical discomfort aside, even though there was technically
some flexibility in the rules that allowed for personal accommodation.[1] It
felt crushing to my sense of autonomy. But to keep wearing garments, I had*

*to turn off the critical voice in my mind that raised those concerns. I needed
to see my frustrations with garments and my period, pregnancy, and nursing as my individual problems that caused feelings of shame. Talking about
them in a group opened up the idea that these problems were not just mine
but that they were systemic. My good feelings about my church community
suddenly felt complicated in my body, but my belief continued to shape my
behavior, providing a restraint against making my own choices.*

INTRODUCTION

Secrecy and silence shape how Mormons experience their garments. Within
Mormon communities, garments are simultaneously hidden from outsiders
yet visible to fellow members because of their familiar clothing lines. The
requirement to wear garments, the visibility of their lines, and the understanding that garments serve as a shorthand for doing Mormon belief in the
correct ways, create a complex dynamic of shared identity and surveillance.
While garments are rarely discussed openly, they remain a central religious
practice that enables Mormons to pursue both assimilation with mainstream Christianity and maintain their distinctive beliefs. Many women
struggle silently with physical discomfort, health issues, and challenges
during pregnancy, nursing, menopause, and illnesses. Some find community
in breaking this silence, while others fear judgment for questioning this
sacred practice. Men's experiences vary based on their type of belief, with
many feeling pressure to wear garments despite their doubts. Whereas
nonconforming believers understand this secrecy as secrecy, conforming
believers typically understand this religious secrecy as a kind of sacredness.
These different experiences with secrecy reveal the power dynamics that
shape Mormon identity, relationships, and daily religious practice.

GARMENTS AND SECRECY IN THE SCHOLARSHIP

The secrecy around garments is an extension of the secrecy around Mormon
temples and their ceremonies. Receiving and referencing garments are part
of these and serve as an extension of these rituals in daily life. As such,
the taboo on speaking and writing about temples is broadly understood
to cover garments as well. Church leaders have, in the past, described this
expectation of secrecy as a kind of special sacredness. The language around

power and control is often obscured, from the viewpoint of church members, through the use of positive euphemisms that invoke ideas of sanctity.

In 1972, LDS Church president David O. McKay wrote an explanation of temples for adult church members where he stated that "the temple is sacred, not secret."[2] At that time, and up until 1990, the endowment ceremony included penalties that detailed the ways in which church members agreed to accept execution if they shared the endowment's details, described in chapter 1.[3] Long after the penalties were removed from the ritual, church leaders have held on to the language of *sacred, not secret* in reference to the temple.[4] Many online Mormon communities have discussed this, with justifications and critiques of McKay's separation of sacred and secret. LDS Church leader (later president) Gordon B. Hinckley said in a church-wide conference in 1990 that "we are under obligation, binding and serious, to not use temple language or speak of temple matters outside."[5] This meaning of this kind of sacredness is always described in direct or indirect terms that speak to secrecy.

Colleen McDannell, a non-Mormon scholar of Mormonism, commented on the issue of religious secrecy after her 1990 conference presentation on garments was described by LDS Church leaders as "offensive" in a statement to the media.[6] She paired the words *sacred* and *secret* in her defense of her academic work, stating,

> To begin with, I acknowledge that I already presume a connection between the sacred and the secret by coupling the terms. Some LDS authorities would deny this connection. Nowhere in the *Deseret News* statement, nor in other aspects of LDS culture, are Mormons told that they should not talk about certain things because they are secret. Instead, matters are not discussed because they are "private," "confidential," or "sacred." However, most of us assume that when we are told not to discuss something it means we are asked to keep it secret, and while we may not understand exactly what the sacred is, we know from everyday life what secrets are.[7]

McDannell saw the ways in which church leaders used the language of sacredness, which recalled a kind of holy mystery, to communicate ideas about secrecy that made secrecy more palatable to church members.

Few Mormon studies scholars have crossed this line. Religious studies professor John Charles Duffy, a former Mormon, wrote about ritual nudity in the early initiatory ceremony. He discussed his choice to refrain from commenting on explicitly forbidden parts of sacred ceremonies but saw other parts as open to study.[8] Mormon scholar Christopher Blythe disagreed with Duffy's choice, describing it as one that inflicted "violence," going on to claim that "the vast majority of endowed Latter-day Saints feel attacked and disrespected when someone divulges what they believe should be held in . . . sacred silence."[9] Blythe did not support this claim with data but went on to insist that scholars should not discuss more than church leaders have said in public, that temple ceremonies are "an internal matter, not for scholars to resolve."[10] Such charges against former members' scholarly work reveal the power associated with belief to exclude the historical work of folks who no longer hold conforming belief, particularly when those scholars are addressing potentially embarrassing elements of church history. Secrecy is then part of a larger strategy to resist the pressure to change.[11] Secrecy around temple ceremonies has helped the LDS Church pursue projects of assimilation with white American Protestants in public while maintaining many distinctive beliefs and practices within its communities.

Foucault's panopticon, where unseen surveillance fosters self-discipline, offers a lens for understanding Mormon garments.[12] Garment lines, visible to community insiders but hidden to others, establish a system of internal and external surveillance. Survey responses indicate that fear of judgment is a key motivator for wearing them. Rosemary Avance argues that this practice internalizes church teaching, leading to self-policing.[13] Consequently, the secrecy surrounding garments, coupled with their visibility within the community, creates a powerful mechanism of institutional control over Mormon bodies.[14]

Blythe's concern for respecting Mormon sacred practices is understandable. There is a long history of outside groups mocking temple ceremonies and the practice of garment wearing. But Duffy's work did not mock nor did it reveal anything that was explicitly secret. For this book, we chose not to include illustrations of garments because we did not want church members to perceive our work as mocking something they hold sacred. Nor did we reveal anything in the temple ceremonies that participants are specifically charged with keeping secret. Instead, we are trying to show how secrecy operates in the lives of church members who wear garments. The suffering documented in our survey data—including medical issues, marital tensions, sexual challenges, and spiritual struggles—cannot be dismissed as merely "internal matters" where there are no clear mechanisms for addressing garment challenges with the institutional church. These are the difficult and interesting problems of living out lives of Mormon belief in a world that does not understand that belief and where there is little understanding of different garment experiences within the church community.

The lived experiences of garment wearers reveal the power dynamics at work within Mormon communities that privilege gender and belief, together with other identities, while silencing difficult experiences under the guise of *sacred, not secret*, at once ignoring and sanctifying personal suffering around the issue. Limiting scholarly discussion to what the LDS Church leaders have publicly addressed would effectively silence the voices of those who bear the heavier burdens in wearing garments, particularly women and nonconforming members. All of this strays into the territory of the uncomfortable, but none of it violates the sacred boundaries that are explicit in the endowment ceremony. Still, we acknowledge that some church members and readers may still feel that this book crosses into forbidden territory.

LIVED EXPERIENCE AND EMBODIMENT

One of the biggest secrets that the survey revealed was the way in which church teaching about garments did not always align with lived experiences of garments for many survey participants. *Lived religion* is an approach to religious studies that prioritizes the meaning making of ordinary religious people instead of religious institutions.[15] So much of Mormon studies emphasizes the institution of the LDS Church as the object of study, but Mormon studies scholar Tona Hangen observed that while the church "exerts strong pressure on its members to conform within a very narrow range of well-defined behaviors and perspectives, there is an unexpected plurality and dynamism in the way believers practice Mormonism."[16] Often, secrecy and silence hide this plurality from church members and outsiders, making the experience of Mormonism appear more unified than it really is.

The LDS Church relied on the lived experiences of Joseph Smith, together with the experiences of later male church leaders, in forming church doctrines and practices. For example, Joseph Smith encountered God the Father, Jesus, and the Holy Spirit as distinct entities, and so Mormons do not hold a trinitarian model of God but instead embrace a *godhead*. In this way, Joseph Smith's personal, lived experiences of God determined many elements of LDS teaching that are still embraced today. The foundational assumption in this belief-forming process is that a particular action will always create the same result. What worked for Joseph Smith, with all of his identities and nineteenth-century context, will work for all people in all places. The LDS Church expects, then, that the doctrines it teaches will be absorbed by its members.

Scholars Grace Ji-Sun Kim and Susan M. Shaw observed that women's lived experiences in many religious institutions were often downgraded or dismissed as memoir, whereas men's lived experiences and insights carried the weight of authority and often became part of institutional theologies.[17] Intersectional approaches, they argued, invited stories of the lived experiences of people from different social locations, while also inviting the kind of systems analysis that produces those different kinds of experiences.[18] Different bodies produce different embodied beliefs because these bodies exist within a religious framework where identity takes on a lot of meaning. Garments, then, are experienced by many different kinds of bodies whose identities take on meaning and exist within systems of power. Hangen noted that garments represent beliefs that are not gendered but are worn by bodies that are gendered.[19] Carol Cornwall Madsen observed that garments are received in a temple ceremony that is segregated by gender.[20] Gender, together with belief, matter in Mormons' lived experiences with garments. Other kinds of identities also matter, but the data emphasized these two identities as being particularly meaningful.

Scholars who have used lived religion as a framework have typically focused exclusively on the experiences of underrepresented identities within underrepresented groups. Nazneen Kane, whose recent research focused on interviews of Mormon women, identified significant limitations to this approach.[21] Drawing on the insights of intersectionality scholar Patricia Hill Collins, Kane observed that a focus on women's lived experiences *only* did not engage the systems of power at work in institutions and communities that work to prioritize the needs of some identities over others.[22] This project seeks to understand the structural piece by analyzing the experiences of four different social locations within Mormonism, using a framework that included both gender and belief.

Embodiment, an extension of the lived religion framework, understands the human body as an active site of knowing, where sensory experiences yield new information.[23] This perspective directly challenges prior scholarly work that emphasized the objectivity of the researcher and the rationality of the mind, often marginalizing the body. Sociologists critique this mind-body dualism through *carnal sociology*, while feminist scholars refer to *embodied epistemologies* to foreground bodily ways of knowing.[24]

Contrary to an LDS understanding that prioritizes the intellect and emotions in belief formation, neglecting the body's active role, scholars Jon P. Mitchell and Hildi J. Mitchell posit the "experiencing body" as the primary site for acquiring religious knowledge and forming belief.[25] They highlight an important point: Institutions like the LDS Church may establish the intellectual content for belief, expect that content to produce good feelings, and set behavioral expectations for members' bodies, but they cannot fully control the experiences and meanings individuals ascribe to these practices. The wearing of garments demonstrates this disconnect, as it can be experienced as a privilege, a burden, and both at the same time.[26]

SURVEY SECRETS

The secrets that participants shared with us ranged from the banal to the terrible. We had assumed that men's experiences with their garments would not be particularly noteworthy, as garments are largely designed to resemble men's secular underwear and accommodate men's underwear needs. But our assumptions here were wrong. The institutional and community expectation of secrecy (keeping garments out of the view of outsiders) and silence (refraining from discussing this practice with other church members) created a burden that different gender and belief groups experienced in different ways. While scholar Christopher Blythe described this as a "sacred silence," Mormon bodies pay different kinds of costs for this silence according to their social location.[27] This chapter highlights the roles of gender and belief type in the lived experiences around garments, silence, and secrecy.

At the end of 2013 and beginning of 2014, Nancy and Jessica were planning a study on garments. Both involved with church at that time, we were garments wearers who held temple recommends. We had our own experiences of physical discomfort with garments and also a growing sense that the itchiness of garments was also irritating our emotional and spiritual lives. We had observed a number of online conversations in the private spaces of Facebook groups where women broke the taboo on speaking about garments. They asked questions about navigating garment wearing during lactation, pregnancy, and menstruation. Women asked for advice about the best fabrics for different weather conditions or the limitations of different garment styles. Such conversations about garments often ran into hundreds of comments, longer than many other kinds of conversations in those spaces. Unlike the in-person conversations that Jessica experienced, no one tried to shut down those online conversations with charges of impropriety. We wanted to see if others beyond our Mormon feminist Facebook groups experienced these same things.

While some researchers had advised us to collect garment data through interviews, we felt that the anonymity of an online survey would allow people to share things they might not share in person. Our survey was wildly popular, and part of that we attribute to people wanting to share their garment secrets with anonymity. They confided their secrets, their personal experiences, with us as fellow Mormons who wanted to better understand this central spiritual practice.

Secrecy is essential to the larger narrative about Mormons and garments. Garments are rarely a topic of open discussion in LDS communities but are a central religious practice. Secrecy allows Mormons to work on dual projects of assimilation with white Evangelical Protestants while at the same time emphasizing denominational distinctives in church curricula. Secrecy allows these two projects to coexist. In the previous chapter, belief was related to how Mormons make meaning of their garments, but the framing of secrecy reveals how Mormons hold beliefs and practices in community and in tension with broader society. Garment wearing is hidden from outsiders, as garments are underwear, but garment lines (like underwear lines) are visible to church community members. In this way, garments are a kind of shared secret identity. In the LDS Church, secrecy is a value that is signaled through the language of the *sacred*.

Jessica's story highlights the ways in which the challenges that women experience with garments and their bodies are often held as private, isolating secrets that may be met with silence and judgment when they share their experiences. Such difficult embodied experiences impacted the belief of many respondents. Many of these themes emerged from the survey question "How does wearing garments make you feel?" Likewise, in answering the question "Why do you wear garments?" many respondents wrote about the ways in which they wore garments to maintain relationships with spouses, parents, and other family and community members and to hold on to social capital in a church community that prioritizes conforming behavior. In answering the question "What do you do when you hear others complain about wearing garments?" speaks to the social costs of breaking this secrecy, this silence around garment wearing.

That different Mormon bodies produce different experiences with garments was highlighted in a 2021 *New York Times* article, described in chapter 1. The article described the ways in which one Mormon woman tried to bring her concerns around garment fit, menstruation, and gynecological health problems to church leaders, who are all men.

> When a church designer finally agreed to meet with [Southam Parker] last year, she showed him 34 PowerPoint slides that explained the garments' many problems for women. The initial result was disheartening, although she was encouraged recently when the church's design team asked her for more feedback. "You're talking about pads and gore," she recalled the man responding at first. The implication was that such earthy topics were inappropriate for discussions of sacred matters.[28]

Society at large also resists discussions of bodily functions and health-related topics in public, but the understanding of garments as *sacred* underwear requiring a *sacred* silence magnifies the problem for some women. For Mormons who menstruate, "pads and gore" *are* part of navigating the spiritual practice of wearing garments. Navigating garments through pregnancy, childbirth, and breastfeeding are also part of Mormon life for many women, together with working through other issues related to health and especially gynecological health. For Mormons who are dealing with pain, body changes, and human reproduction, the gore of the body and the spiritual practice of garments are not separate issues. Secrecy and silence around garments and garment wearing allow male church leaders to remain disconnected from these realities and make it difficult for women to seek help in navigating garment wearing, creating feelings of isolation and disconnection from God and community.

Such issues came up repeatedly in our survey data. Bodies are not a minor issue with garments; they are a central issue. Embodied experiences impact belief, with positive experiences supporting conforming belief and negative experiences challenging conforming belief. This is in line with how Mormons are taught to interpret feelings. Whereas some bodies can easily accept church teaching around garments, many bodies struggle with this.

Bodies are a particularly disruptive force in belief, as embodied experiences with garments generate experiences and meanings outside of institutional control. Different bodies also pay different costs to wear garments, and these costs are particularly hidden from conforming men, who are the decision-makers and gatekeepers in church communities.

Finding information on how race influences the wearing of garments is challenging. The church has a deeply racialized history, particularly concerning Native groups and those of African descent, yet this topic is seldom discussed in church or social contexts. Initiating conversations about race can be particularly difficult in predominantly white spaces, where leadership often emphasizes that the only identity that truly matters is being a *child of God*. Additionally, the culture of secrecy prevalent in Mormonism may contribute to the obscuring of past actions and policies. In online spaces that offer anonymity, Mormon women of color have shed light on a distinctive aspect of wearing garments in relation to darker skin tones. The high contrast between the white fabric and melanated skin makes it more challenging to keep garments concealed. When clothing exhibits any degree of sheerness—something common in many men's and women's shirts—garments are more visible against darker skin than against lighter skin. This seemingly minor issue illustrates how different bodies carry the burden of secrecy in varied ways. People of color often have less access to the community acceptance associated with adherence to Mormon cultural guidelines, such as the need to keep garments hidden. People of color were underrepresented in our survey and this is an important area for future research.

HOW DOES WEARING GARMENTS MAKE YOU FEEL?

In the survey, we asked all participants the following questions: "How comfortable are you when you wear your garments?"; "How does wearing garments make you feel?"; and "How does not wearing garments make you feel?" Women respondents answered additional questions about menstruation, pregnancy, and nursing. Survey questions did not ask specific questions about medical issues, but about two hundred conforming and nonconforming women identified medical problems related to wearing garments, but just one man reported a medical concern. A culture of secrecy and silence around the lived experiences of garment wearing keeps garment decision-makers (conforming men) at the local and general levels ignorant and distant from what people experience with their garments. This ignorance, together with the social cost of complaining, is a burden for those who struggle with wearing garments. At a community level, an individual's struggle with garments is often framed as a personal failure to maintain conforming belief.

Conforming Women

The survey asked participants "How comfortable are you when you wear your garments?" and asked them to rate that comfort on a five-point scale from "Not at all comfortable" (1) to "Very comfortable" (5). Only 58 percent of conforming women gave a "4" or a "5" response. This is a majority of this group, but 43 percent indicated that they had a neutral or uncomfortable experience wearing garments. This is significant for items of clothing that the LDS Church expects people to wear continually, day and night. The survey asked if women wore regular underwear during their periods to help manage menstrual pads or liners. Nearly half of conforming women said yes.

In digging deeper into this question of comfort, the survey asked, "How does wearing garments make you feel?" This question proved to be an important one. For some conforming women, wearing garments was a positive experience. One white conforming woman in her fifties wrote, "I love them; can't imagine not wearing them. They make me feel whole. Also, I find them to be very comfortable and minimize chafing from a bra or waistband." This woman likely wore her garments under her bra and may have tucked the top into the bottoms, a typical practice. Another white conforming woman in her thirties wrote, "Wearing them is like my second skin." For these conforming women, garments maintained positive meanings through positive embodied experiences. Women who experienced a high level of comfort did not often answer the open-ended question about how garments made them feel.

Conforming women who had lower comfort scores were more likely to answer this question. Some conforming women made distinctions between the different kinds of comfort and discomfort that they felt with their garments. They separated the physical discomfort of garments from other kinds of comfort. One mixed-race Native American and white woman in her thirties wrote, "Emotionally I feel safe. Physically I'm a little uncomfortable because of the fit. They don't feel like they were made for my body." While this woman did not detail the specific issues around fit, a white young adult woman explained further:

I feel good when I wear them, but I'm not sure why that is. I also really like not having any underwear lines, which is a plus. After about 2 weeks into my mission in the Philippines, I developed rashes on my backside that ended up lasting my entire mission. I felt like it was due to the lack of airflow to those parts as well as how much heat was being held in because of the garments. That was probably the most negative experience I've had with garments. I was so frustrated because I couldn't do anything about it- I had to keep wearing them.

Her role as a full-time missionary required her to wear garments. She did not believe that she had the option to take them off, even as they were impacting her health. Garments made her feel both good and frustrated, rashy and unable to make different underwear choices. She kept her commitment to wear garments, which returned positive feelings to her, but she also suffered physically because of them.

Some conforming women gave responses to this question that spoke to difficult garment-wearing experiences. A white woman in her thirties wrote that garments made her feel "Frumpy. Claustrophobic. Hot. Like I can't breathe properly. When I first got them they were a reminder [of covenants]. Now they are a hair shirt." This woman was not the only one to describe garments as a hair shirt, an intentionally rough item of clothing worn by religious ascetics to induce physical suffering as a sign of devotion. Institutional messaging around garments does not frame them as causing intentional suffering, but this conforming woman described her experience of suffering within an understanding of physical suffering as an unwanted spiritual practice. Another white woman wrote that garments made her feel

like my body belongs to the men of the church, not myself. I feel hideous, frumpy and ugly in them. They are so uncomfortable and I spend all my time and energy making sure they stay in place. I feel so frustrated and saddened that I resent them so much when they are supposed to be a spiritual help. I also have constant yeast infections during the hot summer months. I have been advised by doctors not to wear them in the summer.

Another white woman wrote,

I hate wearing garments. I despise them. I feel angry and resentful towards the church when I wear them, even when I think about them. They make my life as a woman miserable. They are terribly designed for women's bodies and especially for women's bodily functions (gestation, lactation, menstruation, etc.). They are itchy and hot and uncomfortable. I feel frumpy and unattractive in my garments. I also have problems with recurrent yeast infection and bacterial vaginosis due to garments.

All three of these women referenced garments as "frumpy," indicating that they viewed garments as old fashioned and unflattering. Chapter 1 demonstrated that garments have not kept pace with women's underwear designs but are, rather, more in line with men's underwear trends. As such, these women experienced difficulty moving through different stages of life, including pregnancy, lactation, and menstruation while wearing underwear not specifically designed to facilitate ease with those bodily functions. While breastfeeding, menstruation, and pregnancy have traditionally been taboo topics in American culture, they become additional obstacles to wearing garments, and thereby fulfilling religious obligations, in Mormon communities.

These conforming women described medical conditions, like bacterial vaginosis and yeast infections, that their doctors attributed to garment wearing, with recommendations to adjust garment wearing to their physical needs. Still, these women did not see adjusting garment wearing as a good option for them, with high social costs for not wearing them. Scholar Jana Riess observed that women tended to embrace a more conservative approach to the requirement to wear garments than men but were also more understanding than men of not wearing garments due to medical issues.[29] Women reported other common medical issues included urinary tract infections (UTIs), skin rashes, and overheating. Beyond these common problems, conforming women reported an extensive list of medical problems related to their garments. Many were left to figure out garment wearing on their own, as silence on this issue within the community made it hard for many to access help and understanding.

Many women described garments as creating a lot of additional difficulty and pain during pregnancy, postpartum bleeding, and breastfeeding. Women reported buying larger garments, stretching out the neck for nursing, even cutting elastic on their garments to make them more comfortable. Still, some women reported no problems. One white woman reported that "garments during pregnancy and postpartum were a huge problem for me as well. They caused me physical pain and discomfort." Another white woman wrote that during breastfeeding, garments "frequently stuck to my nipples and caused them to crack and bleed." Another white woman said that she "had to take them off [due to] yeast infections and mastitis." A mixed-race Native American and white woman wrote,

> There was no impact with my first child but I eventually stopped wearing them with my second baby. The elastic on the waistband didn't stretch enough and added to the nausea. It also settled into my scar from my first cesarean section, which was quite painful. I put them on again after I had the baby. I'm still nursing and they've had little impact on my experience with breastfeeding.

Another white woman wrote,

> I usually feel uncomfortable [in my garments]. They're always sliding down from my waist, coming untucked, and in the summer when it's hot I can't stand having to wear another layer of clothing. I didn't wear the tops at all while I was breastfeeding. It simply interfered too much with what I needed to do (feed my baby).

This last woman felt empowered to take her garments off during periods of breastfeeding, but other women did not feel that they could make that choice. LDS Church teaching has emphasized that women are expected to become mothers but also created additional demands, through the requirement to wear garments, on women's bodies during these physically challenging life stages. Many Mormon women described complying with these expectations within a culture of silence, placing additional feelings of isolation to the list of emotions related to garments as they were left to navigate the challenges of wearing garments on their own.

The survey asked respondents how they felt when they were *not* wearing garments. These comments from conforming women were striking. One Latina woman wrote that not wearing garments made her feel "guilty but it's nice to not have my vagina feel like it is on fire or like I have to pee all the time," common symptoms of yeast infections and UTIs. Another white woman reported that her "skin is in better condition because I don't have to deal with all the garment rashes!" These women reported significant physical relief from discomfort, UTIs, and rashes, even though one woman experienced guilt from not obeying the rules. Conforming women must navigate not only societal pressure to conceal these natural processes but also religious requirements to maintain sacred clothing in a pristine state while managing menstrual flow and nursing. This layering of religious and cultural taboos created a unique burden for conforming women as they attempted to fulfill both their commitment to garment wearing and biological necessities.

Other women experienced emotional relief while not wearing their garments. One white woman wrote,

> It's not over simplifying to say that I am always happier [when not wearing garments]. I am able to focus on people and tasks without constantly being distracted by tugging and pulling, itching and tucking. I think about my appearance and insecurities a whole lot less.

This woman felt her garments tugging at her attention and body image, together with dampening her happiness. Another white woman wrote that when she did not wear garments,

> I feel like myself, that I have control of my body, not the men of the church. That I am allowed to be trusted to make correct choices for myself. I feel beautiful and at peace! I have zero yeast infections when I wear regular women's underwear during the summer.

This woman, and many like her, experienced psychological discomfort, in addition to physical discomfort, associated with a loss of control. Taking garments off allowed her to feel like her body belonged to her and that she was allowed to make choices for herself. Many women connected not wearing their garments with feeling better about their bodies and improvements in their physical and mental health.

Conforming women reported a range of embodied experiences with their garments. Some conforming women had exclusively positive embodied experiences, which reinforced their conforming belief. Other conforming women worked to separate out the intellectual and emotional parts of belief, which they viewed as positive, from their negative embodied experiences and related feelings of frustration. This subgroup of conforming women worked to preserve their conforming faith through this intentional separation of bodily experience and cognitive assent, while paying high physical and emotional costs for wearing garments. Other conforming women reported only negative experiences and feelings about garments and connected those negative experiences to changed meanings for their garments.

Nonconforming Men

Nonconforming men reported significantly less comfort with their garments than expected. Only 18 percent of this group described their garments as comfortable. Nonconforming men described far less pain related to garments than conforming women but consistently reported poor fit, overheating, and a general feeling of dissatisfaction with their garments. Even with these physical concerns, many nonconforming men had feelings of safety and security associated with them. One nonconforming man wrote that garments made him feel "safe, yet they are uncomfortable and not well suited to my body type." Another white nonconforming man described that garments made him feel

> sometimes more secure. But exercising publicly is a little embarrassing because others may see what I'm wearing. They are not really comfortable for my body type. They are loose and tight in the wrong places. They are hot. I get overheated and sticky in the summer. It makes me want to limit physical activity in the summer when I'm wearing it.

Both respondents reported conflicted feelings, with safety and security on the one hand and discomfort and embarrassment on the other hand.

Nonconforming belief had a direct impact on the experiences of others in this group. A Black man wrote about the ways in which he felt like his nonconforming belief came into conflict with his garments, as they made him feel "like a liar. Because I'm not that convinced of the gospel, wearing them seems like an affront." The tension between nonconforming belief or a total lack of belief, together with wearing garments, created an uncomfortable friction for this respondent, but he continued to wear them anyway.

Nevertheless, other nonconforming men had strong positive experiences and associations with their garments. One white nonconforming man wrote,

> It really does make me feel special, like I am representing Jesus Christ to myself and maintaining a commitment to get closer to Him because of the symbolism. I have never connected garment-wearing instructions with body image, as I was taught meanings that I feel are much more profound and valid and approved by God than what I have heard my wife or others describe (a focus on skin coverage that to my knowledge has no historical or theological basis whatsoever). The folk tales, announced as official or not, about them

protecting me from harm where others are more exposed to harm do not make sense to me.

This nonconforming man held different meanings for his garments than his wife, which he dismissed as folk beliefs around protection and modesty. His garments made him feel close to God, but he did not believe that garments protected him from harm.

When we asked nonconforming men how they felt when they were *not* wearing garments, many gave answers like this white man: "Comfortable. I physically breathe easier when not wearing the garments. My clothes actually fit and I am not self conscious." Another white nonconforming man reported that

> I used to feel naked without them. But I exercise a lot and my wife and I have sex a decent amount so I'm often not wearing them. Sometimes I will exercise in the afternoon and go the whole rest of the day not wearing them. I just forget.

This final respondent used canonically acceptable reasons to not wear garments (sex and exercise) as his reasons to not wear garments at other times. Both men reported a preference for not wearing garments.

Nonconforming men have mixed experiences with their garments. Many felt some degree of safety or protection from their garments but also overheating and discomfort. While nonconforming men do not reference physical pain in the same way that conforming women do, many nonconforming men described wearing garments at the cost of their physical comfort.

Nonconforming Women

Just 8 percent of nonconforming women described their garments as comfortable. Nonconforming women described many physical difficulties with their garments, even if they still held some spiritual value. The majority (55 percent) wore regular underwear during menstruation to more easily wear pads. These women felt a strong sense of anger and resentment that garments did not work with their bodies but are also an acute awareness of the social costs of not wearing garments. One Asian woman wrote,

> Sometimes I feel protected. Sometimes I feel constrained and resentful. Recently I've had several rashes and infections that prevent me from wearing garments. I feel angry because I feel like I will be judged even though I stopped wearing garments for health reasons.

Another white nonconforming woman described her medical problems in more detail:

> I have a severe chronic illness and my issues with garments started when I started having greater pain when I wore garments. Physically, garments hurt me to wear and keep my body at a higher temperature that increases my pain significantly. I also realized after not wearing them that I had a mild yeast infection for the entire 5 years I had been wearing garments. My body starts to develop that yeast infection again if I wear them for more than a few hours (living in Texas certainly doesn't help the problem). Emotionally, I feel like I am in prison when I put my garments on for family or church. Because I do not believe in them any longer, and view them as a control mechanism, there is always anger simmering beneath the surface when I wear them. It angers me that there is no cultural understanding for not wearing garments when they interfere with a person's health. I should not have to wear undergarments that give me yeast infections and significantly increase my level of pain to be a worthy, righteous person.

This nonconforming woman describes the high cost to her health of wearing garments. Even though she took regular breaks, putting them back on created a feeling of being trapped, which contributed to a loss of belief in their spiritual value. Once she understood garments as part of a system of control, her belief in the power of garments to connect her with God collapsed. While this woman's experience was extreme, other women described similar frustrations around garments and medical problems. Another white woman reported,

> Years of chronic yeast infections led me to finally get to the doctor, where I was diagnosed with lichen sclerosis, an autoimmune disorder of the vagina. While the garments did not cause this disease, they exacerbated it to such an exponential degree that I have permanent scarring so intense it inhibits my sex life. Not only did I stop wearing my garments to preserve my health and safety, but because I feel so deeply betrayed that women's gynecological health is a complete non-factor in how we are taught to wear them.

This woman described being harmed by the LDS Church's silence on issues of garments and women's health. Eventually she stopped wearing garments, but only after her body paid a high cost in physical pain and a loss of sexual pleasure. Additionally, research indicates that lichen sclerosus not only causes significant discomfort but carries serious long-term risks if left untreated, including the potential development of vulvar cancer in some cases.[30]

These experiences reveal a troubling gap in religious guidance around women's health needs—one that forced these women to choose between their religious obligations and their physical well-being only after sustaining lasting harm. These stories demonstrate how institutional silence around women's gynecological and physical health can lead to preventable suffering, as many women may hesitate to modify garment practices even when medically necessary.

Even when women's experiences with garments and their bodies were not so extreme, nonconforming women were direct in their criticisms of garments and the negative impact they left on their lives. One Asian woman lamented, "I hate wearing them. I never had difficulty thinking my body was amazing until I had to look at myself in a mirror wearing garments. For the first time in my life I was ashamed of my body. I feel hideous wearing them." For this woman, garments replaced the positive regard that she felt about her body with shame, creating strong negative feelings about wearing garments. One nonconforming woman described the ways in which garments impacted her mental health when she related, "I only wear them during [temple] ordinances now, due to medical issues. I have struggled for years with anorexia and I hate the extra bulk. It triggers my body image issues. I feel unsexy. When I wore them more regularly, it impacted my gynecological health." Garment wearing created negative feelings and experiences with her body that she linked with disordered eating, an inability to access sexual feelings, and gynecological problems. Another nonconforming woman reported that garments made her feel

> constricted, [garments] distort my body [and make it] difficult to wear clothes that I actually like. They make me feel very unsexy. They are not practical for everyday wear if you are nursing, pregnant or on your period, or in the summer. It's very difficult for me to find clothing that will fit with garments (skirts and shorts always seem to be too short because I am tall, even if they go to my knee). I love the symbolism of the temple garment but I don't understand why a necklace or ring would not work just as well to remind of covenants.

This woman touched on issues of nursing, pregnancy, and menstruation, discussed earlier in the chapter, together with poor fit. Many women described the way that garments made it difficult to access sexual feelings in their bodies and a positive body image. These nonconforming women's relationships with their own bodies were harmed because of wearing garments. The silence around garments made it difficult for women to feel good about their bodies and to access sexual feelings. Far more than giving up autonomy around underwear choices, wearing garments cost these women positive experiences and feelings about their sexual selves.

Other nonconforming women referenced the ways in which garments did and did not work with their body size. One white nonconforming woman observed that

> when I was skinny, they were fine. My body felt great, so garments felt fine. As I've gotten older and fatter, they feel TERRIBLE. I feel dumpy, unfeminine, totally unsexy, and frumpy. They do not give enough support to hold in my fat belly. I really really dislike wearing them.

This woman's experiences with garments changed from positive to negative as her size increased. A different white woman felt that her garments were comfortable on her larger body:

> I guess because when I went through the temple I believed in the gospel very strongly. And even though I have no idea what I believe now, I'm not ready to stop wearing them. Especially because they are more comfortable on my overweight body.

With size, as with other identity categories, there was no universal experience with garments.

Like conforming women, nonconforming women also felt that menstruation, pregnancy, postpartum bleeding, and nursing were all made more difficult with garments. One white woman recounted that she "felt guilty for years for wearing underwear during my period to hold a pad in place. How stupid is that??" This woman felt guilt for finding an adaptation to garment wearing that worked for her but later felt that the guilt was not necessary. One Latina woman remembered,

> I had to wear my husband's garment bottoms because both the pregnancy garments and regular women's garments were HORRIBLE during pregnancy. It was extremely difficult to nurse with the regular tops, the nursing tops were uncomfortable and impractical, and the elastic on the bottom was painful during my postpartum period.

Another nonconforming woman remembered that garments fit "horribly. I stopped wearing them regularly in the later part of my pregnancy. Nursing with garments was a nightmare and was one of the reasons I stopped nursing earlier than I planned." For these and many women, garments created deeply negative experiences with normal bodily changes. Some women described feeling like they were required to prioritize garment wearing above preferred parenting practices. Garment wearing shaped their behavior in ways that they later resented.

When nonconforming women wrote about how they felt when they were not wearing garments, nonconforming women experienced feelings of physical and mental well-being, sexual confidence, and a sense of owning their own body, though sometimes these feelings were tinged with sadness that garments did not work better with their bodies. One Latina woman wrote that she felt

> vulnerable and sad, because I have changed, but happy because I feel like I don't need to [wear them] always and it's my decision. Free to wear more things. Sexier and more confident in society. I feel like I can wear clothes others can. Guilty sometimes, like I'm missing something that feels comforting. Obviously some mixed feelings and emotions.

This woman described the ways in which changes in belief coincided with the decision to no longer wear garments. This decision came with mixed emotions and feelings of loss. A white woman reported feeling

> free. Physically, my body feels slightly better and my vagina feels healthy. Emotionally, I feel free. For the first time in my life, I actually like my body, despite its many flaws. I feel sexy and more able to find guys to interact with. I am not ashamed of my body, both how it functions and how it looks. Wearing garments was contributing to my depression and while I still fight depression, I noticed the darkness lift when I stopped wearing garments at all times. Removing the garment has absolutely increased my mental and physical health and I look forward to being brave enough to stop wearing them completely.

This woman was able to recapture emotional and physical health together with positive feelings and acceptance with her body, including accessing sexual feelings. Still, she described fear over social pressure to wear garments and looked forward to no longer wearing garments at all. One Native American woman reflected,

I used to feel scared. When I first stopped wearing them religiously (pun intended), I had extreme anxiety and was sure I was going to be hit by a car or raped, or something terrible that I would "deserve" because I wasn't protecting myself. I no longer feel that way. Not wearing garments makes me feel free, makes me feel like myself. I feel like I own my own body, for the first time in my life. I feel sexier and more vulnerable when intimate with my spouse.

This woman described the ways in which fear had been a factor in her decision to wear garments but that she eventually grew into feelings of freedom, including improvements in her sexual connection with herself and her spouse. A Native American woman reflected on the way in which taking her garments off did not impact her spirituality. Instead, they helped her to feel

free. Sexy. I do not feel a major shift in whether I have the Spirit with me or not. It was a moot point when I decided to not wear the garment as often. Without the garment my clothes fit better. My mind is off of my body. I am not too hot. I feel eyes on me, however, of other members, judging me and the absence of garment lines. I HATE that my choice of underwear puts my spirituality on display.

This final woman felt as though she could still access closeness with God without garments. She reported improved physical and emotional well-being but was aware of the social costs she was paying in order to make the choice to stop wearing garments.

Unlike conforming women, nonconforming women were much less careful about separating out their cognitive and emotional experiences with garments from the physical experience of wearing garments. Many of these women reported deeply negative experiences and referenced difficult pregnancy and nursing experiences together with other gynecological health issues, menopause, and autoimmune disorders. Many women described garments as disrupting their sexual connection with themselves and with their spouses. All of these embodied experiences made wearing garments more difficult. Some nonconforming women described themselves as previously conforming believers but talked about the ways in which their extreme negative experiences with garments coincided with a change in their belief type.

Conforming Men

Conforming men had the highest comfort rating of any group, with 70 percent reporting that they were comfortable while wearing them and less than 10 percent of respondents reporting discomfort. Many conforming men noted that they did not usually think about their garments because of that high level of comfort. One conforming white man wrote, "For the most part I forget about them, so fine I guess (#maleprivilege)." Another white man commented, "Kind of an odd question. How does wearing any underwear make you feel? Normal." A third white man reported, "It's been long enough that I feel pretty indifferent. Being a guy, I was used to wearing boxer/briefs and a T-shirt before getting my garments. Wearing garments isn't a whole lot different than when I didn't wear them." For these respondents and so many conforming men, garments resembled the underwear they wore before wearing garments, which reinforced the idea that their bodies were normal. It was easy for them to forget about the practice because of the ease with which they wore them.

However, comfort does not describe all conforming men's experiences with their garments. One Native American man described a fit issue: "I have a 29 inch waist and a 48 inch chest. They don't fit very well." He felt that garments did not accommodate his small waist and large chest. One white conforming man wrote that garments made him feel "enclosed in a sort of good way—spiritually. I somewhat remember covenants and wear them as part of that. Also too hot, men's bottoms don't fit right with the fly hole—poor design in my opinion." Another white man shared, "If I wear [garments] 24/7, I sometimes get a rash on my upper thighs and crotch area." These issues of fit, overheating, and skin conditions are common in all four gender-belief groups but least likely to be reported by conforming men.

When we asked conforming men how they felt when they were *not* wearing their garments, their answers surprised us. Asking this question helped conforming men open up a bit more about the challenges they experience with their garments. One white man wrote, "I miss them. But summer makes them difficult to wear. I sometimes sleep without them. I think there needs to be a better explanation on taking them off for health reasons." This respondent recognized that there was a gap in discourse on garments that did not fully account for health and medical problems, which men experienced at much lower rates than women. Another white man reflected, "Sometimes, not wearing garments makes me feel more positive about my body and feel more attractive." These kinds of comments made conforming men sound a lot more like the other three gender-belief groups.

Whereas more than two hundred women, conforming and nonconforming, described UTIs, yeast infections, autoimmune disorders, and other medical problems requiring treatment where wearing garments was a factor in those conditions, just one man reported such a problem. This white conforming man described his circumstances:

> I used to wear them when exercising until I started bleeding in them. I'm a runner, and the friction from the marks against my chest made my chest bleed. I'm now a cancer patient who struggles with incontinence because of the disease, so I have to wear a pad when I run. I can't use a pad with garments because the pad needs a cradle to hold it. Finally, I do need support when I run. That's why I have decided not to wear them when I exercise. I think these are very good reasons, but I still feel less than great about it.

This conforming man identified the same problem with pads that many women also described and he also wished that there were better garment designs to accommodate such needs.

Conforming men reported a high level of comfort with their garments, and some noted that wearing garments was similar to wearing secular underwear. Just one man in our sample reported a serious medical condition that impacted his garment-wearing experiences.

THE SOCIAL MEANING OF GARMENTS

Scholar Colleen McDannell observed that Mormons were adept at spotting even subtle markers of garment wearing.[31] The lace trim on women's garments created noticeable raised lines that are visible at the neck. The legs on some women's styles were prone to rolling up and raised lines on the thighs, though men's garments were fully hemmed. Men's tops resembled a traditional undershirt, but they were conspicuous when worn beneath a white shirt. In this way, garments became a marker of personal righteousness that is continually visible in Mormon communities but generally unrecognized outside of the community.[32] Garments were kept secret and invisible to outsiders but were visible to insiders.

Official teaching about garments identifies them as a symbol of private religious commitment but also frames the relationship between church members and their garments as one that is symbolic of the individual's relationship to the church.[33] Scholars have observed that garments serve as community markers, symbolize the religious commitment of the wearer, and are visible to community insiders.[34] The wearing of garments has been linked to an adult LDS Church member's high standing within their community.[35] Scholars have observed that some Mormons wear garments to please family and friends.[36] Excommunicated members, forbidden from wearing garments, have reported wearing them anyway in an attempt to resist the isolation of not wearing garments.[37] Garments have been a signal of moral and sexual purity,[38] which will be discussed further in chapter 4.

Wearing garments has been a sign that an individual is keeping their temple covenants, a prerequisite for the highest level of heaven in Mormon cosmology. Church teaching has emphasized that individuals will be judged on their own actions, reaching heaven is something that family groups do together, making salvation a family affair. Survey respondents shared many stories of conforming family members pressuring less conforming family members to be more conforming. People who took the survey discussed the pressure to wear garments, and some named the consequences of not wearing them. For the Mormons who discussed this, they worried about losing marriages and easy relationships with family members. People also expressed their fear of losing their place in heaven. We describe these consequences as the *social cost* of wearing garments. Conforming women, nonconforming men, and nonconforming women all named specific relationships in their lives that would be harmed if they did not wear garments.

WHY DO YOU WEAR GARMENTS?

The survey asked participants "Why do you wear garments?" Conforming men viewed their decision to wear garments as primarily one that emerged from their personal private sense of religious commitment but also one that they understood as an LDS community expectation. Conforming women understood their garments in a similar way but were more likely than conforming men to reference the community element and named that there was a high social cost of not wearing garments. Nonconforming men wrote that they mainly wore garments to please their wives and extended family members and expressed fear at the social cost of not wearing garments. Nonconforming men were afraid that their wives would not want to remain married if they did not wear garments or that they would be ostracized from their extended Mormon families if they did not wear garments. Nonconforming women gave similar answers as nonconforming men, noting that they wore them for their husbands, for their parents, and to remain part of their local Mormon communities. Conforming members understood garments as a requirement of the community, but nonconforming members had a clear sense of the potential social costs of not wearing garments, including divorce, estrangement from family, and change in church community relationships. These answers revealed a clear hierarchy of gender and belief at work in Mormon communities and families. These power dynamics were part of a system that was hidden to conforming believers, who focused on their individual choices, and very clear to nonconforming believers who were more sensitive to the social costs of not wearing them.

Conforming Men

Conforming men wrote that they wore their garments to satisfy God's commandments and temple covenants, which they saw as maintaining their relationship with the divine. They expressed a strong internal desire to keep those commitments while also acknowledging that it was a community requirement. One white man described his three reasons for wearing garments as

> 1. Because I've made a covenant to do so, and I believe in that promise that I made and the promises made to me in the temple. 2. Also because it is one of the temple recommend questions and my continued attendance at the temple is important to me. 3. Social pressure is just as big a reason, however; it is immediately very obvious in LDS social situations who is not wearing their garments. And there's a stigma that goes with that.

This conforming man acknowledged that there was a stigma with not wearing garments but did not discuss the more specific social costs of not wearing garments. Another white man further acknowledged the social pressure when he responded to the question by writing, "I am a member of an extremely orthodox religious community wherein wearing garments is an established custom." A third white man explained that he wore garments for "physical comfort, reminder of the temple, and cultural identity."

Conforming men acknowledged a more generalized social pressure that encouraged them to wear garments, while not referencing the particular relational costs of not wearing garments. Conforming men's responses revealed that they did not spend much time navigating the cost of not wearing garments in their own minds.

Conforming Women

The majority of conforming women wrote that they wore garments because of commitments, commandments, promises, and covenants. These women felt bound by the things they agreed to during temple ceremonies and wanted to sustain their relationships with God and community in the way that the LDS Church prescribed. One white woman wrote, "I think garments provide a sense of unity with other members of the LDS Church. Additionally, I chose to wear garments in exchange for temple ordinances, and I believe that is important." For this participant and for many other conforming women, garments benefited the wearer because they offered access to sacred temple rituals that connected families together for eternity. These answers largely restated church teaching.

Conforming women also wrote that they wore garments to avoid conflict in their relationships with other Mormons. One white conforming woman wrote,

> Because it's part of Heavenly Father's plan. Because I want to be obedient and live up to my covenants. Because I have been reprimanded by my mother-in-law and husband when I did not [wear garments]. It would be socially unacceptable if I felt otherwise and followed those feelings.

This particular respondent affirmed her commitment to keep promises made in the temple but also indicated that the costs of not wearing garments have been high for her in the past and that she is unwilling to try that again. This conforming woman named fears of surveillance and judgment by family members.

Another white woman wrote that she wore garments "because I felt like I had to. I wear them a lot less these days though. Sometimes I fear judgment from other church members or family members if they can tell I'm not wearing them." This fear that she described was a powerful force in the lives of conforming women, nonconforming men, and nonconforming women. One mixed-race woman with Asian, Native Hawaiian/Pacific Islander, and white identities indicated that she wore them

> as a reminder of covenants I have made, and oftentimes because of social pressure. Such a big deal is made about wearing them all the time that I feel disobedient when I don't. I don't like the guilt [I feel when I do not wear them] because I feel like our sense of obedience and righteousness should not be tied up in clothing. I think it should be reflected in what we say and do and how we treat others. Some people are vigilant about wearing garments but are also big jerks!

This conforming woman separated conforming belief from garment wearing, noting that garments did not encourage kindness. Another white woman told us she wore garments to attract the kind of husband that she wanted. "I want to get remarried. An LDS guy is more in line with who I am and what I believe. Therefore, it seems important to exhibit what I want in others, particularly a mate."

Conforming women wanted to maintain good relationships with God, their husbands, extended family members, and their Mormon communities. They did not always want to wear garments, but relational pressures encouraged them to keep wearing them.

Nonconforming Men

Some nonconforming men explained that they wore garments out of "habit," "tradition," "social norm," and "custom." One white man wrote, "They mean that I am part of a people, and that I am committed to something greater than myself." This respondent's sense of commitment was not tied specifically to temple ceremonies and covenants but to a broader sense of community. Another white man wrote, "I used to because I believed they were religiously important. These days they are a cultural symbol that are part of being a community member." Nonconforming men were less likely to reference temple covenants as they explained the reasons why they wore garments.

Many nonconforming men gave responses that referenced the role their wives and others played in the decision to wear garments. One nonconforming white man wrote that he wore garments due to "fear of judgment from [my] spouse as well as others and second because I made a covenant to." This relationship with his spouse was the primary reason he wore garments, and keeping his religious commitments was a secondary motivation. Another white man gave more detail when he wrote that he wore garments "because I would lose my family and career if I didn't, as the Church has created a narrative to demonize me with all of those people if I don't conform." This man had a particularly strong fear of losing everything if he did not wear garments.

Other nonconforming men referenced keeping secrets from family in their answers. One white man wrote that he wore garments "to keep family from knowing about my disbelief." Another white man wrote that he wore them "so that I can answer the temple recommend questions truthfully. So that my children and grandchildren will not assume I am an apostate. Sometimes [I wear them] to keep myself warmer in winter." A third white respondent was blunt in his explanation:

They are a means to control members by the LDS leaders at the top. Go to the temple, pay tithing, and get garments. [If you] don't pay tithing, [then] no temple, no family forever, no garments. No garments [means] no admittance to family weddings and events. No admittance to family weddings equals public shame and humiliation. And that, my friends, is extortion.

Some nonconforming men, like the man above, expressed that to wear garments is to get to hold on to their family but that if their family members knew of their unbelief, relationships would become strained and distant. Nonconforming belief was something that nonconforming men wanted to keep secret. Few nonconforming men pointed to their relationship with God in explaining their decision to wear garments.

Nonconforming Women

About a quarter of nonconforming women told us that they wore garments because of temple commitments, commandments, promises, and covenants. They offered these answers at a far lower rate than conforming women. Other nonconforming women wrote that they wore garments "because I was told to" and because of "guilt, fear of punishment." Nonconforming women gave the widest variety of responses to this question.

Many nonconforming women described the different kinds of social pressures they felt while trying to navigate garment wearing. Keeping their nonconforming belief secret was one of these. One conforming woman answered that she wore garments because of "cultural pressure. I don't want to be socially ostracized if it becomes apparent that I do not have a testimony of the LDS church." A Latina woman wrote, "My spouse is very orthodox and it has caused problems in the past when I haven't wanted to wear them. Also, [I wear them because of] cultural pressure." Another white woman explained, "People will know I don't believe or think I am sinning if I take them off. It's an easy way to tell if someone is not temple worthy." One Asian woman gave a different reason, explaining that "because I want to be a good member. I am a late convert (age 27) and didn't serve a mission or marry in the temple so wearing garments is one of the few markers I have." She wanted to be seen as being Mormon and wearing garments was one way that she could claim her religious identity just like longer standing members of her community.

Some nonconforming women described wearing garments only when seeing family in an effort to keep their nonconforming belief hidden. One nonconforming white woman described how she navigated a life where she wore garments only when I am around my parents or at church meetings. I wear them with my parents because I am afraid of them knowing about my changes in beliefs and behaviors because I was always the righteous child and I am afraid of breaking their hearts. I wear them to church when I attend partially to avoid gossip and awkward questions and also to show respect to the traditions of the faith I grew up in and though I don't believe completely, I still see some positive attributes.

This woman wore her garments to protect her parents' feelings and judgment from within her congregation. She wanted to hide her doubts while trying to appreciate some elements of Mormonism. One mixed-race Asian and white woman indicated that she felt "guilty by wearing them and my husband disapproves when I choose not to wear them." For this woman, the guilt came from disappointing God because she was wearing her garments while not believing in the LDS Church. At the same time, she felt compelled to wear them because of her husband.

Whereas some nonconforming women wore garments to keep their religious commitments, many others wore them to maintain relationships with their spouses, parents, and church communities. Nonconforming women were aware of the specific social costs of not wearing garments and were often willing to wear garments at least some of the time to reduce friction in their relationships.

WHAT DO YOU DO WHEN YOU HEAR OTHERS COMPLAIN ABOUT THEIR GARMENTS?

The survey asked participants "What do you do when you hear others complain about their garments?" This question got to the heart of what happens when garment wearers break the secrecy or silence surrounding garments. The answers to this question revealed many of the social costs of not wearing garments, the impact of limited institutional discourse, and a culture of secrecy. Many respondents from different gender and belief groups indicated that they did not respond to complaints about garments, reflecting this idea of "sacred silence" discussed by Blythe.[39] But the meaning of that sacred silence is something that many respondents discussed at length. Our respondents did not describe such complaints as acts of violence, attacks, or disrespect, as Blythe did. Instead, respondents reflected on what they were thinking while hearing such complaints.

Conforming Men

Conforming men struggled to understand why LDS people might complain about their garments. Responses earlier in this chapter and in chapter 2 demonstrated that conforming men paid the lowest belief and embodied costs for wearing garments. At least some conforming men seem unaware of the social cost of not wearing them. One white conforming man wrote that he had not "heard complaints, but if I did, I'd ignore them." Another white man expanded on this silence:

> I generally do not respond. What they do with their garments is not any of my business. I find garments to be extremely unobtrusive to my life, so I worry a bit about someone who struggles with a commandment as simple and easy as "wear this." I struggle so much more with so many other things (things which are "harder," subjectively) that I suppose I don't have any empathy or understanding for those who have complaints about their gar-ments. But, unless they have some sort of question or are actively seeking my opinion, I'm not going to tell anyone what to do with their garments. (Except perhaps my wife, but she doesn't complain [about garments].)

Like many conforming men, this conforming man understood garment wearing as a choice that was easy to the extent that he stated that he does not have "any empathy or understanding" for those who complained. An-other white man responded, "I listen to their complaints and try to under-stand that person. It is not my place to lecture someone else about how seriously they take their temple covenants, so I hold my tongue." For these conforming men, complaining about garments was to hold sacred temple commitments lightly. One mixed-race Native Hawaiian/Pacific Islander wrote that hearing people complain about their garments was

> a little awkward for me. I get that they're a little uncomfortable sometimes, but that's why there are different fabrics and styles. Most of the complaints I've heard are from guys about girls garment checking them, which I think is pretty unfair of them to do.

This respondent was sure that garments came in a wide enough range of fabrics and cuts to accommodate most needs. He reported that he'd heard men complaining about being garment checked by women, meaning that others were looking or feeling for the presence of garments, typically for distinctive hemlines. He assigned to garment-checking behaviors to women even though it is widespread among men and women in the LDS community. Few conforming men indicated that they responded in a different way. One white conforming man wrote that he was "sympathetic. Usually, when I hear complaints, they are often done humorously-as an 'insider' joke or gag."

Nonconforming Men

Nonconforming men responded to this question in a different way. One Native Hawaiian/Pacific Islander wrote that in response to a complaint, he would "just laugh." A mixed-race Black and white man wrote that he would

> smile and nod externally. Internally, I want to tell them to stop complaining and just stop wearing garments if they don't like them. But since I can't bring myself to stop wearing them, I don't feel justified in telling others to do what I cannot.

This respondent expressed frustration with himself for not being able to make the choice to not wear garments. He felt trapped in garment wearing. One white nonconforming man wrote, "I don't 'hear' anyone complain about them. When I read about these complaints [online], I wish they felt free to make another choice, and that garments were worn in the temple and not elsewhere." Again, this respondent discussed the limitations around agency that he and others feel and write about online but rarely talk about in person. Another white man wrote, "Since my faith transition, I would have to say that I wouldn't judge them at all. Prior to that change, I'd have to say that I wouldn't say anything, but I would probably secretly think they need to get over their hang ups." Many of these responses talked around the ways in which nonconforming men felt or sensed the high cost of not wearing garments and the mixed feelings that followed. Many of these answers pointed to shame because they did not resist garment wearing but wanted to.

Conforming Women

Conforming women gave a range of responses to this question of complaints, some of which resemble conforming and nonconforming men. Many conforming women expressed empathy with those who struggled with their garments. One mixed-race American Indian/Alaska Native and white woman wrote, "I've mostly heard people complain about the fit, and I agree. I've also heard complaints about being too hot in the summer, and I just tell them I don't mind." A mixed-race Latina and white woman wrote,

I tend to empathize because I have issues with them too, in regards to the fabric and style. I think they have come a long way and each new fabric and style seem to address common "fit" complaints. If they are complaining about having to wear them in general my reaction is this is something they chose and it's between them and God.

Many of these comments recognized that complaints often come from a place of physical discomfort.

Still other conforming women view complaints as coming from a lack of belief. One white woman wrote, "I assume they're not fully converted to the gospel." Another white woman indicated, "I feel uncomfortable because it is such a sacred and personal thing, and I don't really know how to respond to complaints." Another white woman reported, "I don't hear any complaints. No one around me speaks about this issue." Another white conforming woman explained the challenge of complaining about garments in LDS communities: "Most people I know don't dare complain about garments for fear of appearing like an apostate, unless it's a pregnant or nursing woman and I always fully support them in their complaints." Within the community, being an apostate, or losing one's Mormon beliefs, was one of the worst sins that a person could commit.

Nonconforming Women

Nonconforming women also gave a range of responses to this question of how they respond to complaints, but their answers were different and similar to conforming women. One kind of response unique to this group was that some nonconforming women found community and relief with other complainers who broke the silence on garments. One white nonconforming woman gushed,

> I love to hear other people complain about garments—it's validating and it gives me hope that one day things will change. I also love noticing that other Mormon women aren't wearing their garments either—it makes me feel like I'm not alone.

Another white woman observed that complaining about garments "bonds Mormon women. Everyone complains about fit or length! When I know someone has stopped wearing them, my knee jerk response is to think they are lazy and selfish. I hate that I think that first thing." Where other gender-belief groups experienced inner turmoil, judgment, and some empathy when others complained about their garments, many nonconforming women viewed this complaining as an important moment of connection with other Mormons.

Still other nonconforming women described slightly different responses to complaints. One white woman wrote, "I sympathize with them. I'll try to encourage [them] to stay positive." A mixed-race American Indian/Alaska Native and white woman wrote, "I usually shrug it off. I'm a non-traditional, live-and-let-live kind of Mormon. I think that people usually are pretty good at governing themselves in regards to what they talk about and feel." Nonconforming women described their responses to complaints in ways that did not center fear or discomfort but rather invited connection, conversation, and acceptance in ways that other gender-belief groups did not report. Rather than feeling constrained by the prohibition on discussing garments, nonconforming women viewed complaints as a welcome resistance to community norms.

CONCLUSION

Silence and secrecy around garments insulated conforming men from the lived experiences of others. This harms those in the other three gender and belief groups. Women pay particularly high costs to wear garments through different life stages and medical challenges, and named that garments interfered with sexual feelings and behavior. Women regularly held their suffering in silence for fear of the judgment of complaining, though some nonconforming women found community by hearing others complain about their garments. Nonconforming women, conforming women, and nonconforming men all named that they wore garments to please or avoid conflict with family and community members and were aware of the costs of not wearing garments. Nonconforming believers generally tried to keep their nonconforming belief a secret from family members and they kept that secret through garment wearing. These stories of the lived experiences of Mormons wearing garments revealed the power dynamics in Mormon communities, where conforming men held the fewest secrets and the least shame, but nonconforming men, conforming women, and nonconforming women all paid high costs to keep silent about their experiences and belief with a religious environment ruled by fear.

Given that our survey was conducted online and most respondents were in their childbearing years, we received relatively few comments about experiences with garments during menopause. This is a notable gap in our data, as menopause represents another significant bodily transition that women navigate while wearing garments. The physical symptoms of menopause—including hot flashes, night sweats, changes in vulvar health, and body temperature—regulation issues—likely create additional challenges for garment-wearing women. Future research should specifically investigate how women manage garment wearing during this life transition, as it represents another example of how women must negotiate religious practice through major but ordinary physiological changes.

4

SHAME AND WORTHINESS

Larissa's Story

I was fourteen years old and sitting in the chapel of my church building with the boys and the girls together for a special lesson. Usually, our classes were separated by gender, but today's lesson was going to be an important one. A man who normally taught the boys' class brought in a fancy cake from a bakery, a special and rare treat. "Who wants a piece of cake?" he asked, and all of the teens raised their hands. To our horror, the teacher then took a can of shaving cream and sprayed the shaving cream onto the beautiful cake. "Who would eat this now?" he asked again. There was one goofy kid who said he would still eat it. The teacher continued to pour shampoo on the cake and then sprayed household cleaners into the cake. "Who still wants it?" the teacher inquired. No one wanted the cake anymore. Now that the teacher had our attention, he told us that this was an object lesson to teach us how important it is to stay sexually pure before marriage. Sexual activity, in its many forms, would taint a person to the point where no one would want them. Our purity was one of our most prized possessions and one that must be guarded at all costs. We were instructed that we should say no to sexual activity and that wearing modest clothing would help us remain pure.

This lesson always stood out in my memories because it was unique, because of the special and expensive cake, and because of the messages about modesty and purity that followed. I understood that in this metaphor, I was the cake and the poisonous shampoo and the cleaning products were sexual activity. Sexual purity was not a new message for me at this time in my life but one that I had begun learning in childhood. As a teenager, much of the messaging I received at church was about preparing myself for marriage and motherhood. Even when the lessons focused on Jesus, the learning goal was to become a pure woman so I could be the right brand of wife and mother. From lessons like these, I learned that sexual activity would taint me, and dressing modestly was presented as a key aspect to remaining sexually pure until marriage.

At the time of this lesson, I was in that awkward transition between being a girl and a woman, and my body was already beginning to change. I had recently started getting attention from boys, which resulted in my first boyfriend and my first kiss. I had always been interested in boys and was well aware of my developing sexuality. With these thoughts, feelings, and my changing body, I sometimes worried that I was not righteous enough. As I moved through my teen and young adult years, the quest for purity would always feel just out of reach. Purity, worthiness, and modesty were always represented in a very specific way, but those examples never quite looked like me. I had been taught that purity was about my behavior and within my control, but I was a biracial girl with divorced parents. Modest clothing and abstaining from sexual behavior did not bring me the acceptance and comfort that church leaders and some friends described.

When I started wearing garments as an adult, though, I relied on them to be a powerful symbol of my purity and worthiness. Not only did garments validate my worthiness, but I knew that others could see this and would know that I belonged. Because my garments were serving this affirming role in my life, I did not question my experiences with them.

INTRODUCTION

Garment wearing visibly signals worthiness within Mormon communities, where worthiness is bound up with modesty and sexual purity, thus avoiding shame. Church teachings consistently emphasize these standards of behavior from childhood, reinforced in adulthood by the specific design of garments and ongoing messaging. Temple recommend interviews formally assess worthiness. These early and ongoing experiences link one's body and sexuality with shame and worthiness. Even when deemed worthy, the potential for shame and exclusion persists, as worthiness is perceived as fragile and constantly in peril. While conforming men often experience their garments as affirming their worthiness, the other gender-belief groups report a wider range of experiences, where wearing garments induce feelings of shame. Identities that are not associated with power (e.g., being a woman, experiencing doubt) were associated with feelings of shame even when the behavior conformed to church expectations. This interplay of secrecy and shame impacts sexuality, self-concept, and relationships.

Concerns around worthiness impact different groups in distinct ways, with women and girls bearing a heavy burden around dressing modestly and gatekeeping sexual behavior, and men around avoiding masturbation and pornography. Worthiness opens up a range of volunteer opportunities associated with responsibility and status, but unworthiness limits the ways in which a teenager or adult can participate in the community. Unworthy teenage boys will not be able to bless or pass the sacrament (communion). Unworthy teens of all genders would not be able to participate in temple baptisms or confirmations, special blessings known as *patriarchal blessings*, and could be excluded from class leadership opportunities, church-sponsored dances, church camps, enrollment in church universities, church missionary opportunities, and other spaces where church leaders determine that worthiness is a requirement. Unworthy adults would not be able to be married in the temple, attend the temple weddings of friends and family members, not be able to fill a number of volunteer and leadership responsibilities in congregations, and may not be able to receive in the sacrament. Unworthy adults who have participated in the temple endowment may be asked to refrain from wearing their garments and experience formal church discipline. To be unworthy is to be morally suspect in Mormon communities and forfeit a privileged place in heaven with family members.

GARMENTS AND SHAME

Students of sexual purity culture have likely experienced object lessons like the one Larissa described. Instead of a ruined cake, the lesson might have been about a licked cupcake, a chewed piece of chewing gum, a rose with the petals torn off, and tape that has been used multiple times and lost its stickiness. Such object lessons have been common in both Mormon and

Evangelical purity teachings, and scholars have identified them as sharing many of the same principles and goals.[1] Evangelical purity rings were similar to Mormon *Choose the Right* (CTR) rings, though purity rings were for teenage girls and CTR rings were generally first given to children at age eight.[2] Both groups hoped to curb sexual behavior before heterosexual marriage and emphasized girls' and women's modesty as a way of achieving that, recalling the American religious ideal of the sexless woman, described in chapter 1.[3] While there were similarities between Mormon and Evangelical purity cultures, there were also key differences. Evangelicals encouraged teens to pledge to sexual abstinence before marriage and Evangelical women were encouraged to be sexually available to their husbands. Instead, Mormon teens were interviewed every six months about their sexual practices behind closed doors with local priesthood leaders. In marriage, women were also supposed to be sexually available to their husbands, but garments took on the active role of governing modesty in marriage.[4] Garments also took on the role of creating boundaries around sexual behavior in married couples (see chapter 5).

Wearing garments is a powerful symbol of an individual's *worthiness* in Mormonism. Worthiness is judged by local leaders in formal temple recommend interviews, where church members are found to be *worthy* or *unworthy*. Shame and empathy researcher Brené Brown has discussed the close relationship between feelings of unworthiness and shame.[5] Unworthiness is a state of shame that is supposed to serve as a motivator to change behavior toward worthiness. Scholar Elizabeth Gish pointed to shame as the driving force of Evangelical purity culture.[6] To wear garments in Mormon communities is to be understood as worthy, and not wearing them signals unworthiness. While worthiness entails more than sexual purity, sexual purity is a significant component of the Mormon concept of worthiness.

Modesty is a central practice in the LDS Church that is understood as supporting sexual purity. Church teaching about modesty begins in childhood, intensifies in the teenage years, and continues through adulthood. Garments are the capstone experience of these modesty teachings because garments create modesty boundaries on adult Mormon bodies. They are, in the words of scholar Rosemary Avance, "the foundation for Church teachings on modesty."[7] Avance further observed that "while chaste Mormon bodies are objectified, they are simultaneously resisting objectification through the very act of putting on temple garments and modest attire."[8] Such objectification is associated with feelings of shame. The idea that a woman's worth could be assessed by her clothing has led to habitual body monitoring for Mormon women, the behavioral manifestation of self-objectification.[9] Body monitoring was a concerning behavior that has been associated with eating disorders, anxiety, depression, and sexual dysfunction.[10]

Modesty and sexual purity teachings in the LDS Church contributed to a central paradox at the heart of understanding Mormon bodies: bodies are sacred temples and bodies are dangerous temptations.[11] LDS women consistently reported a hyperfixation on their bodies that stemmed from modesty rhetoric. Women explained that even when they were wearing clothing that was deemed modest by garment standards, they were still adjusting and checking to make sure their garments were not visible. Wearing garments created an ongoing shame-management project in the lives of Mormon women, as the business of adjusting, checking, and self-monitoring of garments was a constant. Complying with modesty standards, then, did not always create feelings of worthiness but often provoked shame, especially from those whose identities have been problematized. Where church teaching emphasized *behavior* as a marker of worthiness, in practice many understood that their *identities* brought on feelings of unworthiness.

Elizabeth Gish found that in the Evangelical purity movement, ideas about purity were often rooted in specific identities in addition to behavior.[12] Research has identified purity culture as a colonizing movement, where the image of purity is associated with white beauty standards, including thinness. Women of color have a long history of having their bodies policed and oversexualized, independent of the clothing they wear. Whereas white women have the ability to change their clothing to appear more acceptable within purity culture, this acceptability is elusive for nonwhite women who cannot take off the aspects of their appearance, such as racial differences, that have been associated with unworthiness.[13] If white garments symbolize an idealized notion of purity and whiteness, then putting garments on the bodies of people of color can be seen as a contemporary form of colonizing behavior. The internalization of white beauty standards has strong implications for the well-being of those that cannot conform to community expectations. Larissa's ongoing research on the impact of garments on body image and sexuality, which had a larger sample population of women of color, confirms garment wearing as a racialized experience for many women.

GARMENTS AND MODESTY

The survey asked each participant a series of questions, including "What do LDS Church teachings teach you about your body?"; "Why do you wear garments?"; "What do your garments mean to you?"; and, where relevant, "Why did you stop wearing garments?" Whereas church teaching has remained largely consistent on bodies and modesty, each of our four groups gave different responses to this question, reinforcing the significance of gender and belief identities in the LDS Church. Respondents from all four groups referenced modesty in their answers. Nonconforming believers were more likely to see the negative impact of church teaching, though conforming women were also able to name some of those same negative impacts. One of the important findings from the responses below is that shame and feelings of unworthiness were not just associated with behaviors that transgressed community expectations around garments and sexuality. Survey respondents also reported feeling shame from repeated modesty lessons (conforming and nonconforming women), experiencing sexual desire (nonconforming men), and wearing garments (conforming and nonconforming women, nonconforming men). Because women's clothing choices are understood in church teaching as restraining men's sexual behavior, when some women disclosed being sexually assaulted to church leaders in interviews, they received church discipline as a consequence of that disclosure. Typical punishments included being unable to take communion, known as *the sacrament*, and being unable to say prayers or speak in church meetings. Women who had that experience felt shame over being misunderstood and punished for being abused. For those who experienced shame around wearing garments, the act of needing to cover their bodies in church-mandated ways felt shameful.

Conforming Men

Conforming men received mostly positive messages about their bodies from the LDS Church. They learned that bodies are sacred, that sexual behavior should be saved for marriage, that sexuality is for procreation and furthering marriage relationships. They also noted that sex outside marriage was held as a serious sin within the LDS Church and that masturbation was forbidden. Some conforming men also commented about women's bodies and modesty even though the question asked about the respondent's own body. Nonconforming men did not do this.

Conforming men gave a narrower range of responses than the other three groups. One white conforming man wrote that he learned "not much. That life is a sacred gift. That any sexual uses need to be within marriage, worked out between wife and husband." A second white man wrote that he learned "that sex is the second worst sin after murder, which worried me greatly before my current marriage." These responses largely repeated church messaging, unfiltered through personal experience, though one white man did share more personally:

> As a man I have been taught I should keep the Word of Wisdom[14] because my physical body is a blessing I sought in the pre-existence[15] but I don't remember ever hearing any teachings that would make me feel ashamed of my body. We played shirts and skins basketball games at the church for youth activities. Away from the church we went skinny dipping at scout camp and laughed at the guy whose suit came off when the scouts were water skiing but never thought there was any modesty issue about these. They were naughty the same way fart jokes are naughty but revealing our bodies didn't have anything to do with our morality.

The Word of Wisdom references the LDS Church's health code that prohibits consuming coffee, tea, alcohol, tobacco, and harmful drugs. He did not connect church teaching on bodies with messages of shame and referenced experiences of breaking modesty rules in church activities, which no one saw as a problem. Most meaningfully, he did not receive the message that his body put him in moral peril but that these incidences of immodesty were innocent and harmless.

Few respondents discussed race in their answers. One white man commented that he learned that "white = delightsome. Bodies are important for exaltation. Bodies are important for learning." This participant referenced language from pre-1981 editions of the Book of Mormon that described white skin in favorable terms compared with darker skin colors (2 Nephi 30:6). As described in the first chapter of this book, the LDS Church had a long history of excluding Black members from priesthood and temple worship and taught against miscegenation.[16]

Conforming men made a surprisingly wide range of comments about the relationship between garments and modesty. Some conforming men referenced that garments kept them modest and protected them from having sex outside of marriage. One white conforming man in his thirties wrote,

I do believe there's a level of protection that comes from wearing garments, but not that they're "magic." They're not going to stop a bullet, they're not going to save me from a fire. But they'll discourage me from being immodest, getting put into immoral situations.

References to immodesty and immorality directly discuss sexual behavior, as LDS teaching typically references sex with euphemisms. In this way, this man described his garments as a tool of purity culture, not for teenagers, but for (mostly) married adults to prevent sexual behavior outside of marriage.

Other conforming men resisted the idea that garments were about modesty. One white conforming man was frustrated that other Mormons seemed to be concerned with the sleeve and leg lengths of garments. He wrote that garments were

a teaching tool. I just wish they were made with more modern fabrics and shortened to be more practical. It's the marks that are important, not the boundaries caused by the length. The new modesty rage about being covered at temple length all the time, even children, is a classic Mormons-going-overboard movement. [They are] suppressing nudity instead of sexuality, which hurts body image.

This participant saw the meaning of the garments in the sacred marks that they held, which was an unusual response. Only a few respondents in the whole survey referenced garment marks in discussing experiences or meaning of garments. This respondent resisted the idea that garments were about modesty or restraining sexual behavior, but he did acknowledge that LDS modesty culture contributed to poor body image.

In discussing garments and modesty, some conforming men expressed real dissatisfaction with their garments, which was another surprise. One white conforming man in his forties, who no longer wore garments at the time of the survey, noted that he did not connect them with modesty. He wrote,

I hate them. Always have. They were stifling to me and uncomfortable. They are ugly and very poorly made. They are impractical. I do not associate them with modesty at all. I can't stand them on women either—the best way to make a woman unattractive. I feel guilty saying all that, but it's the truth of how I feel.

He named physical discomfort, frustration, poor fit, and excess heat. He also commented that garments made women sexually unattractive and that he did not associate them with modesty. This conforming man rejected garments, their meaning, and wearing them, indicating that they had not served a positive role in his life but still felt guilt about rejecting them.

Few conforming men gave lengthy answers with detailed and complex explanations. One white conforming man in his thirties described comprehensively the positive abstract meanings of garments while pointing to the negative impact that garments had on his and his wife's body image and the shame they feel about their bodies. Garments made him feel

> divided: on one hand they help me feel committed to my temple covenants and I appreciate the tactile reminder of those covenants and the symbol of Adam and Eve receiving their garments from the Lord, presumably from a slain sheep, the first sacrifice as a symbol of the atonement. I appreciate the symbols in them and the symbolism of the [temple] veil and passage into the Celestial kingdom through an encounter with the Lord that that represents. At the same time, they serve as much as a shield to my body as a protection of it (as discussed in the temple), meaning they keep me from identifying with my body and being comfortable with it: there's always a rather baggy, uncomfortable, and frequently hot covering that keeps me from having visual or tactile contact with my own body. I never see my body, so I can never learn to be comfortable with it; instead it remains something to cover and hence something to be ashamed of. On a practical level, they can also add physical discomfort (bottoms that are too hot/don't breathe) and, even for me as a man, be difficult on the bottom to find a pair that are comfortable (not too tight) but don't hang below near knee-length shorts. Although not inclined to be what LDS generally consider immodest, I don't appreciate that the garment, which should function as a reminder of my temple covenants, is generally treated instead as a de facto modesty enforcer; I don't appreciate this about my wife's garments either, as I feel it eliminates some tasteful clothing options for her just to keep the garments covered and, hence, contributes to her own distaste for her body, which I feel is much greater than my distaste for my body. I feel she would be more comfortable with who she is and how she is built if she were able to expose her shoulders or lower thighs, let them be seen publicly, and normalize that part of her body in her mind.

Few conforming men were so self-reflective or concerned about the experiences of their wives in their responses. This conforming man recognized that the requirement to cover his body with garments continually generated feelings of shame about his body. He used the language of policing in describing the relationship between garments and modesty. He understood his wife as being even more negatively impacted.

Nonconforming Men

Nonconforming men were taught that it was their responsibility to keep their bodies healthy and strong by avoiding drugs, tobacco, and alcohol. They were also taught that their bodies were temples that should be kept sacred by embracing sexual purity, including abstaining from sexual thoughts and masturbation. These men reported internalized shame from these teachings, where their bodies and sexuality were not their own but held by the LDS Church and God.

Nonconforming men gave a much greater variety of responses about church teaching on bodies. Some of the responses echoed official church teaching, like "[My body is] a gift from God, that it's something to protect and keep sacred" and "It's a temple." One Black nonconforming man wrote, "My body's value and beauty is not about the way it looks. It is not about conforming to the kind of beauty we see in the magazines." A number of comments reflected the shame respondents experienced or witnessed about sexual behavior. One white man wrote that his body "is to be covered and that my body and its needs are inherently evil." One white nonconforming young adult man wrote that he was taught to feel

> ashamed of my own sexual responses and to feel a need to suppress all sexual response until after marriage. That I shouldn't masturbate, that if I was having an erection then I was already in a spiritually suspect state of mind.

Sexual purity messaging in the LDS Church does not just focus on partnered sexual behavior but also on masturbation and suppressing sexual thoughts.[17] Teenagers experienced specific questions about masturbation in interviews with local leaders that generated significant shame. The strong anti-sex message of church teaching was confusing to some.

Other nonconforming men focused on the ways in which shame about modesty and sexual purity impacted women. A mixed-race American Indian and white man in his thirties wrote that he learned his body is "a temple. However the focus on sexual purity is not always interpreted by the youth that way. If they are told to be modest many times that leads to girls questioning what is wrong with their bodies that creates the need to cover it up." This respondent connected modesty with women's shame and the ways in which he saw teenage girls learning to understand their bodies as morally suspect. A white man in his thirties framed his answer entirely in terms of modesty messages directed at women:

> Be attractive, but not too attractive, but just kind of modestly attractive, but don't overdo it or else the men won't be able to control themselves, but a little bit because you get the man you dress for. And modesty and body image is definitely about what you wear and not who you are.

A number of these comments connected church teaching on modesty to shame, experienced by both men and women. This respondent observed the ways in which teenagers learned to judge each other's worthiness through their clothing choices. This surveilling behavior was a direct outgrowth of modesty teaching.

Still others commented on the need for good bodies to be thin and able bodies. One white man wrote that he was taught his body was "a wonderful thing, but you must take care of it. If you are overweight, you are not being a good steward of your body." A Black nonconforming man also wrote,

> Based on the Church's emphasis on sexual purity, you're better off being unattractive because it reduces your likelihood of ruining that purity if others don't find you attractive. As a guy, there is a strong undercurrent of physicality. Scouts and many Young Men's activities are physical in nature: hiking, camping, sports. If you are not physically able to participate in said activities, you are not a "good" Mormon man. Since we are taught (perhaps more culturally than doctrinally) that we find that one perfect, attractive, beautiful, nurturing woman to marry and have copious offspring with, it places a strong focus on physical beauty, both for males and especially, females.

These men absorbed messages about physical activity and body size. Still others had a different experience. One Pacific Islander wrote, "Nothing much really. I guess, being Polynesian, body image isn't exactly high priority and Polynesian culture in this instance supersedes religion." For this last respondent, his cultural values about bodies were more important to him than religious teaching.

Some respondents discussed the impact of additional identities on their understanding of their bodies. One white gay man responded with a different answer. He learned that his body is abnormal, fundamentally flawed (not masculine enough) and naturally evil ("the natural man is an enemy to God"[18]). I'm gay—so these messages were drilled into me very actively and systematically from a very young age, particularly from male leaders and Boyd K. Packer's[19] very dangerous pamphlet "For Young Men Only" . . . leading to 7 years of bulimia later in life for which I am only now seeking treatment.

This respondent internalized negative messages and shame about his gay identity as a child and teenager were harmful to his developing sense of self.

Nonconforming men also gave a wide range of comments on the connection between garments and modesty. Some felt that garments covered more of the body than was necessary for decency. One white man in his forties wrote, "I do not believe that there is anything particularly 'divine' about the cut and coverage of the garment. I believe men and women can be completely modest with bare shoulders and knees." Another white man in his thirties indicated that his garments represented "damaging messages that I am trying to overcome surrounding sexuality and modesty." A final respondent in his thirties indicated,

> I no longer believe that it is God requiring [garments]. . . . It is my view that garments have become a retrenchment of body shaming/policing as part of misguided modesty rhetoric. I'm not certain of God and God's involvement in human affairs, but I do feel fairly certain the decision to mandate wearing garments at all times was made entirely by a few men.

This respondent saw a clear connection between body shame, surveillance, and modesty and named church leaders as the source of this practice. For many nonconforming men, garments were a symbol of the ways in which the LDS Church interfered in their lives in ways that they did not welcome.

Conforming Women

Conforming women reported receiving many conflicting teachings about their bodies. A common response from conforming women was that they would then try on their own to separate out which messages truly came from the church from others that were cultural practices around church teaching. They connected positive outcomes with church teaching and negative outcomes with culture. Some women focused on teachings about their bodies that centered on being made in the image of God, that appearance did not indicate a person's value, that sex was pleasurable, and that God intended for them to experience joy and pleasure in their bodies. Many women described being taught that motherhood was their destiny and main goal in life. Other conforming women reported absorbing more negative messaging from church teaching. These women described an intense focus on modesty, where the boundaries of modesty seemed to shift at different times, fear that their bodies held too much sexual power over men, that sexual abuse was their own fault.

Conforming women's range of responses to this survey question is captured in some of the following responses. One white woman wrote that she learned "that my body is awesome! That it is a gift, and I should do things to respect and be thankful to my body. Also, that sex is pleasurable and that bodies should have lots of sex in the bonds of marriage." Very few respondents in the survey absorbed such sex-positive messages. One Latina woman wrote, "Depending on the Young Women's presidency, boundaries of clothing changed. Sleeveless was ok with one group and gossiped about with another. Shorts had to reach fingertips one year and then two inches above the knee another. I was confused as a teen." One white woman wrote, "As a rape victim that experienced church discipline for my rape . . . I have a lot of issues with church teachings about women's bodies, modesty, and rape/chastity." In the survey, conforming and nonconforming women discussed their experiences with sexual abuse and sexual assault and how those impacted experiences with garments and temple recommend interviews, but men did not.

Conforming women communicated their commitment to the church while identifying problems with garments and church messaging about modesty. Two of the most common kinds of responses in describing teaching about bodies were "It is a temple" and "It is sacred." Many other responses included variations on these statements but with additional commentary unique to this group. One white woman in her thirties wrote,

> I don't like being told that showing a little skin, cleavage, or leg is wrong. I don't like that girls are taught that if they dress "sexy" they are causing impure thoughts in the opposite sex. I do like the idea that my body is a temple and is special just for me. I do like a discussion that I had with other women about the amazing ability our bodies have to create life and how that makes us closer to the Savior.

When these women express complaints, like the complaint about the sexualization of women's bodies expressed in this last comment, they were likely to return to elements of the practice that worked for them. Conforming women did not tend to make critiques of the LDS Church without also making statements that demonstrate their loyalty to the institution. Because of this, conforming women wrote lengthier responses than the men to the open-ended survey questions and showed a greater awareness of how other women might also respond differently to the same question. A white woman in her thirties captured this issue in her comment:

> I feel super lucky that modesty teachings did not make me feel ashamed of my body. The church has taught me that I should respect my body and by some miracle I retained that instead of shame or feeling like I needed to cover up or that my body was sinful. Not sure how I got so lucky?

Even as she stated that she was taught to respect her body, this woman showed an awareness of and sensitivity to the prevalence of body shame that other Mormon women carry. A small minority of responses to this question revealed the harm of church teaching without caveats. A white woman in her thirties wrote that she learned her body "is shameful, lust-inducing, something to hide and a burden to overcome."

The topic of disability came up but infrequently in answering this question about body teachings. One white woman wrote,

> My body is a remarkable and miraculous gift. It has the potential to create life, to nurture, to gain strength, and to heal itself. Having a physical body is a huge step toward becoming like Heavenly Father, because he also has a body. All disease and disability can be conquered, whether in this life or after resurrection.

This woman saw her belief system as fixing, instead of accommodating, bodies with disabilities. Church teaching about the afterlife included the idea that heaven is a place for resurrected physical bodies and that all disability would disappear due to divine healing.[20]

Conforming women understood the relationship between garments and modesty in a variety of ways. One white woman in her thirties wrote about how garments offered clarity about modesty: "I also appreciate the fact that when I wear [garments] I have a guideline for a certain level of modesty. That makes things easier sometimes." For this woman, garment hemlines gave her specific guidelines around modesty, which she was grateful for.

Another white woman in her thirties agreed with church messaging about garments and modesty when she wrote,

> From the beginning I understood that they were a representation of the covenants I made in the temple. Garments are a very personal reminder of who I am and what I've promised. I wear them out of obedience, gratitude, modesty, protection. I've never been resentful of garments. I look at them as a blessing.

This woman named the many benefits she received from wearing garments and saw them as a net positive in her life. She used the language of identity, obedience, blessing, and protection.

Conforming women also held more complicated relationships with their garments and modesty. One white young adult woman wrote,

> They were once such a source of pride to me, a reminder of the covenants I held so dear and a symbol of how important I was to Heavenly Father. Now they are simply a comfort to me- keep me warm, keep my thighs from chafing. I also feel they mean to keep me ashamed of my body by keeping me modest.

In church teaching, pride is associated with feeling superior to others. This woman invoked pride to describe how garments made her feel more important to God than others who did not wear garments. She described some practical benefits to wearing garments but also described the requirement to cover her body for modesty as a practice that produced shame.

A number of respondents wrote about double standards in garments and modesty for men and women. One young adult Black woman wrote,

> The big question of the day is about modesty in women, and the double standard afforded to men. . . . I am surprised by the number of people who make fun of Mormons for thinking that a girl showing her shoulders is sexy and will lead a boy to hell. The church teaching for me is a little more simple and not as crazy: we encourage youth to wear modest clothes to prepare them for wearing garments. Seems pretty simple to me.

This woman understood modesty for teens as being primarily about preparing them to wear garments in adulthood, an end in and of itself, without seeing garments as part of a larger project of sexual purity. In her mind, the emphasis on the modesty of teenage girls was misplaced because both genders would one day wear garments. One white woman in her thirties explained this differently: "I feel like there is a large discrepancy between male/female garments. I feel like women's garments are designed to enforce greater expectations of modesty than men's are." This respondent felt the unfairness of the double standard. In online forums, many women have commented on the different leg lengths for men and women, noting that women's garment legs are often longer than men's garment legs. Rose Marie Reid's gendering of men's and women's garments in the middle of the twentieth century, as described in chapter 1, paved the way for them to be used to map out modesty in separate ways on men's and women's bodies, with extra coverage for women's bodies.

Other conforming women explicitly rejected the idea that garments were about modesty, noting that garment designs had changed in the past and that modesty was not a virtue with a fixed meaning throughout the church's history. One Asian woman in her thirties reflected,

> I am struggling to develop a healthy relationship with my garments. My spirituality, access to the spirit and daily habits are no different than before I was endowed. I don't have the affirming experiences that others have with their garments. I don't believe they are about preserving modesty (although I feel there is a lot of focus on that aspect) because styles and standards for garments have changed over the years. I have a hard time believing that what they are supposed to symbolize needs to be so literal and so intrusive in order to benefit from it or remember the promises associated with it. So, as I said, I wear them because I promised I would, but outside of feeling almost constantly depressed about them, what they mean to me mostly is almost a ticket into the temple for worship.

This woman resisted the idea that garments were about modesty because she understood that there had been changes to garments in the past. Garments, in her mind, did not represent some kind of eternal and unchanging truth about modesty, so they were not about modesty. She experienced this conflict in her body over shifting meanings of garments over time but saw the benefits of wearing garments in terms of access to the temple. Another white woman in her thirties felt like the invasive discomfort she experienced with garments undermined positive functions and meanings:

> They do not work for me in my life, my belief in their ability to protect, while real for some, I do not feel overshadows my need to feel comfortable,

in charge of how I cover my own body, in charge of who gets input on very personal matters like what kind of underwear I should wear while menstruating, exercising, sleeping or even having sex. These are not questions that should be for cultural consumption or public input, and whatever modesty is gained in covering up your garments is almost certainly immediately lost by incessantly talking about things as private as your own underwear.

This participant understood the concept of modesty more broadly than just covering up specific areas of the body. She felt that policing bodies in public with both garment and modesty rhetoric defeated a more central sense of private devotion and decorum.

Nonconforming Women

Nonconforming women reported that the LDS Church taught them primarily negative things about their bodies and sexuality. These women absorbed the message that their bodies belonged to God, the LDS Church, and their husbands. They were taught that their bodies were objects of sexual temptation for men and that it was girls' and women's jobs to protect men's sexual purity by wearing modest clothing, stopping sexual thoughts, and abstaining from all sexual behavior. Nonconforming women learned that they held all of the responsibility for maintaining men's sexual purity and associated these impossible expectations with shame.

Some nonconforming women learned that their bodies were tools for managing and rewarding men's sexual purity. In the survey data, one mixed-race white and Asian nonconforming woman wrote that she was taught that her body was "a gift, a sort of loan from God . . . that contained a prize for your husband's virginity" and that she should use it "to manage men's sexuality via your corporeal behaviors (no sexy body language, no breastfeeding in church)." Women struggled with feelings of not owning their body while needing to cover and use their bodies to control men's sexual behavior.

Nonconforming women understood that their garments enforced modesty standards. However, many nonconforming women's responses reflect a lived experience that modest dress in women did not effectively control men's sexual behavior despite church teaching. They resented this myth that they were responsible for men's actions in this way and the considerable time spent in church meetings reinforcing these myths. These responses were more critical than conforming women and did not typically contain additional statements demonstrating loyalty to the LDS Church. A white woman in her thirties wrote that the church taught her to

> cover up! My shoulders, breasts, legs, even arms should be covered. I am going against God if I do not follow these "laws." That if I dress provocatively, I am responsible for men and their sexual reactions. That I deserved to be raped because of the way I dressed. That men can dress how they like, but women have multiple rules about their dress. If I wear anything other than a dress or skirt at church, I am being disrespectful and even disobedient.

Although her comment about rape may sound extreme, a number of non-conforming women tied modesty teachings to rape and sexual assault. Some of these responses expressed a church teaching that practicing modesty would prevent sexual assault, and other responses indicated that modesty did not prevent their sexual assault.

A few conforming women discussed the relationship between women's bodies, size, and shame. Of these, most of them stated that women's bodies needed to be thin to be judged as good. One white nonconforming woman wrote,

> That the female body is shameful and causes men to sin. That the way to make it a little less shameful is to make it thin. Anyone who is righteous enough and works hard enough can be thin and if you are not, you are not righteous enough. Cover everything up because it is your responsibility to keep men righteous. If men think or act inappropriately or abusively, it is your fault for enticing them.

In this response and others like it, modesty included the idea that women's bodies should not take up space, that thin women's bodies were disciplined bodies.

Like some conforming women and nonconforming men, nonconforming women resented the connection between modesty and garments. One white conforming woman in her thirties complained,

> I really do like the physical reminder of the covenants I made in the temple. I just wish there was another way. Why does my modesty have to be so rigidly enforced? Can't I be trusted to keep my covenants and be modest if I don't wear the exact underwear that a bunch of men tell me I have to wear? If I could silk screen the symbols onto my own underwear, I would do

it in a heartbeat. If I could alter my garments to be better fitting and more comfortable without fear of judgment or discipline, I would do it.

For this respondent, garments were a symbol of the church's lack of trust in her sexual decision-making abilities as an adult woman. The requirement to wear garments to ensure modesty signaled the church having control over her body in a way that she did not like.

Nonconforming women discussed modesty as a double standard with different expectations for men and women. One white young adult woman wrote,

> When I discovered that the LDS was a) not aligning with my integrity and the things I believe in, b) was not truthful about their history, c) propagated unhealthy modesty rhetoric, more often targeted to women than men, I no longer wanted to wear my garments because I felt they were more oppressive and negative for me than uplifting and spiritual.

Modesty rhetoric that emphasized rules for women's bodies was a deal-breaker for some nonconforming women. The lack of symmetry in discussions around men's and women's bodies helped some women understand wearing garments as a harmful practice.

Respondents saw modesty as one more meaning heaped onto the pile of many meanings for garments. For some, this collapsed the meaning of garments to make them meaningless. One Asian woman said that one of the reasons she no longer wore garments was because of "the arbitrary design that 'fostered modesty' aka a singular cultural standard of modesty despite them being a reminder of covenants that had little to do with hemlines." For this woman, putting too much meaning on garments created a lot of confusion and frustration. Another white woman in her sixties agreed, observing that

> there is so much emphasis in the church on "modesty" and a lot of encouragement for young women and girls to wear clothing that would cover garments, even though they are not endowed and are not close to the minimum age for being endowed. In my opinion, this over-emphasis has detracted from the significance of garments as a symbol of the Atonement and of covenants.

Garments, in the understanding of these women, were never about modesty. The initiatory and endowment ceremonies introduced and described the meaning of garments but did not reference modesty like it was used in church teaching elsewhere. Conversations about modesty detracted from the other meanings of garments.

Still some nonconforming women felt like garments let them know if they were wearing too little clothing. One young adult white woman indicated, "I wear them out of loyalty to a Mormon heritage and out of preference. I feel they help me feel more secure in my body image that I wish to convey by indicating if my outfit is incomplete or immodest or too see-through." This woman's experience was much closer to that of conforming women. The experiences of each of the four gender-belief groups were not singular but ranges of experiences.

Nancy's Story

When I was a graduate student in England, my closest friends were two other Mormon women who were also graduate students. The two other women had recently given birth to their first children, and we were sitting together and talking at one of their homes. The friend who had given birth most recently was describing the difficulty of navigating the challenges of a postpregnancy body. She was breastfeeding her newborn and still bleeding from the delivery. Her body felt hot and uncomfortable continually, while also exhausted from middle-of-the-night feedings. She told us that she had not yet put her garments back on after taking them off to give birth at the hospital. She was not sure when she would be ready to put them back on.

My husband and I were hoping to become pregnant at this time, and I listened to this conversation with curiosity. I empathized with my friend and saw the difficulty of caring for a newborn while trying to manage bodily discomfort. The challenges she faced would soon be my own. At the same time, I also felt dread. I knew that whatever physical challenges I experienced after giving birth in the future, I would need to wear garments regardless of the difficulty. But I had never heard women talk openly of how to manage these challenges in a faithful way.

I saw my friend as someone who claimed more autonomy for herself than I felt capable of and I worried about what I would have to endure at an already difficult time. I wanted to support her but also felt inclined to judge her for not following the rules, even if this adaptation seemed reasonable and temporary. She was more capable of resisting the judgment of others than I was. Still, the lack of open discussion around adapting garment wearing to the needs of the body unsettled me. This left me wondering why things had to be this way and why I already knew that I would not be able to relax my practice of garment wearing when I had a baby.

Reflecting back on this conversation many years later, I recognized my poor boundaries and I knew that my friend's underwear decisions were her own. At that time, I felt like all Mormons needed to make the same choices around wearing garments and that a different choice might cause something bad to happen. The specific nature of these ominous bad things were unclear to me, but it felt more comfortable, more secure and reassuring to me to imagine my whole church community making the same choice.

SURVEILLANCE

Survey data showed that this impulse to surveille the garment wearing of others and to encourage everyone to make the same choices around garments was widespread in Mormon communities. This is not a case of individuals choosing their behaviors but rather a system producing group behaviors. Shame was an important motivator within the system, both in the feeling itself and in fearing the feeling. This shame produced informal systems of surveillance (garment-checking behaviors) in addition to the formal systems of surveillance (temple recommend interviews) required by the LDS Church.

Surveillance was a key feature of Foucault's panopticon for understanding the way that power operated through in modern societies. The visibility of garments to church members meant that Mormons were checking each other for garments. Foucault observed that inmates in the panopticon would conform to expectations not because of a fear of formal punishment so much as a fear of being surveilled by others.[21] Garment wearers were motivated by this fear of informal surveillance and rarely expressed concerns about not being deemed worthy in a temple recommend interview. While church teaching described wearing garments as a personal decision between the wearer and God, church members wrote survey responses about their fear of social judgment when answering the question about why they wore garments. Through this pervasive fear of surveillance, generating compliance with church expectations, garment wearing was continually reaffirmed as a norm in Mormon communities. This system of surveillance affirmed the church's power of Mormon bodies.

In addition to the open-ended question "Why do you wear garments?" where participants told us about garment-checking behaviors, the survey asked two questions: (1) "Have you ever looked to see if someone was wearing garments?" and (2) "Have you ever felt that someone was looking to see if you were wearing garments?" Conforming men and women admitted to garment checking other Mormons at similarly high rates and nearly all participants in these two groups answered these two questions. However, far fewer conforming believers had observed someone else garment-checking them. This meant that while conforming believers overwhelmingly engaged in garment-checking behaviors, they were much less aware of others garment-checking them.

Nonconforming believers approached this question in a different way. About half of nonconforming men and nonconforming women did not answer this survey question. We hypothesized that nonconforming believers were uncomfortable admitting to this behavior because it came across as judgmental. Nonconforming men and women often felt judged, and answering the question may have felt tantamount to admitting hypocrisy, and so they chose not to answer. Nonconforming believers were much more likely than conforming believers to report that they had observed other people garment checking them. Among nonconforming believers, there is a greater awareness of checking behaviors in general.

Conforming Men

Few conforming men discussed garment-checking behaviors or expressed an awareness of the social consequences of not wearing garments. One white conforming man wrote, "I believe in the covenants I made in the temple and I think my family and neighbors would be able to tell and judge me if I didn't wear them." He wore garments because of his conforming belief but also expressed a fear of being judged unworthy. Still another white conforming man said that he wore garments because "it is a personal commitment that I have made with my Heavenly Father. I've gone days without wearing my garments when visiting Hawaii, because I was in a swimsuit the whole time, but I didn't feel like I was being judged by anyone for it." While this was not a common theme in conforming men's responses, a few did express confidence that other LDS Church members were not judging them when they did not wear garments and seemed to be unaware of the practice.

Nonconforming Men

Nonconforming men discussed garment-checking behaviors and family judgment with a specificity that spoke to personal experience. One white man wrote that he wore garments "because I have to in order to attend family events. I am manipulated into wearing them. If I don't, people notice, therefore I am publicly shamed. I would not wear them if the LDS Church didn't use them for extortion." This man named shame and fear of shame as specific motivators for him to wear garments. Another white man explained that he wore garments because "I would be judged by neighbors and eventually tattled on to my bishop if I do it very often." Another white nonconforming man recognized that garment-checking behaviors were normal. "I think it's a natural part of our culture to look at those who are Mormons not wearing their garment as people who might not be as faithful, or it is used as a signifier of where someone is at in their belief." Still another nonconforming white man expressed concern that those *outside* the LDS Church would see his garment lines when he wrote, "I'm afraid that a portion might show, letting others know I'm Mormon." This man expressed shame around garments as a marker of religious identity. Whereas some acknowledge that this behavior might be normal within the community, many nonconforming men wore garments because of a fear of surveillance.

Conforming Women

Conforming women had a wide range of comments related to garment checking. Some conforming women, like a minority of conforming men, indicated that they worried about being judged and reassured themselves that no one was judging them for wearing or not wearing garments. One conforming woman wrote, "I feel conspicuous not wearing my garments (somehow that it's super obvious, even though I know no-one's actually looking or judging)." She acknowledged that people might check but resisted the idea that checking was tied to judgment.

Many conforming women indicated that they wore them because of their beliefs about garments and also because of a fear of shame and perceptions of unworthiness. One Asian woman wrote, "I wear them because I am commanded to by the ordinances I've made in the temple. I also wear them because I don't want other members checking to see if I wear them." The second part of this comment speaks to the way in which garment wearing is normal in LDS communities but not wearing garments is a visible difference and draws attention. A mixed-race Asian and white woman wrote, "I wear them on Sundays at church, I know people secretly check to make sure people are wearing them." She saw garment-checking behaviors as secretive, but others did not see it in the same way. Another mixed-race Asian and white woman wrote that she wore garments because it is part of the whole package of being Mormon. I covenanted and I take that seriously. Additionally, I know I would be super judged if I stopped wearing them. On the positive side, I do like the meaning behind the markings: constant nourishment, honor in obedience.

This survey participant understood the social costs of not wearing garments but still found value in wearing them and keeping her commitments.

Still others expressed a lot of fear. One white woman wrote that she wore them "because my mom would probably cry if I stopped. Because I would get judged by friends. Because what if I get struck by lightning when I'm not wearing them. I hate that these are my reasons." This conforming woman was afraid of being judged as unworthy by friends and family members and a general sense that God might also recognize her unworthiness and seek retribution. Others expressed a fear of divine judgment more directly. One white woman wrote, "I feel I made a commitment and I do feel a bit awkward when I break that, even if the church is false, I believe it is true and that I was making that promise to God. I think he will hold me to that promise just for making it, and judge me on my beliefs." For so many conforming women, fear of shame and unworthiness, from verdicts human and divine, was a motivating factor in their choice to wear garments.

Nonconforming Women

Nonconforming women told us that they wore their garments largely because of a fear of surveillance. One nonconforming woman wrote, "I wear garments in front of my parents only because my mother will check to see if I am wearing them or not. I am inactive and haven't had the heart to tell her yet and hurt her." Another nonconforming woman wrote, "I wear them on Sundays at church, I know people secretly check to make sure people are wearing them." Both respondents wore their garments selectively to avoid scrutiny. A third nonconforming white woman stated that she wore garments because

> right now, they're an obligation. I worry, if I stop wearing them full-time, of judgment or social repercussions or of having someone pat my back and make a judgment based on whether or not they feel the back neckline of my garment top.

The "pat my back" part of this response pointed to this as something that had happened to this woman, not just something she worried might happen. Garment surveillance took the form of looking for garment lines for some, but others surveilled garments through touch. Another white woman told a particular story of being judged by her family. She wore garments because

> I feel like I'm supposed to, that I am committing a great sin if I don't. I don't judge anyone who doesn't [wear garments], but I am too afraid not to. Even when I feel it would be appropriate to not wear them (e.g., moving boxes upstairs for several hours, walking in 100+ degree heat, dancing) I worry about being seen by someone who will judge me. I found out my family sat around discussing how my husband was dragging me down spiritually, as evidenced by my panties (used in conjunction with garments during my period) poking out from the top of my pants. I guess some part of me also worries that some horrible thing could happen to me if I remove the protection of the garment.

This woman's family judged her when they saw evidence of this woman wearing regular underwear together with her garments. Like others, she expressed a fear of further social costs, including possible divine retribution for not wearing garments.

CONCLUSION

Garments did not start out as a tool for policing modesty or promoting purity culture, but they inherited these meanings and functions as the LDS Church pursued assimilation with white Evangelicals. Garments, modesty, and purity culture became linked by the mid-twentieth century, when LDS Church teaching started to emphasize modesty as one of the practices that supported sexual purity. Many survey respondents from all four groups linked modesty teaching, modesty in practice, and garment wearing to shame about bodies and negative body image. The LDS Church's purity system, with its formal surveillance methods, generated feelings of shame around modesty not only for teenagers but, through the religious technology of garments, for married Mormon adults. This panoptic system, with its formal means of surveillance, encouraged church members to engage in informal surveillance of garments. Many Mormons reported wearing garments because of their fear of surveillance and the shame of being judged unworthy.

5
OBEDIENCE AND CONTROL

Jessica's Story

In 2005, I was fully invested in church and family. I dressed very modestly, had small children, and my husband did the same. A few years prior to this, I had a crisis of faith as I attended the temple weekly. As I became more familiar with the role of Eve in the creation narrative of the endowment ritual, I started to understand that the endowment described a God who loved me less because I was a woman. For my life of belief, obedience, worthiness, and respecting the sacred, I would get to serve my husband eternally, where for the same cost, my husband would get the opportunity to be like God. I really struggled with this disparity and became obsessed with finding resources that would help me reconcile my understanding of a loving God with the one who loved women less. The only way I could see through this belief dilemma was to be a perfect Mormon and hope for the best in the afterlife. I tried not to think about it too much, as it was so upsetting.

On this particular cold spring Utah day, I was wearing a light blue turtleneck and a loose maxi skirt. I went to see the stake president to complete the annual (now every two years) ritual of renewing my temple recommend. I had to complete this a few weeks early because I was traveling across the country to attend a family wedding, where the recommend was a requirement for being able to attend the ceremony. This was a standardized process where my male leader was supposed to ask a set of yes/no questions from a list in the church-authorized handbook. Before this instance, I never had a leader deviate from the handbook.

This stake president asked me if I wore my garments appropriately, and I knew that this question was a required part of the interview, even if it made me uncomfortable to have to answer questions about my underwear. He stopped and stared at me. He then started to ask for explicit details about when and how I took my garments off during sex. I was caught completely off guard and tried to give strategic answers that would hopefully satisfy his questions and preserve some of my privacy. But he was not easily satisfied. He pushed for graphic details, requiring me to walk through a typical sexual encounter with my husband, step by step. I was horrified by what he was asking but also needed his signature on my temple recommend. If I did not answer his additional questions, he could deem me unworthy and I would experience many shameful consequences. I felt compelled to give him the details he wanted, as I did not see any other option. Time seemed to pass so slowly as the stake president asked more and more unexpected questions. He was interrogating me like I had committed a serious sexual sin. I was confused and upset but felt powerless to make him stop. Surely my clothes signaled a modest life. Couldn't he see that I was a committed mother to young children? Was I not doing enough to be a good member of the church? I left this interview with so much shame but uncertain of what I had done wrong. The garment question had opened a door for ecclesiastical surveillance of my sexual behavior and I felt compelled to comply or risk being excluded from a family wedding.

The whole experience felt so gross that I just wanted to forget about it. I kept this incident secret from my husband. Prior to this interview, I wore garments day and night, as instructed, including when I exercised, and was careful about only removing garments just prior to sex. This interview increased my anxiety about wearing garments, and I became fixated on delaying removing garments and then put them right back on afterward. I was afraid of further questioning by this leader and any other who might choose to ask such questions in the future. I internalized the church's authority over my body, even in my own bed, and did not feel like I could make my own choices about how and when I wore garments.

For a long time, I assumed that the sexual and ecclesiastical abuse that I experienced in this encounter was unique. About five years later, my husband

and I were having dinner with another Mormon woman who had lived in the same area. She shared a similar story about the same local leader. Both of our husbands were shocked to hear the same story from both of us. While searching for community around Mormonism and feminism, I heard familiar stories of women experiencing a similar kind of invasive questioning of their sexual behavior in and outside of marriage during temple recommend interviews. I realized then, many years later, that the system had facilitated this, that the stake president was using his power to exert control over me and to make me feel shame about my sexual behavior in marriage for his own gratification.

Although this story does not describe a typical temple recommend interview, it does reflect the ways in which church leaders formally police the boundaries of sexuality through required interview questions about garments and other questions about keeping the law of chastity (maintaining expectations around sexual purity). The expected answers in the interviews are yes/no, but confessions are also part of the interview process.[1] This particular leader went beyond the standard questions and used the temple recommend as leverage to get personal information, but there were no checks on his power. I had been trained, through years of church teaching and practice, that I was supposed to obey my church leaders. I now understand that obedience really means that I was supposed to submit to their control.

INTRODUCTION

Earlier scholars have commented on the way in which the LDS Church lays claim to Mormon bodies by covering the genitals of those bodies.[2] Within Mormon communities, the language of *obedience* masks a system of *control* over bodies that is enforced through garment wearing, formal interviews where church leaders ask about garment wearing and sexual purity, and informal surveillance by family and community members. All of this concern over wearing garments and sexual behavior creates, for many Mormons, a deep anxiety around bodies and sexuality, primed through experiences of shame. The interview process itself, where church leaders act as gatekeepers to essential religious and social participation through required questions about underwear and sexual behavior, creates a power imbalance that makes meaningful resistance impossible for those who need or want a recommend. Members must submit to whatever level of questioning occurs or risk being denied access to family weddings, temple worship, and full community participation. Temple recommend interviews are spaces where male leaders exert inappropriate surveillance and control over intimate details of their lives, whether they adhere to the list of required questions or not. Through garments and interviews, the church maintains surveillance over church members' sexuality, creating lasting impacts on the relationships with self, spouse, and community. Garments are a religious technology that restrains sexual behavior, which is not just about maintaining the celibacy of single adults but also about controlling sexual behavior in married adults.

GARMENTS AND CONTROL

The framework for understanding garments and control relies on an understanding of belief and gender as central identities that shape the experiences of Mormons. Conforming believers place significant trust in the LDS Church that making individual ongoing commitments to its teachings and practices, including the wearing of garments, will produce a privileged salvation and a life that feels safe and comforting. Nonconforming believers understand that conforming believers are deeply invested in this project of salvation but do not trust the LDS Church to the same extent. They can often see the system of control at work in garments, and that leaves some uneasy. Men, whose bodies make up the priestly class of the church, have their underwear needs met in garments. Women have different underwear needs, and some women report having their needs met with garments and others report significant medical, menstrual, pregnancy, lactation, and other health issues related to their garments.

For each of these four groups, themes of secrecy, shame, and control show up in different ways. Conforming believers discuss these issues in the language of sacredness, worthiness, and obedience, and this language makes it easier for them to frame garment wearing in agentic and beneficial ways, a positive return on the personal sacrifice of wearing garments. Nonconforming believers are more likely to name secrecy, shame, and control in describing their garments and to understand garment wearing as part of navigating a social system with demanding requirements for belonging. Men are generally fine with their garments unless they feel a strong tension with the social system that requires them to wear garments; then they are resentful of the church's control over their bodies. Women have very mixed experiences with their garments, which are largely determined by the ways in which their individual bodies interface with garments to produce comfort or discomfort and health or harm. Negative experiences with discomfort and harm highlight the isolating impact of secrecy, clarify body shame, and reduce individual choice.

The above matrix of garment experiences sit within histories of modesty and sexuality rhetoric, institutional decisions around garments, and a concern about the intimate activities of Mormon bodies, as having an impact on the LDS Church's ability to be seen as legitimate by its conservative Evangelical peers. In nearly all episodes of garment history, church leaders opted for greater control over Mormon bodies by creating more restrictions around garment production, emphasizing and tightening rules, and institutionalizing surveillance through interviews. They did this even as garment design evolved over time to cover less of the body. Church leaders grew the meaning of garments so that they would be so heavy with eschatological, moral, and social meaning that to stop wearing them would be tantamount to identifying oneself as a bad Mormon or shedding a Mormon identity. The practice of wearing garments helped the church align with Evangelical sexual norms while also maintaining a distinct identity.

One of the few things that all four gender-belief groups agreed on is that garments hindered sexual behavior, both for single and married adults. Constant surveillance of the body and sexual behavior, described by Foucault's panopticon and achieved through garments, normalized the objectification of Mormon bodies. Within the expectation that they do not experience sexual desire, women experience significant disconnect with their bodies, making it difficult to access sexual pleasure. Men described their wives' bodies as less attractive in garments, leading to reduced sexual behavior. Isolation, body shame, and surveillance were not an erotic combination for many survey participants. Put more directly, church members understand that the requirement to wear the church's underwear gives the church ownership over their sexuality. Conforming believers are more likely to accept this as a reasonable cost for salvation. Nonconforming believers are more likely to see this as a personal loss. Nonconforming men reject the control but do not critique the underlying church teachings that support it. Nonconforming women are the most likely to critique both, rejecting church teaching that supports practices they experience as harmful.

Emerging work on Evangelicals has indicated that there are poor sexual outcomes for women who experienced sexual purity messages as teenagers.[3] There are many similarities and some significant differences between Mormon and Evangelical purity cultures. Many Mormons have likely experienced a much more intense version of purity culture than many Evangelicals. Hopefully, further research will explore the health and sexual outcomes for Mormons of all genders.

CONTROLLING SEXUALITY

The survey did not ask open-ended questions about sexuality, but respondents volunteered a lot of information about the most private parts of their lives. The institutional church's anxiety about sexuality and women's bodies is transferred to those bodies in ways that are disruptive. Some conforming women are able to understand this anxiety as having a positive influence in their lives, but others are not. Nonconforming women emphasized the ways in which this anxiety, as expressed through garments, created feelings of being disconnected with their sexual feelings. Nonconforming men also pick up on this anxiety and name the ways in which it has harmed their sexuality within marriage. Conforming men's answers reflect much less anxiety but also some negative impacts on their sex lives from wearing garments. Conforming men have absorbed LDS Church messaging that women's bodies control men's sexual behavior. Many nonconforming and conforming men reported that seeing their wives in garments decreases their own sexual desire. Nonconforming men see this as the church controlling their bodies and sexuality through garments.

Nonconforming Women

For nonconforming women, garments interfered with their connection to their bodies. This lack of connection to the self made it difficult to connect sexually with their husbands. At the same time, many nonconforming women understood their garments as a sign of their commitment to their marriage and wanted to demonstrate that commitment to their husbands. One white woman wrote, "In good moments, they remind me of my marriage and the importance of that relationship." Another white woman explained that she wore garments because I said I would and I'm expected to. Because garments and what they represent are important to my husband, and it's a way I can show I'm committed to our marriage even though I have issues with the temple. Because I would feel weird and guilty not wearing them, even though I don't think there's anything inherently important about them.

For these women, garments held the same symbolism as a wedding ring and trusting in the goodness of those relationships, even if other garment meanings did not resonate with them.

Many nonconforming women mentioned their husband in talking about their bodies and garments. Many nonconforming women struggled with feelings of not owning their bodies, with the belief that God and/or a husband was the main beneficiary of these women's bodies. In the survey data, one mixed-race white and Asian women wrote that she was taught that her body was "a gift, a sort of loan from God . . . that contained a prize for your husband [that was your] virginity" and that she should use it "to manage men's sexuality via your corporal behaviors (no sexy body language, no breastfeeding in church)." Her understanding of her experience aligns with church teaching but uses cynical language. She did not want her body to be a reward for her husband's good behavior; she wanted to feel like it belonged to her. Another white woman wrote,

> It is something to be ashamed of and covered up. The relationship between my body and sexuality is to be feared and locked away. . . . I need to cover my body in the right way in order to not make men lust after me, but at the same time, desire me so I can one day attract a husband.

This woman's relationship with her body and sexuality was ruled by secrecy, shame, and fear. She saw it as her job to dress in such a way as to both repel men but also attract a husband. Church teaching left these women feeling as though they did not own their bodies but were obligated to cover their bodies in ways that would control men's sexual behavior.

Nonconforming women reported that garments made them feel disconnected from their bodies and their sexual selves. One white woman wrote, "I found them desexualizing. I felt disconnected from my sexuality and body. I felt entombed in them." This woman evoked images of death in describing the way her garments made her feel both trapped and sexually lifeless. Another white woman commented,

Wearing them makes me feel disconnected from my body. It makes me feel like I cannot access my sexuality, because garments are a stark reminder of chastity. They make me feel like my sexuality is stifled and it has been a huge stumbling block in my marriage and in conceiving children.

For this woman, garments were a successful reminder of sexual purity but one that she could not turn off. This caused a strong sexual disconnect with her body that made it difficult for her to create the family she desired. Another nonconforming woman reported that garments created difficulty with sex. She wrote, "I also don't really feel that sexy while wearing them. I always need more foreplay when I've been wearing garments all day than I do when I wear regular underwear." Like the previous woman, garments created significant distance from her sexual self, something that Rosemary Avance found in her research.[4]

For some, garments worked in a different way to prevent sexual activity. One white woman described a period of prolonged sexual inactivity:

I don't feel good about my body and I can't wait until nighttime to take them off (to prevent yeast [infections]) but all the while I feel guilty because that's what I've been programmed to feel. My husband and I have been married for 6 years but haven't had sex for nearly 5 because my garments make me feel very unsexy.

This respondent prioritized her health and did not wear garments at night, but the result was overwhelming feelings of guilt and her sexual relationship with her husband suffered. For many nonconforming women, garments in their marriage created a double bind: husbands wanted their wives to wear garments as a symbol of their marriage commitment, but garments made sexual activity difficult or impossible. The idea of marriage that garments represented did not include sex for some nonconforming women.

Other nonconforming women drew connections between garments and previous experiences of sexual abuse in ways that were unexpected. One mixed-race Native American, Black, and white woman wrote that she "was molested from age 10 and raped when I was 14, and so to me they also offer a shield between my body and the world." This respondent used the language of protection in describing her garments, drawing feelings of safety from them.

Nonconforming women with LGBTQ+ identities described their experiences with garments. One white nonconforming woman wrote that she stopped wearing her garments when "I resigned from the church after I came out as gay." Like many other LGBTQ+ respondents in the survey, she saw her sexual orientation and Mormon identity as incompatible. For her, being gay meant no longer wearing garments. Future research should explore more deeply the experiences of LGBTQ+ members with garments. While this study captured some perspectives from gay and lesbian members who described garments as incompatible with their sexual orientation, a more focused analysis could examine how garments intersect with various aspects of LGBTQ+ identity. Such research should investigate how garments are coded as embracing binary gender norms and heterosexuality, together with specific challenges for transgender members, and examine how garment requirements impact LGBTQ+ members' ability to maintain church membership. Understanding these intersections would provide valuable insight into how this distinctly Mormon practice, already linked to sexuality, affects this population within the church community.

Some women were put off by garments because of their ties to polygamy and the sexual behavior of Joseph Smith, whose polygamous wives included teenage girls. One white nonconforming woman wrote, "As soon as I learned about Joseph Smith's polygamy, polyandry, and marriage to teenage girls by coercion, I couldn't put my garments on again. I threw them away." The historical connection of garments to Joseph Smith's polygamy was offensive and a deal-breaker. Another white nonconforming woman also referenced eternal polygamy in her explanation of why she stopped wearing garments:

> When I realized that the church still practices polygamy through sealings of men to multiple women and I allowed myself to confront the things that were upsetting to me in the temple (specifically the fact that women are to "hearken" to men while the men hearken directly to God), I just took off my garments and it was so empowering and wonderful.

The contemporary practice of LDS polygamy that she referenced is where a man can hold sealings to multiple wives at the same time if those wives die or if he divorces them. The belief is that he will be able to claim all of those wives in the afterlife. This is the polygamy through sealings that she references. Many women share this fear of eternal polygamy, discussed by author and poet Carol Lynn Pearson.[5]

Nonconforming women experienced distance from their bodies and sexual desire in wearing garments. Wearing garments created an impediment to feeling connected to the self, to their sexuality, and to their husbands. These kinds of disconnection reduced sexual activity for some women and made it much more difficult to access for others. Respondents in this group did not make positive comments about the way that garments impacted their sexuality.

Nonconforming Men

Nonconforming men felt that church leaders controlled their sexuality. They understood that garments and women's modesty served the larger goal of men's sexual purity. Garments reminded these men that the only appropriate sexual partner is their wives. At the same time, nonconforming men saw their wives as less sexually attractive while wearing garments. Many respondents expressed shame over masturbation, forbidden by church teaching.

Nonconforming men saw their garments as something that connected them to their wives. One white nonconforming man described his garments as "part of my identity as a Mormon and they remind me of the covenants that I have made, in particular my marital covenants." One Pacific Islander wrote that garments "help remind me of my sealing day to my wife, beyond that not much." A different white man reported that his garments were a "reminder of [my] current weak faith and they remind me to not have an extramarital sexual affair." Another white man explained, "I wear garments for the sole purpose of keeping peace with my wife. It would be a tremendous blow to my wife if I quit wearing them." Still another white participant had a slightly different take, noting that his garments reminded him of his "commitment to my monogamous marriage."

Like many nonconforming women, many nonconforming men viewed garments as an impediment to sexual connection with their wives. One white man wrote that wearing garments with his wife was "like getting into bed with Elder Ballard between us."[6] A different white man wrote that his garments "detracts from my sex drive. My own garments and those of my wife take away nearly all sex appeal." Another white man wrote, "If there were no garments I'd probably have a few more kids." For nonconforming men, wearing garments reduced sexual desire and limited sexual activity with their wives.

Nonconforming men received positive messages about the value of their bodies but stated that they did not own their sexuality. A white man wrote, "Generally, my sexuality does not belong to me. I have been taught to surrender that authority to local leaders who I am supposed to ask questions and make confessions to." Formal surveillance of sexual behavior through interviews made this man feel that his sexuality had been given over to church leaders. Another white man reflected, "All of the negative talk around these subjects from church leaders makes us feel that sex is a bad thing." This last point is confusing to many who feel that sexual behavior with their wives should not be tainted in this way.

A number of nonconforming men discussed their garments as being out of alignment with their gay identity. A Black gay man stated that he no longer wore garments because "I'm gay, and I'm no longer active in the church." One white gay man explained in more detail:

> I am gay and because of extraordinarily painful experiences I underwent navigating the impossible coexistence of my authentic sexuality/self and the church's dangerous teachings on homosexuality, I am no longer an active member of the faith. Taking off my garments was the first step in making this transition, and I cannot explain how liberated I felt when I stopped wearing them. The temple garment always made me feel trapped, awkward, ugly and it was a constant reminder that my body was not my own—that in some way I had pledged it to someone/something else. Getting rid of my garments was painful in a certain sense, but ultimately led me to where I am now—seeking intensive treatment for an eating disorder that kept me feeling similarly trapped and disgusted with my own body. I've learned now to accept myself more and that my body is not in fact inherently evil. The freedom and power I feel without garments has meant the world to me, though naturally it also became a way for my active LDS family to check in on my "worthiness" as I was exiting the faith. (I used to wear a white t-shirt underneath my clothes at home so I could trick my family into thinking I was still wearing garments; the day I stopped doing that was the day I learned how to better be myself and how to stick up for my own beliefs, which do not include garments at all.)

This man described garments producing feelings of lack of ownership and disgust with his body, which held him in a cycle of disordered eating. Removing garments created feelings of liberation and healing.

A few nonconforming men also referenced polygamy in relation to garments. One white nonconforming man gave a long list of reasons as to why he no longer wore his garments, but among them was this comment: "It's not fair to make people wear what was originally a secret polygamy garment. It's not right." The particular legacies of polygamy and secrecy in his garments was off-putting.

For nonconforming men, garments encouraged them toward fidelity in marriage while also reducing sexual desire. A number of gay men described the ways in which garments were incompatible with their sexual orientation and removing garments meant leaving the church. Throughout their comments, nonconforming men described the sexual and relational costs of wearing and not wearing garments. Unlike nonconforming women, nonconforming men did not elaborate on the disconnection to self that they feel through garments.

Conforming Women

The range of conforming women's experiences with garments and sexuality was wider than that of nonconforming men and women. Conforming women wrote about how garments impacted their relationship to their own sexuality. They described how garments impacted sexual behavior and desire in marriage but affirmed the need to wear them as a symbol of commitment to their marriage for their spouses.

Some conforming women received solidly positive messages about their sexuality. Conforming women's range of responses to this survey question is captured in some of the following responses. One white woman, also quoted in chapter 4, wrote that "sex is pleasurable and that bodies should have lots of sex in the bonds of marriage." Very few survey respondents referenced sexual pleasure in such a positive way. A more typical positive response included that the purpose of women's sexuality was to become pregnant and grow families within marriage. One conforming Latina woman wrote that she learned that her body "is the vessel through which children are born, families grow, and marriage bonds are reinforced through sexual intimacy." Many conforming women commented on aspects of modesty and modesty's relationship to poor teaching on sexuality. A mixed-race Asian Pacific Islander conforming woman wrote, "I feel like there is a push to cover up and hide our bodies rather than celebrate them. I also think our culture avoids talking about sexual desire in a healthy manner, which leads to a lot of problems." Still other conforming women were more critical, often as a result of negative personal experiences. One white woman, who discussed her rape and subsequent church discipline, concluded, "The intense focus on my virginity/virtue belonging to my future husband was very damaging." Where conforming women generally resisted being directly critical of church teaching, experiences of mishandled sexual abuse and rape brought out many direct critiques.

Like nonconforming men and women, conforming women reported that garments reminded them of their commitment to their husbands. One white woman wrote, "They remind me of the most important things in my life: my belief in God, my commitment to the LDS church, and my promise of fidelity to my spouse." One white woman who had lost her husband reported that "I felt like I needed to wear them as a covenant to my late husband and the promises we made." For this woman, the promise of life after death and her eternal marriage to her deceased husband were alive and at work in her garments.

Garments as a reminder of marriage did not translate well to sexual activity for conforming women. One white woman commented, "Nothing like garments to kill the mood when you're trying to get it on with your husband." Another white woman wrote, "I have no problem wearing garments most of the time, but I feel like they kind of put a damper on sexy time with the husband. I don't necessarily feel attractive once the rest of the clothes are off, and it doesn't allow for a smooth transition to sex." Both of these comments spoke to the way in which garments bookended sexual encounters and reduced sexual desire and impacted sexual behavior in a negative way. This sense that garments interfered with initiating sexual behavior was consistent among conforming and nonconforming women and nonconforming men.

When conforming women sensed that garments were hindering their sexual relationships with their husbands, they sometimes made choices outside of the rules to try and accommodate sex. Sometimes this worked, but sometimes it backfired. One white woman detailed her experience with this:

> I wear garments because I'm supposed to wear them and my husband wears them. For the longest time when we were having sex the second he finished, before pillow talk or anything, he'd put them back on. He felt so terribly guilty to have them off. This made me feel awkward. He thought that it wasn't reasonable to spoon sans garments. A few times I tried to be sexy and I skipped wearing them when going on a date with my husband. He found out and instead of being turned-on or playful he was disgusted and wouldn't touch me. This made me feel like my value as a wife was tied to my obedience to wearing garments.

For this woman, there was no choice that she could make around garment wearing and sex that would address the problems of control. If she complied with expectations, she felt that her connection with her sexual desire was reduced. If she did not comply, then her husband was turned off by her nonconforming behavior. She did not like that her value to her husband was in her willingness to accept the church's control of her body through garments.

Like nonconforming women, many conforming women lamented their own loss of sexual feelings while wearing garments. One white woman reported, "I feel like they undermine a woman's sexuality. I FELT less desirable to my husband when wearing them." This participant had an awareness of her reduced sexual attractiveness to her husband when she wore garments. Instructions on only garments off immediately prior to sex and put them back on right after likely contributed to this dynamic. An Asian woman observed that garments were "not sexy, but protected" her body." This participant named feelings of sexiness as the cost she paid for spiritual protection. Another white woman admitted, "I don't feel attractive or alluring to my husband in my garments." A mixed-race Black and white woman noted that garments did not make her feel "sexy or cute." Conforming women did not indicate that garments helped them feel confident in their sexuality and many observed that garments reduced the sexual desire of their husbands.

Just one conforming white woman reported that her husband looked sexually attractive to her in garments. She wrote, "Frankly, I think my husband is extremely sexy in his garments so if anything, wearing garments has encouraged marital intimacy! I'm sure we might be an outlier in this situation, but I felt the need to weigh in on that bit." She was right; she was an outlier in the survey data but likely representative of some women's perspectives and experiences.

For some conforming women, garments reminded them of polygamy. One conforming woman described her decision-making process with wearing garments. She wrote,

> Sometimes they remind me of Christ and of His constant companionship, of his grace and the strength available through the atonement. This is when I wear them. Sometimes they remind me of the very painful covenants I made in the temple (hearkening to my husband, giving myself away at sealing).

They remind me of the threat of eternal polygamy and make me feel like I do not belong to myself. This is when I do not wear them.

This "threat of eternal polygamy" is one that upsets many conforming and nonconforming women, who worry that garments lock them into an idea of the afterlife that they do not find appealing.

These concerns about eternal polygamy point to a deeper pattern in conforming and nonconforming women's responses. Nonconforming women's critiques extended beyond institutional control over their bodies to challenge the underlying theology that justified that control. Their rejection of garments often stemmed from deeper theological disagreements about eternal polygamy, gender hierarchy in temple ceremonies, and the fundamental premise that God requires specific underwear as a marker of faithfulness. For many nonconforming women, their growing theological doubts centered on teachings about gender, divine valuation of women, the need for constant regulation of female bodies, and eternal polygamy. While nonconforming men expressed concerns about institutional control over their bodies and sexuality, they rarely questioned these deeper theological implications about gender hierarchy or eternal marriage structures. For nonconforming women, rejecting garments can represent a rejection of both the control mechanism and the theological framework used to justify that control.

Conforming Men

Conforming men gave a narrower range of responses than the other three groups. Several men repeated church teaching on sexuality. One white conforming man wrote that he learned "that any sexual uses [of my body] need to be within marriage, worked out between wife and husband." Another white conforming man wrote, "The human body includes sexuality for the purposes of procreation AND for developing loving bonds and closeness with your mate. Sexuality is a wonderful, beautiful and sacred aspect of life- within the bonds of marriage." These men repeated elements of church teaching without commenting on personal experience. For another white man, church teaching sounded more threatening. He wrote that he learned that "masturbation is reviled and men shouldn't be called on missions if they do it." Generally speaking, conforming men were less likely to share personal experiences.

Some conforming men reported the ways that their garments did or do not make them feel connected to their sexuality. One white man wrote, "I've worn them so long it just feels normal—I'm lucky enough as a man that garments don't really affect how good-looking or sexy I feel." This respondent was sure that garments did not impact his connection to his sexual self. Another white man expressed that "body image to someone who is faithful has nothing to do with garments." This response indicated that garments and conforming belief protected the wearer from possible harms from garments. There is some judgment embedded in this kind of comment, which holds garments as a kind of abstract idea instead of as an embodied daily practice that might cause legitimate challenges for fellow church members. A third respondent had a different experience, writing that his garments made him "feel old—older than I am. Like I'm wearing my grandfather's underwear. Which, I suppose I am." This speaks to the history of garment fashions following contemporary men's fashions in underwear but often several decades behind. Another respondent noted that "they keep me from identifying with my body and being comfortable with it." This last respondent's comment recalled the responses of conforming and nonconforming women, though this was not a common comment among conforming men.

Conforming men also saw their garments as a symbol of their marriage covenants. One white man wrote that they meant that he was "committed to the church and my wife." Another white man wrote, "I promised to be faithful to my beautiful wife, I promised to honor my body, to serve God, and to wear my garments as a constant reminder of what I choose. Why wouldn't I wear my garments?" For these men, garments represented honorable goals in life, including sexual fidelity, and were a positive reminder of those good goals. A third white man wrote, "My wife and I both wear them to remind us of the covenants that we made. It bonds us and keeps us on the same page where we understand each other and more importantly what we want to teach our children." Many respondents framed this reminder of the marriage covenant in positive terms.

Even as conforming men had positive association with the marriage covenant for their garments, they were mostly disappointed at the excitement-dampening role of garments in their sexual experiences. One white man wrote, "I want to find my wife attractive, sexy. Garments do not help this cause at all and my wife is attractive." For this man, garments disrupt his sexual response to his wife. Another white man observed that garments had a

> negative impact on our intimacy, as they also have in the initiating stage of intimacy: they are not attractive, and getting them off quickly makes us feel more comfortable having sex but also results in a focus on the garments during foreplay rather than on each other.

This is an important insight into the specific ways in which garments created a boundary around sexual behavior. This respondent felt that garments were an off-putting distraction during foreplay.

Conforming men discussed issues of timing and putting garments back on at the end of sex. Another respondent wrote, "After intercourse I have at times been upset at the nagging voice of our conscience (or social pressure) telling me and my wife to put them back on quickly rather than spend the night sleeping naked together." This respondent experienced that feeling of needing to put garments back on as a kind of loss of intimacy. At the same time, a different white man really resists this kind of mentality about garments and sex: "My view is that if anyone thinks they need to wear garments while having sex or in leading up to sex, they have been horribly misinformed." This respondent highlighted one of the main problems around garments, where silence and secrecy lead to shame, which allowed for a high degree of institutional control around bodies and sexual behavior. There were many allusions, in our survey and in social media, to older generations wearing garments during sex and bathing. As has been illustrated elsewhere in this book, it is not clear where people should go for better advice or to find the authority to make decisions for themselves within a system that prizes institutional control.

Just as there was a lone conforming woman who thought her husband's garments were sexy, there was a lone conforming man who reported that his wife's garments were sexy. This white man wrote, "My spouse's garments enhance intimacy. My wife looks sexy and desirable in her garments. They are delightful and she is more attractive to me. This is an unexpected fringe benefit, for I am not talking about some 'spiritual' element here—she looks sexy in them." This kind of comment is definitely an outlier but important to include to demonstrate the range of responses, as nonconforming men and women did not make any comments like this.

Conforming men held positive associations with their garments, which reminded them of marriage and the happiness they felt in marriage. They still felt the same challenges with garments and sexual behavior that Mormons in other gender-belief groups experienced.

CONCLUSION

Garments serve as a physical and metaphorical boundary around Mormon bodies, acting as a constant reminder of the church's influence over the lives of its members. As garments reinforce church teaching, they generate feelings that influence behavior. Feelings of secrecy and shame leave garment wearers vulnerable to control. Conforming believers often frame this control in positive ways that reflect the language of *obedience*, which is emphasized in church teaching. Nonconforming believers often feel controlled through garment wearing. Men commented on their wives being less attractive in garments. Women felt disconnected from their bodies and sexuality because of garment wearing. All four gender-belief groups indicated that garments reduced sexual behavior in married relationships by interfering with the initial and end stages of sexual activity. The recurring themes of secrecy, shame, and control expose a systemic issue that transcends individual experiences. The emotional and relational consequences of such practices underscore the tension between personal belief and institutional authority, where the line between spiritual guidance and coercive control becomes blurred.

CONCLUSION

Nancy and Jessica's Story

We started the garment survey on the heels of a different project that surveyed the Mormon feminist community in 2013. We were capturing the perspectives of a group that was inside the LDS Church but often viewed as outsiders within the faith community. We felt like we were airing our faith community's dirty laundry as we published journal articles on the topic. In that airing, we discussed the ways in which men and women were not equal within the gender complementarian systems of the LDS Church. "Equality is not a feeling" was a rallying cry of the Mormon feminist movement in the 2010s, which challenged the comments by some conforming women who told us that they felt that they were equal to men.[1] Their lived experiences in the church felt affirming to their identities and they did not desire to look beyond those good feelings. For those of us who were advocating for change, including ordination for women, good feelings did not address systemic inequality between genders, let alone LGBTQ+ inclusion or racial equality.

At that time, we were both temple-recommend holding conforming Mormon women who experienced a growing discomfort with church teaching on gender. In 2013, we surveyed the Mormon feminist community and published a journal article later that year. Our survey asked Mormon feminists to explain their religious belief and practices and their reasons for identifying as Mormon feminists. The survey received more than 1,800 responses. So many Mormon feminists at that time were also conforming women who attended church regularly and were involved in volunteering for their local congregations, just like us. By writing the article, we wanted to publicly claim these seemingly conflicting identities, in both Mormonism and feminism, that Mormons and secular feminists told us was impossible.

Working on that project felt both exciting and dangerous. It felt exciting to explore and explain these identities and our LDS community and to a wider audience. At the same time, we both felt that this was also dangerous in a religious culture that was often hostile to those who critiqued the LDS Church and its members. We knew that if our local congregations read our work, people would perceive us as nonconforming believers and we would lose whatever status and social capital we held as conforming women.

After those first articles were published, our collaboration felt like it had momentum. We decided to continue working on other projects and scouted around for topics. Jessica encountered a call for papers in a fat studies journal, and we decided to do a survey related to body image and garments. At that time, there had been a number of lengthy online forum discussions in Mormon feminist spaces about garments. As we were meeting to write and revise papers, these posts came up regularly in our discussion. As our own belief questions started to become more important to us, garments were a more regular topic of conversations between the two of us. In those conversations, it seemed like we had a lot of unexpected and strong feelings about garments. We realized that we associated our garments with feelings of dread, but that experience was confusing. Even though it was a forbidden topic, we decided to do another survey to find out if other Mormons were experiencing anything similar.

When the garment survey closed in June 2014, we were surprised with the sheer volume of responses but realized that people really wanted to tell their stories. It seemed as though many shared their garment experiences in an anonymous survey to alleviate the burdens of secrecy and shame.

Over the next two years, we both became nonconforming believers and then left the LDS Church. Like so many other nonconforming Mormons, we started to understand our own agency in a different way. When we started writing about Mormon feminists in 2013, we felt like we had agency to influence and change church structures. We were invested in the LDS Church, and the LDS Church would be forced to reckon with peer-reviewed research on its own people. Although we feared local reprisals for writing about a controversial topic, we also felt like we were using our agency to do good in the church. In becoming nonconforming Mormons, we started to see the limits of that agency, both the agency we had as nonconforming believers but also new clarity with the agency we had as conforming believers. We had always had so much less power in the church than we believed. There was no amount of feeling equal that created structural power for women in a system that embraced a gendered hierarchy as something divinely ordained. Neither of us could continue to believe in a God who ordered the universe in that way.

Larissa's Story

In my years as an active, temple-recommend holding, conforming Mormon woman, I never questioned garments or pushed against the admonition to wear them day and night. I did not find meaning in my garments as a symbol of my covenants, but I did find meaning in them as a symbol of in-group belonging. Garments were inconvenient and often uncomfortable, but I did not have awareness of significant body issues while wearing them. The fact that I have never been pregnant may have protected me from these issues, as I did not experience the struggle of wearing garments during pregnancy and breastfeeding.

My movement away from Mormon conformity began in my early thirties, when I adopted my daughter and son, who are Black. Although I am a mixed-race person of color, I knew that I would not fully understand what my Black children would experience. I worked tirelessly to learn about racial issues and racial identity development for my children. I knew that my kids would have questions about the church's history with racial discrimination and I wanted to be prepared to have honest conversations. A deep dive into the racial history of the church eventually led me to look at other social hierarchies in the church, especially gender and the treatment of women. My Mormon feminist phase lasted for many years, and I might still be in that place if it weren't for a wake-up call that changed things for me.

The year 2020 brought a global pandemic, nationwide protests against police brutality, and a divisive presidential election. By the end of the year, I was ready to turn the page and start fresh, but in December of that year, I was diagnosed with breast cancer. I was still in my thirties and healthy. It was jarring. After six months of doctor visits, tests and scans, medications, and multiple surgeries, I was in therapy trying to process what had happened. Before I had breast cancer, I believed that I was a young and vibrant woman, but postcancer, I had the overwhelming feeling that I was sick and broken. I was adjusting to a new body after a double mastectomy that had forced me to reckon with what my breasts meant to me and what their role was in my expression of femininity. Like many cancer survivors, I was experiencing sexual dysfunction as a result of various medications and the psychological effects of cancer treatment. What I wanted more than anything was to feel like I had the power to reclaim my body from the cancer that had taken so much.

I wanted to feel young, and free, and vibrant again, and in the course of my recovery, I found that I could not feel those things anymore while wearing my garments. In the weeks after surgery, I had been wearing compression clothing to manage the swelling. This was the first extended time that I had gone without wearing garments. When it came time to put them back on, I couldn't believe how overstimulating they felt on my body. I couldn't tolerate what felt like stifling, uncomfortable layers anymore. I wanted to wear clothes that made me feel free in my body. I wanted my body back, and it wasn't mine when I was wearing garments. I knew that I would never choose to wear garments if I didn't have to.

Letting go of my garments didn't immediately change my belief, but it was a pivotal aspect of my transition from nonconforming believer to nonbeliever, essentially leading me to separate from the beliefs and practices of Mormonism. Breast cancer had led me on a journey to reconnect with my body. As I worked in therapy to understand the ideas I had been taught about my body and sexuality, I came to understand how garments had been an integral part of my personal experience.

INTRODUCTION

The complex relationship between Mormons and their garments is deeply intertwined with the concept of agency. Within the LDS Church, this same term is used to describe the power that an individual holds to make conforming choices. Within academic discourse, agency is often described as an individual's power to make choices, and different disciplines and scholars tailor their definitions in different ways. Although there is a lot of work on the question of women's agency in religious communities, there is often an assumption that agency is not an issue for religious men. As the chapters in this book have examined garments in relation to gender and belief with regard to secrecy, shame, and control, it is clear that agency is an important issue for women *and* men in Mormonism. A man's belief type (conforming or nonconforming) also shapes his experiences and feelings about his choices to wear or not wear garments and the social *costs* that he will have to pay to enact those choices. Belief type impacts an individual's experiences and feelings around the issue of agency, obscuring or revealing the system of control at work and in their lives as they do or do not experience different kinds of social and personal costs. Examining the costs and benefits associated with wearing garments illuminates the nuanced ways Mormons navigate faith, identity, and agency within a religious framework that emphasizes obedience and conformity.

AGENCY

Where LDS Church members reference *obedience* and *control* in discussing their decisions around garment wearing, scholars of religion use the language of *agency*. The concept of agency tries to understand the ways in which women in gender-traditional religions make choices and claim their own authority. The ways in which scholars of religion define, describe, and categorize agency has been controversial. Historian Catherine Brekus commented on the ways in which agency literature traditionally understood agency as "emancipation, liberation, and resistance," though the histories of women in Mormonism play out in complex ways that are often not well described by scholars.[2] Pushing against this, Saba Mahmood described agency as "the political and moral autonomy of the subject" in her study of the women's mosque movement in Egypt, while Orit Avishai articulated agency within a framework of "doing religion" by performing religious identities shaped by religious discourse in her study of Jewish Israeli women.[3]

Amy Hoyt called for scholars to move beyond a victim/empowerment framework for discussing religious women's agency.[4] Some have understood Mormon women's agency as compliance with church expectations where women benefit from compliance.[5] There are many examples of Mormon women experiencing this kind of social and religious benefit in this book. Others have commented that working Mormon women and single Mormon women were more likely than other kinds of Mormon women to resist gender norms.[6] Recent work by Caroline Kline noted that Mormon women of color from Botswana, Mexico, and the United States used their agency in a variety of conflicting ways for the purpose of nonoppressive connected-ness.[7] These perspectives on agency considered women's individual actions. Nazneen Kane was concerned that while such approaches had value, they also "obscured and minimized" institutional systems of power.[8] To rectify this, Kane drew on the work of intersectionality scholar Patricia Hill Collins, whose work examines the structural oppressions of racism and sexism.[9]

Both approaches, reflecting individual experience and structural analysis, are important to understanding Mormon women's experiences with their garments. A further critique of agency scholarship, though, is the way in which there is an assumption that gender-traditional religions privilege all men in uncomplicated ways. Just one study of Mormonism examined men's agency in expectations around grooming.[10] One of the ideas that this book has tried to get at is the way in which power works in Mormon communities and how those experiences of power, located in identities related to belief and gender, impact individual decisions. By comparing the experiences of four different gender-belief groups in wearing garments, we have captured that sense of the centrality of gender and belief in the Mormon experience. Further research is needed to investigate the roles of other intersections of identity in LDS communities. Race and sexual orientation are particular areas of interest within Mormon studies, but gender identity, disability, and socioeconomic status are also understudied identities that need attention.

AGENCY AND ITS COSTS

When Nancy and Jessica were conforming women, the work of Orit Avis-hai and Saba Mahmood were particularly important to our thinking about women and agency at that time, but the commentary by Kelsy Burke was also on our minds.[11] Burke's substantive review summarized the trend in gender and religious studies to describe *all* women's actions as agentic, grouping them under four general models: resistance,[12] instrumental,[13] em-powerment,[14] and compliance.[15] Amy Hoyt described Mormon women's agency as a spectrum, where women negotiate between self, community, and family, often accepting gendered expectations and resisting them at the same time.[16] Studies of women's agency in gender-traditional religions by Saba Mahmood and Orit Avishai build on postcolonial critiques of Western feminists' theories and marked a turning point in the discussion of religious women. This literature focuses on the benefits that women receive from such participation and identifies various locations of women's agency within

Islam and Judaism. Their research pushed against negative stereotypes and reductive views of religious women as "doormats" and "pawns in a grand patriarchal plan."[17] We loved their work in part because we had experienced these stereotypes as religious women. We particularly appreciated the way that these scholars advocated a more nuanced understanding of why women continue to participate in religious structures, asked the scholarly community to take religious women seriously, and viewed religious women as whole people who make nuanced and complex decisions.

We started to understand that the concept of agency was central to our large garment survey dataset, but raising children and the demands of work pushed us to take a break for a few years. We returned to it in 2018 and submitted the paper "Mormon Women, Their Garments, and the Problems of Agency" to a series of journals, receiving both desk rejections and full reviews. Whereas one reviewer was exceptionally angry over our choice of research topic, many offered excellent advice and encouragement, though not an acceptance. At that time, we could not explain the full range of responses we were seeing in the survey data with agency theory from Mahmood, Avishai, and others.

This focus on agency also created problems as we tried to understand the role of belief in our data. To create space for complexity in the lives of religious women, Mahmood and Avishai did not address questions about religious women's loss of agency or the limitations of that agency. Some Mormon women embraced their agency to make conforming choices around garment wearing and found satisfaction in that, but others experienced a lot more difficulty in making conforming choices and handled that in a variety of different ways.

Other projects we worked on highlighted the ways Mormon men and women negotiated their choices within an environment of rules and strong expectations.[18] In thinking about this negotiation process, we started thinking not only about benefits experienced navigating choices but also about the social and personal *costs*. Mahmood and Avishai both discuss benefits, which was an important piece of the agency puzzle, but there is no real recognition of costs in the processes of enacting agency and how different people with different social locations might pay different costs for the same choice.[19]

We took to heart Nazneen Kane's observation that a focus on women's lived experiences *only* did not indict the systems of power at work in institutions and communities that prioritize the needs of some identities over others.[20] The conclusion of this chapter and this book draws together a discussion of *costs* as a way to understand the ways in which Mormons with different identities pay different costs for garment wearing. While there are clear social costs to *not* wearing garments, understood in all gender-belief groups, the costs of *wearing* garments is often hidden to different gender-belief groups due to issues of secrecy, shame, and control. The less social power an individual holds in the LDS Church, the more likely that individual has to bear hidden costs, which often produce feelings of isolation, shame, and loss of autonomy.

Garments impact belief groups in different ways, with conforming believers claiming agency to make their conforming choices and non-conforming believers navigating the limitations on their choices. The following sections summarize the observation about the costs of agency for each gender-belief group.

Nonconforming women paid high costs to both *wear* garments and *not wear* garments. They were aware of garments as a social system of control that was not designed to benefit them but placed high expectations on them. They were deeply aware of the social costs of not wearing garments and were quick to critique a culture where individuals policed each other's underwear choices. When they wore garments, they paid costs related to isolation, shame, feeling controlled by church teaching, local leaders, and family, and community surveillance of their garments. They were also aware of the many embodied costs of wearing garments for women, including discomfort, infections and medical issues, garments not working well with different life stages, and reduced sexual desire and activity. When nonconforming women encountered other Mormons who broke with religious expectations and complained about their garments, they felt connected to those complaining individuals, relieving feelings of isolation and shame.

Of all four groups, nonconforming women had the biggest range of responses for every open-ended survey question. Their answers to questions like "What do your garments mean to you?" and "How does wearing garments make you feel?" were more likely to describe personal experiences and feelings and less likely to repeat church teaching. A number of nonconforming women wrote lengthy stories in the survey about their garments, bodies, and beliefs. Many of these stories indicated that at least some nonconforming women used to be conforming women, indicating that a change in belief type was part of their journeys.

Nonconforming men also described high costs to both wear and not wear garments. Men who felt compelled to wear garments to meet religious and social expectations often felt shame around not being able to make choices about their own underwear. This group was the most likely to use the word *controlled* to describe how wearing garments made them feel, and they often felt trapped within a system. Nonconforming men did not experience the physical discomfort and medical issues that many women experienced, but they described high emotional costs. Like conforming and nonconforming women, nonconforming men often felt that garments were a symbol of not owning their bodies and that represented an acute loss.

Conforming women paid a complex mix of costs to wear and not wear garments. They tended to believe that their choices were their own and not influenced by outside forces. Their compliance with religious and social expectations *felt* agentic and positive because they were meeting expectations of *obedience*. Still, many conforming women paid a high cost to wear garments with regard to issues of discomfort, garments not being well suited to different stages of life, sexual desire, and sexual activity. They typically framed these challenges as *sacrifices* that returned some benefits to them, but they did not question the system that required such sacrifices. They often experienced spiritual, social, and marital benefits from accepting these sacrifices as necessary in their lives.

Of all four groups, conforming men paid the lowest cost to wear garments. They generally did not pay physical costs associated with fit, discomfort, medical issues, or life stages. Some conforming men were aware of the social costs of *not* wearing garments, though others were unaware. As a group, they did not know about the costs that conforming women, nonconforming men, and nonconforming women paid in order to *wear* garments. The silence surrounding garments kept conforming men ignorant of these costs. Silence and ignorance preserved conforming men's judgmental feelings toward those who struggled with wearing garments and maintained their misunderstanding that complaints about garments stemmed from a lack of belief or commitment. This lack of awareness about costs, combined with the social and religious power of this group, gave conforming men a significantly different experience with their garments. Conforming men had good or neutral feelings about their garments, did not describe feelings of shame, had few physical issues, and tended to think about their garments as representing abstract truths that did not impact their bodies. If they were aware of any costs of wearing garments, they were most likely to be aware of sexual costs.

CONCLUSION

Garments in Mormon culture function not only as a religious symbol but also as a form of religious technology that shapes the feelings and experiences of the wearer, which has the effect of reducing sexual feelings and behavior. Where church teaching on wearing garments frames the practice as reflective of one's relationship to God, garments work as a system of social control within Mormon communities.

This control mechanism, part of daily life, is steeped in beliefs that tie sexuality directly to sin and purity. The historical progression of Mormon garments from simple undergarments to complex symbols of faith illustrates a broader religious strategy to maintain control over the sexual behaviors of its members. The religious requirement to wear garments embeds deep obligations to maintain worthiness (shame) and obedience (control) to the LDS Church. In this system, garments imprison Mormon bodies, creating a system of formal and informal surveillance that any community and family member can participate in. Fear of surveillance keeps garment wearers compliant while the system ignores the physical, emotional, and sexual suffering of the inmates. Where obedient Mormon teenagers are instructed to save all sexual behavior for marriage, garments disrupt the sexual relationships of conforming and nonconforming married Mormons. Garments, then, are part of a distinctive church practice that understands sexual behavior, even within monogamous heterosexual marriage, as dangerous and in need of tight control.

Garments in Mormon culture function not only as a religious symbol but also as a religious technology that shapes the feelings and experiences of the wearer, which has the effect of reducing sexual feelings and behavior. This effect is evidenced across all four gender-belief groups studied, though experienced differently based on social location. While conforming men generally reported positive associations with garments, they noted reduced sexual desire when seeing their wives in garments. Both conforming and nonconforming women reported feeling disconnected from their sexuality and bodies while wearing garments, with one participant describing feeling "entombed" in them. Nonconforming men often felt their garments created barriers to intimacy with their wives.

Where church teaching frames garment wearing as reflective of one's relationship to God, emphasizing themes of covenant, protection, and modesty, garments actually work as a sophisticated system of social control within LDS communities. This control operates through formal mechanisms like temple recommend interviews, where leaders question members about their garment-wearing habits, and informal surveillance through "garment-checking" behaviors by family and community members. The survey revealed that many members wear garments primarily to maintain relationships and avoid judgment rather than for spiritual reasons.

The historical progression of Mormon garments from simple undergarments to complex symbols of faith illustrates the church's broader strategy of assimilation. What began as progressive underwear aligned with health reform movements in the 1840s transformed into a tool for controlling sexuality as the Mormon church sought to distance itself from polygamy and align with white Protestant sexual norms. By the mid-twentieth century, garments had become central to enforcing Protestant ideals of sexual restraint and establishing Mormons as properly disciplined white Christians.

The costs of wearing or not wearing garments vary significantly based on social location within Mormon communities. Conforming men, who hold the most institutional power, generally reported the fewest costs and greatest benefits from garment wearing. In contrast, women across belief types described significant physical costs including medical issues, complications during pregnancy and nursing, and reduced sexual intimacy. Nonconforming believers of both genders reported high emotional costs, wearing garments primarily to maintain family relationships while experiencing feelings of shame and loss of agency. These differential costs reveal how power operates through seemingly neutral religious practices.

The intersection of gender and belief fundamentally shapes garment experiences, though other identities including race, sexuality, disability, and class further complicate these dynamics. The normalization and privileging of conforming men's experiences has led to garment designs and policies that fail to address women's needs. LGBTQ+ members report particular challenges reconciling garments with their identities, though this remains an area needing further study. The secrecy surrounding garments has historically kept these varied experiences hidden, though social media and online communities are increasingly providing spaces for members to share their struggles.

Looking beyond Mormonism, this study offers important insights into how religious institutions maintain control through everyday practices and sacred clothing. Like Islamic hijab or Jewish tzitzit, garments make religious commitments tangible and visible to the community while simultaneously enabling surveillance. However, garments are unique in how they specifically target and constrain sexual expression even within sanctioned marriage relationships. This suggests that controlling sexuality remains central to maintaining religious authority, even as specific methods evolve.

Recent changes in church policy regarding garments, including modified temple-recommend questions, new medical exemption guidelines, and new sleeveless garments demonstrate ongoing tension between institutional control and individual adaptation. While these changes acknowledge some practical challenges of garment wearing, they ultimately reinforce rather than relax institutional authority over church members' bodies. At the same time, wider access to information and community through social media is slowly eroding the secrecy and shame that have historically maintained compliance.

This research points to several areas needing further study, including experiences of people of color and LGBTQ+ members, impacts of garments on mental health and body image, and comparative analysis with other religious groups' practices of bodily control. Methodologically, this study demonstrates the value of examining both individual experiences and institutional power structures while considering how different social locations shape religious practice and experience.

Garments represent a uniquely Mormon practice that evolved from progressive origins into a sophisticated technology for controlling members' sexuality. Through mechanisms of belief, secrecy, shame, and surveillance, garments help maintain institutional control over Mormon bodies while simultaneously signaling Mormon assimilation with mainstream Evangelical sexual norms. Understanding the varied costs different groups pay to participate in or resist this system reveals broader patterns of how religious institutions maintain power through everyday practices of bodily control. As Mormonism continues to navigate tensions between tradition and adaptation, group identity and individual choice, garments remain a crucial site for examining questions of agency, identity, and institutional authority in religious life.

APPENDIX

This section contains additional information about the 2014 survey, including tables with demographic information about the anonymous survey participants and a list of survey questions whose responses informed this study. The original survey included additional questions, but this study does not address that data.

Gender-Belief Groups

	Conforming Women	Nonconforming Women	Conforming Men	Nonconforming Men	Total
Count	2,387	1,225	481	436	4,529
Percent	52.7	27.0	10.6	9.6	

Note: This table gives further data about each group. Due to rounding, percentages may not total 100.

Gender-Belief Groups and Age

Age	Conforming Women	Nonconforming Women	Conforming Men	Nonconforming Men	Total
N/A	11	27	3	6	47
18–30	761	345	100	81	1,287
31–40	1,085	554	203	198	2,040
41–50	298	187	98	91	674
51–60	168	80	55	41	344
61–70	55	27	19	17	118
71–80	7	5	2	2	16
80+	2	0	1	0	3

Gender-Belief Groups and Race

Race*	Conforming Women	Nonconforming Women	Conforming Men	Nonconforming Men
American Indian/ Alaska Native	19	16	3	5
Asian	18	24	2	4
Black/ African American	14	7	3	3
Hispanic/Latino	64	30	10	11
Native Hawaiian/ Pacific Islander	10	8	4	3
Middle Eastern	2	4	0	0
White	2,232	1,159	460	414

* Survey participants were able to select more than one race category.

Gender-Belief Groups and Marital Status

Marital Status	Conforming Women	Nonconforming Women	Conforming Men	Nonconforming Men	Total
N/A	11	27	3	8	49
Divorced	86	79	12	21	198
Married (first marriage)	1,836	862	370	309	3,377
Remarried	168	97	37	39	341
Separated	15	22	3	1	41
Single	256	132	54	54	496
Widowed	15	6	2	4	27

Gender-Belief Groups and Household Income

Income	Conforming Women	Nonconforming Women	Conforming Men	Nonconforming Men	Total
N/A	35	40	11	9	95
Less than $10,000 per year	85	34	17	11	147
$10,001–$30,000 per year	263	119	48	28	458
$30,001–$50,000 per year	437	179	54	57	727
$50,001–$70,000 per year	460	207	85	85	837
$70,000–$90,000 per year	355	196	102	65	718
More than 90,000 per year	752	450	164	181	1547

Gender-Belief Groups and Education

Education	Conforming Women	Nonconforming Women	Conforming Men	Nonconforming Men	Total
N/A	12	29	5	7	53
Less than a High School Diploma	4	0	1	1	6
High School Diploma	340	144	43	40	567
Associate's Degree/ Vocational Training	443	210	53	44	750
Bachelor's Degree	1,124	499	163	144	1,930
Master's Degree	379	272	119	112	882
Doctoral Degree	85	71	97	88	341

SURVEY QUESTIONS USED IN THIS STUDY

Even though this survey included more questions than those listed below, these were the questions that were important to this study:

Demographic information, including gender, age, race and ethnicity, marital status, yearly household income, and educational attainment

Belief statements (rated on a Likert scale of 1–5) that contributed to the belief index:

> There is a God.
> There is life after death.
> I have an opportunity to be exalted in the celestial kingdom (heaven).
> Jesus is the divine son of God.
> The LDS Church is the restored church.
> The LDS Church today is guided by a prophet/revelation.
> Thomas S. Monsoon is a true prophet of God.
> The Book of Mormon is the word of God.
> The Doctrine and Covenants contains revelations from God.

Related LDS practice questions:

> Have you received your endowments?
> Do you currently wear garments?
> Why do you no longer wear garments?
> How comfortable are you when you wear your garments?
> How does wearing garments make you feel?
> How does not wearing garments make you feel?
> How comfortable are you when you wear your garments?
> Why do you wear garments?
> What do your garments mean to you?
> If you are a woman, how did garments impact your pregnancy and nursing experience?
> When you hear someone complain about their garments, how do you respond?
> Have you ever looked to see if someone was wearing their garments?
> Have you ever felt that someone was looking to see if you were wearing garments?

NOTES

Introduction

1. Erin Gloria Ryan, "Mormon Ladies Click Tongues Disapprovingly at Ann Romney's Lack of Temple Garments," Jezebel, September 27, 2012, https://jezebel .com/mormon-ladies-click-tongues-disapprovingly-at-ann-romne-30775836; Lisa Butterworth, "Ann Romney, Gossip and Judgement: It's Time to Admit We Have a Problem Mormon Ladies," *Feminist Mormon Housewives* (blog), September 27, 2012, https://www.feministmormonhousewives.org/2012/09/ann-romney -gossip-and-judgement-its-time-to-admit-we-have-a-problem-mormon-ladies/.

2. Luke Perry, *Mitt Romney, Mormonism, and the 2012 Election* (New York: Palgrave Macmillan, 2014), 65–84.

3. Carlos E. Asay, "The Temple Garment: 'An Outward Expression of an Inward Commitment,'" *Ensign*, August 1997, 18–23.

4. Asay, "The Temple Garment," 18–23.

5. Nazneen Kane, "'Priestesses unto the Most High God': Gender, Agency, and the Politics of LDS Women's Temple Rites," *Sociological Focus* 51, no. 2 (2018): 97–110; Edward L. Kimball, "The History of LDS Temple Admission Standards," *Journal of Mormon History* 24, no. 1 (1998): 135–76.

6. David John Buerger, "The Development of the Mormon Temple Endowment Ceremony," *Dialogue: A Journal of Mormon Thought* 20, no. 4 (1987): 33–76; Douglas Davies, *The Mormon Culture of Salvation* (Farnham, UK: Ashgate, 2000), 81; Evelyn T. Marshall, "Garments," in *Encyclopedia of Mormonism*, ed. Daniel H. Ludlow (New York: Macmillan, 1992), 2:534–35; Adam J. Powell, "Covenant Cloaks: Mormon Temple Garments in the Light of Identity Theory," *Material Religion* 12,

no. 4 (2016): 457–75; Stephen C. Taysom, *Shakers, Mormons, and Religious Worlds* (Bloomington: Indiana University Press, 2011), 95.

7. David O. McKay, "The Purpose of Temples," *Ensign*, January 1972, 38; Gordon B. Hinckley, "Keeping the Temple Holy," *Ensign*, April 1990, 49; Shanna Butler, "How to Talk about the Temple," *New Era*, January 2006, 44.

8. Karen Duffin, "The Box," *Moth Radio Hour* (podcast), May 25, 2021, https://themoth.org/stories/the-box.

9. John-Charles Duffy, "Concealing the Body, Concealing the Sacred: The Decline of Ritual Nudity in Mormon Temples," *Journal of Ritual Studies* (2007): 1–21; Jean A. Hamilton and Jana Hawley, "Sacred Dress, Public Worlds: Amish and Mormon Experiences and Commitment," in *Religion, Dress and the Body*, ed. Linda B. Arthur (Oxford: Berg, 1999), 31–52; Colleen McDannell, *Material Christianity: Religion and Popular Culture in America* (New Haven: Yale University Press, 1995), 198–221; Kane, "Priestesses unto the Most High God," 97–110.

10. Kane, "Priestesses unto the Most High God," 97–110; Kimball, "The History of LDS Temple Admission Standards."

11. Asay, "The Temple Garment," 18–23.

12. Asay, "The Temple Garment," 18–23.

13. Asay, "The Temple Garment," 18–23.

14. Asay, "The Temple Garment," 18–23; *True to the Faith*, 173.

15. Asay, "The Temple Garment," 18–23; *True to the Faith*, 173.

16. *True to the Faith*, 173.

17. Asay, "The Temple Garment," 18–23.

18. Jana Riess, *The Next Mormons: How Millennials Are Changing the LDS Church* (New York: Oxford University Press, 2019), 65–66.

19. *True to the Faith*, 173.

20. *True to the Faith*, 124.

21. Rosemary Avance, "Worthy 'Gods' and 'Goddesses': The Meaning of Modesty in the Normalization of Latter-day Saint Gender Roles," *Journal of Religion and Society* 12 (2010): 13.

22. Newsroom Staff, "Church Updates Temple Garment Video," October 22, 2014, https://newsroom.churchofjesuschrist.org/article/church-updates-temple-garment-video.

23. Laurie Goodstein, "Mormons Expel Founder of Group Seeking Priesthood for Women," *New York Times*, June 24, 2014.

24. McDannell, *Material Christianity*, 198–221.

25. Alexandria Griffin, " (In)visible Piety: Reading Mormon Garments through Hijab" (MA thesis, Claremont Graduate University, 2014), 15; Kane, "Priestesses unto the Most High God," 97–110.

26. Hamilton and Hawley, "Sacred Dress, Public Worlds," 32–33.

27. Riess, *The Next Mormons*, 7, 246.

28. Buerger, "The Development of the Mormon Temple Endowment Ceremony," 33–76.

29. Sarah Jane Weaver, "'Mormon' Is Out: Church Releases Statement on How to Refer to the Organization," Church News, August 16, 2018, https://www.church ofjesuschrist.org/church/news/mormon-is-out-church-releases-statement-on -how-to-refer-to-the-organization?lang=eng.

Chapter 1. A Short History of Garments

1. Steven L. Shields, *Divergent Paths of the Restoration* (Bountiful, UT: Restoration Research, 1982), 17–18.

2. Richard T. Hughes, "Soaring with the Gods: Early Mormons and the Eclipse of Religious Pluralism," in *Mormons and Mormonism: An Introduction to an American World Religion*, ed. Eric Alden Eliason (Urbana: University of Illinois Press, 2001), 24; Peter J. Thuesen, *Predestination: The American Career of a Contentious Doctrine* (New York: Oxford University Press, 2009), 100–135; John G. Turner, *The Mormon Jesus: A Biography* (Cambridge, MA: Harvard University Press, 2016), 5.

3. Buerger, "The Development of the Mormon Temple Endowment Ceremony."

4. David John Buerger, *The Mysteries of Godliness: A History of Mormon Temple Worship*, 2nd ed. (Salt Lake City: Signature Books, 2002), 145; Duffy, "Concealing the Body, Concealing the sacred," 1–21; Powell, "Covenant Cloaks," 467.

5. Christine Talbot, *A Foreign Kingdom: Mormons and Polygamy in American Political Culture, 1852–1890* (Urbana: University of Illinois Press, 2013), 36.

6. Talbot, *A Foreign Kingdom*, 22.

7. Buerger, "The Development of the Mormon Temple Endowment Ceremony," 33–76.

8. Buerger, *The Mysteries of Godliness*, 142; Buerger, "The Development of the Mormon Temple Endowment Ceremony," 33–76.

9. "Priesthood Garment History," p. 11, Mace K. Church Papers, Accn 1914, Box 1, Folder 2–2, Special Collections, J. Willard Marriott Library, University of Utah.

10. John C. Bennett, *The History of the Saints: An Exposé of Joe Smith and Mormonism* (Boston: Leland and Whiting, 1842), 248.

11. Laura George, "Austen's Muslin," in *Crossings in Text and Textile*, ed. Daneen Wardrop and Katherine Joslin (Lebanon: University of New Hampshire Press, 2015), 75.

12. Buerger, *The Mysteries of Godliness*, 142–43.

13. "Priesthood Garment History," Mace K. Church Papers, Accn 1914, Box 1, Folder 2–2, Special Collections, J. Willard Marriott Library, University of Utah.

14. Buerger, *The Mysteries of Godliness*, 145; Duffy, "Concealing the Body, Concealing the Sacred," 1–21; Powell, "Covenant Cloaks," 467.

15. D. Michael Quinn, *The Mormon Hierarchy: Origins of Power* (Salt Lake City: Signature Books, 1994), 114–15; Benjamin F. Johnson, *My Life's Review: The Autobiography of Benjamin F. Johnson* (Provo: Grandin Book, 1997), 96; Cheryl Bruno, Joe Steve Swick III, and Nicholas Literski, *Method Infinite: Freemasonry and the Mormon Restoration* (Sandy, UT: Greg Kofford Books, 2022), 251.

16. Buerger, *The Mysteries of Godliness*, 142–43; "Priesthood Garment History," Mace K. Church Papers, Accn 1914, Box 1, Folder 2–2, Special Collections, J. Willard Marriott Library, University of Utah.

17. Buerger, *The Mysteries of Godliness*, 142–43.

18. Ana Stevenson, "'Symbols of Our Slavery': Fashion and the Rhetoric of Dress Reform in Nineteenth-Century American Print Culture," *Lilith: A Feminist History Journal* 20 (2014): 6.

19. Patricia A. Cunningham, and Gayle Strege, *Reforming Fashion, 1850–1914: Politics, Health, and Art* (Columbus: Ohio State University, 2000), 8; Amy Kesselman, "The 'Freedom Suit': Feminism and Dress Reform in the United States, 1848–1875," *Gender & Society* 5, no. 4 (1991): 496–98.

20. Stevenson, "Symbols of Our Slavery," 7.

21. Stevenson, "Symbols of Our Slavery," 8.

22. Cunningham and Strege, *Reforming Fashion*, 8.

23. Cunningham and Strege, *Reforming Fashion*, 8.

24. Bruno, Swick, and Literski, *Method Infinite*, 235.

25. William Morgan, *Illustrations of Masonry by One of the Fraternity Who Has Devoted Thirty Years to the Subject* (Batavia, NY, 1826), 18; Bruno, Swick, and Literski, *Method Infinite*, 325.

26. Emily J. Bailey, "Seventh-day Adventist Dress: "An index to the heart," in Marie W. Dallam and Benjamin E. Zeller, eds, *Religion, Attire, and Adornment in North America* (New York: Columbia University Press, 2023), 27.

27. Emily J. Bailey, "Seventh-day Adventist Dress: An Index to the Heart," in *Religion, Attire, and Adornment in North America*, ed. Marie W. Dallam and Benjamin E. Zeller (New York: Columbia University Press, 2023), 30–32.

28. Joan Kendall, "The Development of a Distinctive Form of Quaker Dress," *Costume* 19 (1985): 58.

29. Mattingly, *Appropriate[ing] Dress: Women's Rhetorical Style in Nineteenth-Century America* (Carbondale: Southern Illinois University Press, 2002), 31; Stevenson, "Symbols of Our Slavery," 8.

30. Theodore Weld in G. H. Barnes and D. L. Dumond, eds., *Letters of Thedore Dwight Weld, Angelina Grimke Weld, and Sarah Grimke, 1822–1844* (Gloucester, UK: Peter Smith, 1965), 508; Mattingly, *Appropriate[ing] Dress*, 31; Stevenson, "Symbols of Our Slavery," 8.

31. Mattingly, *Appropriate[ing] Dress*, 31; Stevenson, "Symbols of Our Slavery," 8.

32. Michel Foucault, *Discipline and Punish: The Birth of the Prison*, trans. Alan Sheridan (New York: Vintage Books, 1995), 200.

33. Foucault, *Discipline and Punish*, 201.

34. Victoria Tensi, "'Taking Every Thought Captive': A Microanalysis of How Control Mechanisms Operate within Evangelical Purity Culture" (PhD diss., George Washington University, 2023).

35. Gerda Lerner, *The Creation of Patriarchy* (New York: Oxford University Press, 1986), 139.

36. Linda B. Arthur, "Introduction: Dress and the Social Control of the Body," in *Religion, Dress and the Body*, ed. Linda B. Arthur (Oxford: Berg, 1999), 1.

37. Mattingly, *Appropriate[ing] Dress*, 31; Stevenson, "Symbols of Our Slavery," 8.

38. David Morgan, *The Thing about Religion: An Introduction to the Material Study of Religions* (Chapel Hill: University of North Carolina Press, 2021), 70.

39. George D. Watt, ed., *Journal of Discourses, 26 vols.* (Liverpool: Latter-day Saints' Bookseller's Depot, 1854–86), 9:376; Buerger, *The Mysteries of Godliness*, 145.

40. Watt, *Journal of Discourses*, 11:10; Buerger, *The Mysteries of Godliness*, 145.

41. Johnson, *My Life's Review*, 96; Bruno, Swick, and Literski, *Method Infinite*, 251.

42. Johnson, *My Life's Review*, 96; Bruno, Swick, and Literski, *Method Infinite*, 251.

43. Thomas Kearns, "Endowment Oaths and Ceremonies," *Salt Lake Tribune*, February 9, 1906, 8.

44. Bruno, Swick, and Literski, *Method Infinite*, 327.

45. Bennett, *The History of the Saints*, 38.

46. Buerger, *The Mysteries of Godliness*, 146.

47. Buerger, *The Mysteries of Godliness*, 146.

48. Mace K. Church Papers, Accn 1914, Box 1, Folder 2–2, Special Collections, J. Willard Marriott Library, University of Utah.

49. "Priesthood Garment History," p. 2, Mace K. Church Papers, Accn 1914, Box 1, Folder 2–2, Special Collections, J. Willard Marriott Library, University of Utah.

50. McDannell, *Material Christianity*, 211–14.

51. Mark A. Scherer, *The Journey of a People: The Era of Restoration 1820–1844* (Independence, MO: Community of Christ Seminary Press, 2013), 398.

52. Buerger, *The Mysteries of Godliness*, 145–46.

53. Turner, *Brigham Young*, 3–4; Talbot, *A Foreign Kingdom*, 1.

54. Sarah Barringer Gordon, "The Liberty of Self-Degradation: Polygamy, Woman Suffrage, and Consent in Nineteenth-Century America," *Journal of American History* 83, no. 3 (1996): 815.

55. Talbot, *A Foreign Kingdom*, 2–3.

56. W. Paul Reeve, *Religion of a Different Color: Race and the Mormon Struggle for Whiteness* (New York: Oxford University Press, 2015), 2–3.

57. Reeve, *Religion of a Different Color*, 17.

58. Amanda Hendrix-Komoto, *Imperial Zions: Religion, Race, and Family in the American West and the Pacific* (Lincoln: University of Nebraska Press, 2022), 9.

59. Michael Austin and Ardis E. Parshall, eds., *Dime Novel Mormons* (Draper: Greg Kofford Books, 2017), x–xv; Craig L. Foster, "Victorian Pornographic Imagery in Anti-Mormon Literature," *Journal of Mormon History* 19, no. 1 (1993): 125; Tammy Heise, "Marking Mormon Difference: How Western Perceptions of Islam Defined the "Mormon Menace," *Journal of Religion and Popular Culture* 25, no. 1 (2013): 82–97.

60. Reeve, *Religion of a Different Color*, 12; Hendrix-Komoto, *Imperial Zions*, 9.

61. Armand L. Mauss, *The Angel and the Beehive: The Mormon Struggle with Assimilation* (Urbana: University of Illinois Press, 1994), 3–4.

62. Mauss, *The Angel and the Beehive*, 36–37.

63. Armand L. Mauss, "Sociological Perspectives on the Mormon Subculture," *Annual Review of Sociology* 10 (1984): 437–60.

64. It is difficult to characterize the unidentified Presbyterian group, though given the other two denominations included in Mauss, it was likely a forerunner of the Presbyterian Church in America (founded in 1973, later than Mauss's study), which is the largest conservative Calvinist denomination in the United States.

65. Mauss, *The Angel and the Beehive*, 8–9.

66. Cristina Rosetti, "'Hysteria Excommunicatus': Loyalty Oaths, Excommunication, and the Forging of a Mormon Identity," *Journal of Mormon History* 47, no. 3 (2021): 22–43.

67. Edward Leo Lyman, ed., *Candid Insights of a Mormon Apostle, 1889–1895* (Salt Lake City: Signature Books, 2010), 497.

68. Leonard John Nutall, *Diaries of L. John Nuttall*, vol. 3, December 8, 1890, p. 227, Special Collections, J. Willard Marriott Library, University of Utah.

69. C. Willett Cunnington and Phyllis Cunnington, *The History of Underclothes* (New York: Dover Publications, 1992), 176.

70. Buerger, *The Mysteries of Godliness*, 129.

71. Joseph F. Smith, "Fashion and the Violation of Covenants and Duty," *Improvement Era*, August 1906, 812–15; McDannell, *Material Christianity*, 214.

72. "Incorporations," *Salt Lake Herald-Republican*, June 15, 1910, 11.

73. Buerger, *The Mysteries of Godliness*, 154.

74. Cunnington and Cunnington, *The History of Underclothes*, 129.

75. Buerger, *The Mysteries of Godliness*, 138, 150.

76. "Priesthood Garment History," Mace K. Church Papers, Accn 1914, Box 1, Folder 2–2, Special Collections, J. Willard Marriott Library, University of Utah.

77. Jill Fields, "Erotic Modesty: (Ad)dressing Female Sexuality and Propriety in Open and Closed Drawers, USA, 1800–1930," *Gender & History* 14, no. 3 (2002): 501, 508.

78. Jennie Lindbergh, "Buttoning Down Archaeology," *Australasian Historical Archaeology* 17 (1999): 50–57.

79. Buerger, *The Mysteries of Godliness*, 138, 150.

80. "Temple Garments Greatly Modified, Church Presidency Gives Permission, Style Change Optional with Wearer," *Salt lake Tribune*, June 4, 1923; Buerger, *The Mysteries of Godliness*, 151–52.

81. "Temple Garments Greatly Modified."

82. "Temple Garments Greatly Modified."

83. "Priesthood Garment History," Mace K. Church Papers, Accn 1914, Box 1, Folder 2–2, Special Collections, J. Willard Marriott Library, University of Utah.

84. Juanita Brooks, "A Close-Up of Polygamy," *Harper's* 168 (1934): 299–307.

85. Brooks, "A Close-Up of Polygamy," 303.

86. "Priesthood Garment History," p. 7, Mace K. Church Papers, Accn 1914, Box 1, Folder 2–2, Special Collections, J. Willard Marriott Library, University of Utah.

87. "Priesthood Garment History," p. 24, Mace K. Church Papers, Accn 1914, Box 1, Folder 2–2, Special Collections, J. Willard Marriott Library, University of Utah.

88. "Priesthood Garment History," p. 25, Mace K. Church Papers, Accn 1914, Box 1, Folder 2–2, Special Collections, J. Willard Marriott Library, University of Utah.

89. First Presidency (Heber J. Grant, J. Reuben Clark, and David O. McKay) to Hyrum B. Calder and counselors, March 25, 1938, in Devery Anderson, *The Development of LDS Temple Ceremonies* (Salt Lake City: Signature Books, 2011), 245–46.

90. Anderson, *The Development of LDS Temple Ceremonies* 245–46.

91. Kimberly A. Miller-Spillman and Andrew Reilly, *The Meanings of Dress* (London: Bloomsbury Academic, 2019), 200.

92. Buerger, *The Mysteries of Godliness*, 153–54.

93. Buerger, *The Mysteries of Godliness*, 153.

94. Buerger, *The Mysteries of Godliness*, 153.

95. Buerger, *The Mysteries of Godliness*, 154.

96. "The Message of the First Presidency to the Church," *Improvement Era*, November 1942, 758; James R. Clark, ed., *Messages of the First Presidency of the Church of Jesus Christ of Latter-day Saints* (Salt Lake City: Bookcraft, 1965–75), 6:176.

97. J. Reuben Clark, "In These Times," *Improvement Era*, May 1943, 314.

98. Katie Clark Blakesley, "'A Style of Our Own': Modesty and Mormon Women, 1951–2008," *Dialogue: A Journal of Mormon Thought* 42, no. 2 (2009): 20.

99. Blakesley, "A Style of Our Own," 21.

100. Blakesley, "A Style of Our Own," 21.

101. Avance, "Worthy 'Gods' and 'Goddesses,'" 12.

102. Sara Moslener, *Virgin Nation: Sexual Purity and American Adolescence* (New York: Oxford University Press, 2015), 16–17.

103. Moslener, *Virgin Nation*, 16–17.

104. Moslener, *Virgin Nation*, 16.

105. Robert Stapes, "The Myth of Black Sexual Superiority: A Re-examination," *Black Scholar* 9, no. 7 (1978): 16; Frantz Fanon, *Black Skin, White Masks* (New York: Grove, 1967), 177.

106. Taylor G. Petrey, *Tabernacles of Clay: Sexuality and Gender in Modern Mormonism* (Chapel Hill: University of North Carolina Press, 2020), 27.

107. Petrey, *Tabernacles of Clay*, 20.

108. Patrick Q. Mason, "The Prohibition of Interracial Marriage in Utah, 1888–1963," *Utah Historical Quarterly* 76, no. 2 (2008): 108–31.

109. Matthew L. Harris and Newell G. Bringhurst, eds., *The Mormon Church and Blacks: A Documentary History* (Urbana: University of Illinois Press, 2015), 164.

110. Max Perry Mueller, "Playing Jane: Re-presenting Black Mormon Memory through Reenacting the Black Mormon Past," *Journal of Africana Religions* 1, no. 4 (2013): 513–61; Gregory A. Prince, Darius A. Gray, and Margaret Blair Young, "'Let the Truth Heal': The Making of Nobody Knows: The Untold Story of Black Mormons," *Dialogue: A Journal of Mormon Thought* 42, no. 3 (2009): 74–99; see also W. Paul Reeve, "A Century of Black Mormons," digital exhibition, J. Willard Marriott Library, University of Utah, https://exhibits.lib.utah.edu/s/century-of-black-mormons/page/credits.

111. Jennifer Craik, *The Face of Fashion* (London: Routledge, 1994), 115–52; McDannell, *Material Christianity*, 215.

112. Roger K. Petersen and Carole Reid Burr, "A Genius for Beauty: Swimsuit Designer Rose Marie Reid," in *Mormons and Popular Culture: The Global Influence of an American Phenomenon*, ed. J. Michael Hunt (Westport, CT: Praeger, 2013), 224; Gavin Feller, "Conceal, Enhance, Expose, Perfect: A Mid-Century Mormon Swimsuit Designer's Feminine Bodily Discipline," *Journal of the American Academy of Religion* 89, no. 4 (2021): 10.

113. Petersen and Burr, "A Genius for Beauty," 201; Feller, "Conceal, Enhance, Expose, Perfect," 10; McDannell, *Material Christianity*, 216.

114. Feller, "Conceal, Enhance, Expose, Perfect," 5.

115. "Temple Garments," *Sunstone Magazine*, January/February 1980, 49.

116. McDannell, *Material Christianity*, 216.

117. Amy DeRogatis, *Saving Sex: Sexuality and Salvation in American Evangelicalism* (New York: Oxford University Press, 2014), 42–47.

118. Will Durant and Ariel Durant, *The Lessons of History* (New York: Simon and Schuster, 1968), 35–36.

119. Church Educational System, *Eternal Marriage Student Manual* (Salt Lake City: Church of Jesus Christ of Latter-day Saints, 2003), 221.

120. Gordon B. Hinckley, "From My Generation to Yours, with Love," *Improvement Era*, December 1971, 71–73; Gordon B. Hinckley, "Reverence and Morality," General Conference, April 1987, https://www.churchofjesuschrist.org/study/general-conference/1987/04/reverence-and-morality?lang=eng#p56; Neal A. Maxwell, "Behold the Enemy Is Combined," General Conference, April 1993, https://www.churchofjesuschrist.org/study/general-conference/1993/04/behold-the-enemy-is-combined-d-c-38–12?lang=eng#p28; Jeffrey R. Holland, "Personal Purity," General Conference, October 1998, https://www.churchofjesuschrist.org/study/general-conference/1998/10/personal-purity?lang=eng#p5.

121. Church Educational System, *Eternal Marriage Student Manual*, 221.

122. *For the Strength of Youth* (Salt Lake City: Church of Jesus Christ of Latter-day Saints, 1990), 14–16.

123. *For the Strength of Youth*, 15.

124. O. Kendall White Jr., "A Review and Commentary on the Prospects of a Mormon New Christian Right Coalition," *Review of Religious Research* 28, no. 2

(1986): 180–88; Anson Shupe and John Heinerman, "Mormonism and the New Christian Right: An Emerging Coalition?" *Review of Religious Research* 27, no. 2 (1985): 146–57; Merlin B. Brinkerhoff, Jeffrey C. Jacob, and Marlene M. Mackie, "Mormonism and the Moral Majority Make Strange Bedfellows? An Exploratory Critique," *Review of Religious Research* 28, no. 3 (1987): 236–51.

125. Ronald Priddis, "The Development of the Garment," *Seventh East Press*, November 11, 1981, 5.

126. Priddis, "The Development of the Garment," 5.

127. Priddis, "The Development of the Garment," 5.

128. First Presidency and Quorum of the Twelve Apostles, "Statement on Symposia," *Ensign*, November 1991, https://www.churchofjesuschrist.org/study/ensign/1991/11/news-of-the-church/statement-on-symposia?lang=eng.

129. Colleen McDannell, *Sister Saints: Mormon Women since the End of Polygamy* (New York: Oxford University Press, 2018), x; Sara M. Patterson, *The September Six and the Struggle for the Soul of Mormonism* (Salt Lake City: Signature Books, 2023), 112.

130. Colleen McDannell, "Sacred, Secret, and the Non-Mormon," *Sunstone Magazine*, April 1997, 41–45.

131. Asay, "The Temple Garment," 18–23.

132. Asay, "The Temple Garment," 18–23.

133. Newsroom Staff, "Church Updates Temple Garment Video."

134. Goodstein, "Mormons Expel Founder of Group Seeking Priesthood for Women."

135. Asay, "The Temple Garment," 18–23; Newsroom Staff, "Church Updates Temple Garment Video."

136. John-Charles Duffy, "Elders on the Big Screen," in *Peculiar Portrayals: Mormons on the Page, Stage, and Screen*, ed. Mark T. Decker and Michael Austin (Logan: Utah State University Press, 2010), 136.

137. Dai Newman, "Flaying the Second Skin: Mormon Underwear and Intersectionality," *Quotidian: A Curated Blog about Everyday Religion*, August 26, 2016, https://www.quotidian.pub/flaying-the-second-skin-mormon-underwear-and-intersectionality/.

138. Newman, "Flaying the Second Skin."

139. Vice Staff, "Mormon-Themed Porn Is Apparently a Booming Business," *Vice*, December 5, 2014, https://www.vice.com/en/article/kwp97y/mormon-themed-porn-is-apparently-a-booming-business.

140. Vice Staff, "Mormon-Themed Porn Is Apparently a Booming Business," 2014; Isha Aran, "Inside the World of Mormon Porn," Fusion.net, July 17, 2015, https://web.archive.org/web/20160118063126/http://fusion.net/story/166513/mormon-lds-porn-sex/.

141. Aran, "Inside the World of Mormon Porn."

142. Stephen Dark, "Mormon-Themed Porn Unites Sex, Faith, and Celluloid," *City Weekly*, July 20, 2015, https://www.cityweekly.net/BuzzBlog/archives/2015/07/20/mormon-themed-porn-unites-sex-faith-and-celluloid.

143. Ruth Graham, "Among Mormon Women, Frank Talk about Sacred Underclothes," *New York Times*, July 21, 2021, https://www.nytimes.com/2021/07/21/us/mormon-women-underclothes.html.

144. Natalie Brown, "Why LDS Women Turn to the Media," *By Common Consent* (blog), July 23, 2021, https://bycommonconsent.com/2021/07/23/why-lds-women-turn-to-the-media/.

145. Annette Dennis, "Put Ye on the Lord Jesus Christ," General Conference, April 2024, https://www.churchofjesuschrist.org/study/general-conference/2024/04/14dennis?lang=eng#p14.

146. Peggy Fletcher Stack, "LDS Leaders Alter Temple Recommend Questions to Make It Clear: No Room for Personal Interpretation on Garments," *Salt Lake Tribune*, April 13, 2024, https://www.sltrib.com/religion/2024/04/13/lds-leaders-alter-temple-recommend/.

147. *General Handbook: Serving in the Church of Jesus Christ of Latter-day Saints* (Salt Lake City: Church of Jesus Christ of Latter-day Saints, 2024), section 38.5.8.

148. Peggy Fletcher Stack, "Sleeveless LDS Garments Are Coming to the U.S. Here's When," *Salt Lake Tribune*, October 17, 2024, https://www.sltrib.com/religion/2024/10/17/heres-when-sleeveless-lds-temple/.

149. Peggy Fletcher Stack, "What LDS Women Are Saying about New Sleeveless Garments: Yes, You Will Be Able to Wear Tank Tops," *Salt Lake Tribune*, March 29, 2025, https://www.sltrib.com/religion/2025/03/29/new-lds-sleeveless-garments-are/.

150. Avance, "Worthy 'Gods' and 'Goddesses,'" 12.

Chapter 2. Garments, Belief, and Gender

1. David Morgan, *Images at Work: The Material Culture of Enchantment* (New York: Oxford University Press, 2018), 2.

2. Morgan, *Images at Work*, 2.

3. Morgan, *Images at Work*, 2.

4. Kimberlé Crenshaw, "Demarginalizing the Intersection of Race and Sex: A Black Feminist Critique of Antidiscrimination Doctrine, Feminist Theory and Antiracist Politics," *University of Chicago Legal Forum* (1989): 139–67.

5. Patricia Hill Collins, *Intersectionality as Critical Social Theory* (Durham, NC: Duke University Press, 2019), 1–3.

6. Susan Shaw, "Susan Shaw: Intersectional Theology Ep. 6," *Madang* (podcast), May 18, 2021, time stamp 21:53.

7. Chiung Hwang Chen and Ethan Yorgason, "Intersectionality," in *The Routledge Handbook of Mormonism and Gender*, ed. Amy Hoyt and Taylor E. Petrey (New York: Taylor and Francis, 2020), 38.

8. Chen and Yorgason, "Intersectionality," 42.

9. Kelsy C. Burke, "Women's Agency in Gender-Traditional Religions: A Review of Four Approaches," *Sociology Compass* 6, no. 2 (2012): 123.

10. "The Family: A Proclamation to the World," *Ensign*, November 1995, 102.

11. Grace Ji-Sun Kim and Susan Shaw, *Intersectional Theology: An Introductory Guide* (Minneapolis: Fortress, 2018), 20.

12. Abby Day, *Believing in Belonging: Belief and Social Identity in the Modern World* (New York: Oxford University Press, 2011), 5–7.

13. Day, *Believing in Belonging*, 8–15.

14. Robert A. Orsi, "Belief," *Material Religion* 7, no. 1 (2011): 10–16.

15. Orsi, "Belief," 11–13.

16. Kimball, "The History of LDS Temple Admission Standards," 135–76.

17. Kimball, "The History of LDS Temple Admission Standards," 135–76.

18. Newsroom Staff, "Temple Recommends Change from Yearly to Biennial," *Church News*, October 26, 2002, https://www.thechurchnews.com/2002/10/26/23241403/temple-recommends-change-from-yearly-to-biennial.

19. Jon P. Mitchell and Hildi J. Mitchell, "For Belief: Embodiment and Immanence in Catholicism and Mormonism," *Social Analysis* 52, no. 1 (2008): 79–94.

20. The LDS Church's canon of scripture includes the Bible but also includes the following texts: the Book of Mormon, the Doctrine and Covenants, and the Pearl of Great Price.

21. Russell M. Nelson, "Closing Remarks," Church of Jesus Christ of Latter-day Saints, accessed May 13, 2021, https://www.churchofjesuschrist.org/study/liahona/2019/11/57nelson?lang=eng.

22. Katie L., "Pastoral Care Basics and Resources for LDS Bishops and Other Leaders," *Feminist Mormon Housewives* (blog), November 9, 2018, https://www.feministmormonhousewives.org/2018/11/pastoral-care-basics-and-resources-for-lds-bishops-and-other-leaders/; ELLEK, "What Church Leaders Don't Understand about the Power Dynamics in Worthiness Interviews," *Exponent* (blog), December 17, 2019, https://www.the-exponent.com/what-church-leaders-dont-understand-about-the-power-dynamics-in-worthiness-interviews/.

23. Bruce A. Chadwick, Brent L. Top, and Richard J. McClendon, *Shield of Faith: The Power of Religion in the Lives of LDS Youth and Young Adults* (Salt Lake City: Deseret Book, 2010), 350.

24. See appendix A.

25. Riess, *The Next Mormons*, 31–33.

26. Amy K. Hoyt and Sara M. Patterson, "Mormon Masculinity: Changing Gender Expectations in the Era of Transition from Polygamy to Monogamy, 1890–1920," *Gender & History* 23, no. 1 (2011): 72–91; Patterson, *The September Six and the Struggle for the Soul of Mormonism*, 128.

27. Asay, "The Temple Garment," 18–23.

28. Asay, "The Temple Garment," 23.

29. Kane, "Priestesses unto the Most High God," 97–110.

30. McDannell, *Material Christianity*, 211–14.

31. McDannell, *Material Christianity*, 211–14.

32. Foucault, *Discipline and Punish*, 195–228.

33. Foucault, *Discipline and Punish*, 201.

Chapter 3. Secrecy and Sacredness

1. Asay, "The Temple Garment," 18–23.

2. McKay, "The Purpose of Temples," 38.

3. Buerger, "The Development of the Mormon Temple Endowment Ceremony," 55.

4. Butler, "How to Talk about the Temple," 44.

5. Hinckley, "Keeping the Temple Holy," 49.

6. McDannell, "Sacred, Secret, and the Non-Mormon," 41–45.

7. McDannell, "Sacred, Secret, and the Non-Mormon," 41.

8. Duffy, "Concealing the Body, Concealing the Sacred," 1–21.

9. Christopher James Blythe, "The Sacred, the 'Secret,' and the Sinister in the Latter-day Saint Tradition," in *The Routledge Handbook of Religion and Secrecy*, ed. Paul Christopher Johnson and Hugh B. Urban (Milton Park, UK: Routledge, 2022), 231.

10. Blythe, "The Sacred, the 'Secret' and the Sinister," 231.

11. McDannell, "Sacred, Secret, and the Non-Mormon," 41.

12. Foucault, *Discipline and Punish*, 200–201.

13. Avance, "Worthy 'Gods' and 'Goddesses,'" 13.

14. Duffy, "Concealing the Body, Concealing the Sacred," 1–21.

15. Robert A. Orsi, *The Madonna of 115th Street: Faith and Community in Italian Harlem, 1880–1950* (New Haven: Yale University Press, 2010), lxi–lxii.

16. Tona Hangen, "Lived Experience," in *The Oxford Handbook of Mormonism*, ed. Terryl Givens and Philip L. Barlow (New York: Oxford University Press, 2015), 210.

17. Kim and Shaw, *Intersectional Theology*, 19–21.

18. Kane, "Priestesses unto the Most High God," 97–110.

19. Hangen, "Lived Experience," 210.

20. Carol Cornwall Madsen, "Mormon Women and the Temple: Toward a New Understanding," in *Sisters in Spirit: Mormon Women in Historical and Cultural Perspective*, ed. Lavina Anderson and Maureen Ursenbach Beecher (Urbana: University of Illinois Press, 1987), 80–110.

21. Kane, "Priestesses unto the Most High God," 97–110.

22. Kane, "Priestesses unto the Most High God," 99.

23. Robert A. Orsi, "The Study of Lived Religion," in *Lived Religion in America: Toward a History of Practice*, ed. David D. Hall (Princeton: Princeton University Press, 1997), 7.

24. Victoria Pitts-Taylor, "A Feminist Carnal Sociology? Embodiment in Sociology, Feminism, and Naturalized Philosophy," *Qualitative Sociology* 38, no. 1 (2015): 19–25.

25. Mitchell and Mitchell, "For Belief," 81.

26. McDannell, *Material Christianity*, 221.

27. Blythe, "The Sacred, the 'Secret' and the Sinister in the Latter-day Saint Tradition," 231.

28. Graham, "Among Mormon Women, Frank Talk about Sacred Underclothes."

29. Riess, *The Next Mormons*, 66.

30. Pedro Vieira-Baptista, Faustino R. Pérez-López, María T. López-Baena, Colleen K. Stockdale, Mario Preti, and Jacob Bornstein, "Risk of Development of Vulvar Cancer in Women with Lichen Sclerosus or Lichen Planus: A Systematic Review," *Journal of Lower Genital Tract Disease* 26, no. 3 (2022): 250–57.

31. McDannell, *Material Christianity*, 198–221.

32. Powell, "Covenant Cloaks," 457–75.

33. Asay, "The Temple Garment," 18–23.

34. Asay, "The Temple Garment," 18–23; Avance, "Worthy 'Gods' and 'Goddesses,'" 1–20; Hamilton and Hawley, "Sacred Dress, Public Worlds," 31–52; Powell, "Covenant Cloaks," 457–75.

35. Avance, "Worthy 'Gods' and 'Goddesses,'" 13; Davies, *The Mormon Culture of Salvation*, 119; Powell, "Covenant Cloaks," 457–75; Hamilton and Hawley, "Sacred Dress, Public Worlds," 31–52.

36. McDannell, *Material Christianity*, 207.

37. McDannell, *Material Christianity*, 220.

38. Asay, "The Temple Garment," 18–23; Clate W. Mask, "Standing Spotless before the Lord," *Ensign*, May 2004, 92.

39. Blythe, "The Sacred, the 'Secret' and the Sinister," 231.

Chapter 4. Shame and Worthiness

1. Madison Natarajan, Kerrie G. Wilkins-Yel, Anushka Sista, Aashika Ananth-araman, and Natalie Seils, "Decolonizing Purity Culture: Gendered Racism and White Idealization in Evangelical Christianity," *Psychology of Women Quarterly* 46, no. 3 (2022): 316–36.

2. Moslener, *Virgin Nation*, 141–47.

3. Blakesley, "A Style of Our Own," 20–53; Kelsey Sherrod Michael, "Wearing Your Heart on Your Sleeve: The Surveillance of Women's Souls in Evangelical Christian Modesty Culture," *Feminist Media Studies* 19, no. 8 (2019): 1129–43; McDannell, *Sister Saints*, 80–82; Colleen McDannell, "Mormon Gender in the Mid-Twentieth Century," in *The Routledge Handbook of Mormonism and Gender*, ed. Amy Hoyt and Taylor E. Petrey (New York: Taylor and Francis, 2020), 152–54; Moslener, *Virgin Nation*, 16.

4. Avance, "Worthy 'Gods' and 'Goddesses,'" 15.

5. Brené Brown, *Daring Greatly: How the Courage to Be Vulnerable Transforms the Way We Live, Love, Parent, and Lead* (New York: Penguin, 2015), 71–74.

6. Elizabeth Gish, "'Are You a "Trashable" Styrofoam Cup?' Harm and Damage Rhetoric in the Contemporary American Sexual Purity Movement," *Journal of Feminist Studies in Religion* 34 no. 2 (2018): 5–22.

7. Avance, "Worthy 'Gods' and 'Goddesses,'" 3.

8. Avance, "Worthy 'Gods' and 'Goddesses,'" 16.

9. Laura Vandenbosch and Steven Eggermont, "Understanding Sexual Objectification: A Comprehensive Approach toward Media Exposure and Girls' Internalization of Beauty Ideals, Self-Objectification, and Body Surveillance," *Journal of Communication* 62, no. 5 (2012): 869–87.

10. Barbara L. Fredrickson and Tomi-Ann Roberts, "Objectification Theory: Toward Understanding Women's Lived Experiences and Mental Health Risks," *Psychology of Women Quarterly* 21, no. 2 (1997): 196.

11. Avance, "Worthy 'Gods' and 'Goddesses,'" 1–20; Kelli Potter, "Trans and Mutable Bodies," in *The Routledge Handbook of Mormonism and Gender*, ed. Amy Hoyt and Taylor E. Petrey (New York: Taylor and Francis, 2020), 539; Jill Peterfeso, "From Testimony to Seximony, from Script to Scripture: Revealing Mormon Women's Sexuality through the Mormon *Vagina Monologues*," *Journal of Feminist Studies in Religion* 27, no. 2 (2011): 31–49.

12. Gish, "'Are You a "Trashable" Styrofoam Cup?," 6.

13. Natarajan et al., "Decolonizing Purity Culture," 321.

14. The Word of Wisdom outlines the LDS Church's dietary restrictions, forbidding members to drink tea, coffee, and alcohol. See John E. Ferguson III, Benjamin R. Knoll, and Jana Riess, "The Word of Wisdom in Contemporary American Mormonism: Perceptions and Practice," *Dialogue: A Journal of Mormon Thought* 51, no. 1 (2018): 39–78.

15. The LDS Church teaches that humans existed in a heavenly space before being born on earth, known as the *preexistence*. See Charles R. Harrell, "The Development of the Doctrine of Preexistence, 1830–1844," *Brigham Young University Studies* 28, no. 2 (1988): 75–96.

16. Mason, "The Prohibition of Interracial Marriage in Utah," 108–31; Petrey, *Tabernacles of Clay*, 20.

17. *For the Strength of Youth*, 14–16.

18. Book of Mormon (Mosiah 3:19).

19. Boyd Packer (1924–2015) was an apostle in the church who preached against LGBTQ+ identities, intellectualism, and feminism. Boyd K. Packer, "Talk to the All-Church Coordinating Council," May 18, 1993, https://bookofmormonevidence .org/intellectuals-feminist-and-same-sex-issues/.

20. Joseph F. Smith, *Gospel Doctrine*, 5th ed. (Salt Lake City: Deseret Book, 1939), 23.

21. Foucault, *Discipline and Punish*, 196–99.

Chapter 5. Obedience and Control

1. Peterfeso, "From Testimony to Seximony," 40.

2. McDannell, *Material Christianity*, 220.

3. Joanna Sawatsky, Rebecca Lindenbach, Sheila Wray Gregoire, and Keith Gregoire, "Sanctified Sexism: Effects of Purity Culture Tropes on White Christian Women's Marital and Sexual Satisfaction and Experience of Sexual Pain," *Sociology*

of Religion (2024): srae031; Sheila Wray Gregoire, Rebecca Gregoire Lindenbach, and Joanna Sawatsky, *The Great Sex Rescue: The Lies You've Been Taught and How to Recover What God Intended* (Grand Rapids: Baker Books, 2021), 18; Linda Kay Klein, *Pure: Inside the Evangelical Movement that Shamed a Generation of Young Women and How I Broke Free* (New York: Simon and Schuster, 2019), 27.

4. Avance, "Worthy 'Gods' and 'Goddesses,'" 12n14.

5. Carol Lynn Pearson, *The Ghost of Eternal Polygamy: Haunting the Hearts and Heaven of Mormon Women and Men* (Chicago: Pivot Point Books, 2016), 6–8.

6. M. Russell Ballard (1928–2023) was an apostle in the LDS Church and was in his eighties at the time of the survey.

Conclusion

1. Joanna Brooks, "Equality Is Not a Feeling," *Religion Dispatches*, October 8, 2013, https://religiondispatches.org/equality-is-not-a-feeling/.

2. Catherine Brekus, "Mormon Women and the Problem of Agency," in *Women and Mormonism: Historical and Contemporary Perspectives*, ed. Kate Holbrook and Matthew Bowman (Salt Lake City: University of Utah Press, 2016), 24.

3. Saba Mahmood, *Politics of Piety* (Princeton: Princeton University Press, 2005), 7; Orit Avishai, "'Doing Religion' in a Secular World: Women in Conservative Religions and the Question of Agency," *Gender & Society* 22, no. 4 (2008): 412–13.

4. Amy Hoyt, "Beyond the Victim/Empowerment Paradigm: The Gendered Cosmology of Mormon Women," *Feminist Theology* 16, no. 1 (2007): 89–100.

5. Reid Leamaster and Andres Bautista, "Understanding Compliance in Patriarchal Religions: Mormon Women and the Latter Day Saints Church as a Case Study," *Religions* 9, no. 5 (2018): 143–60.

6. Reid J. Leamaster and Rachel L. Einwohner, "'I'm Not Your Stereotypical Mormon Girl': Mormon Women's Gendered Resistance," *Review of Religious Research* 60, no. 2 (2018): 161–81.

7. Caroline Kline, *Mormon Women at the Crossroads: Global Narratives and the Power of Connectedness* (Urbana: University of Illinois Press, 2022), 8.

8. Kane, "Priestesses unto the Most High God," 99.

9. Collins, *Fighting Words*, 136.

10. Michael E. Nielsen and Daryl White, "Men's Grooming in the Latter-day Saints Church: A Qualitative Study of Norm Violation," *Mental Health, Religion & Culture* 11, no. 8 (2008): 807–25.

11. Kelsy C. Burke, "Women's Agency in Gender-Traditional Religions: A Review of Four Approaches," *Sociology Compass* 6, no. 2 (2012): 122–33.

12. Mary Fainsod Katzenstein, *Faithful and Fearless: Moving Feminist Protest Inside the Church and Military* (Princeton: Princeton University Press, 1998), 8.

13. John P. Bartkowski and Jen'nan Ghazal Read, "Veiled Submission: Gender, Power, and Identity among Evangelical and Muslim Women in the United States," *Qualitative Sociology* 26 (2003): 71–92.

14. R. Marie Griffin, *God's Daughters: Evangelical Women and the Power of Submission* (Berkeley: University of California Press, 1997), 13–15.

15. Hoyt, "Beyond the Victim/Empowerment Paradigm," 89–100; Avishai, "Doing Religion," 409–33.

16. Hoyt, "Beyond the Victim/Empowerment Paradigm," 89–100.

17. Avishai, "Doing Religion," 410; Mahmood, *Politics of Piety*, 1.

18. Nancy Ross, Jessica Finnigan, Heather K. Olson Beal, Kirsty Money, Amber Whiteley, and Caitlin Carroll, "Finding the Middle Ground: Negotiating Mormonism and Gender," in *Voices for Equality: Ordain Women and Resurgent Mormon Feminism*, ed. Gordon Shepherd, Lavina Fielding Anderson, and Gary Shepherd (Draper: Greg Kofford, 2015), 319–35.

19. Avishai, "Doing Religion," 422; Mahmood, *Politics of Piety*, 16.

20. Kane, "Priestesses unto the Most High God," 99.

BIBLIOGRAPHY

Anderson, Devery. *The Development of LDS Temple Ceremonies*. Salt Lake City: Signature Books, 2011.

Aran, Isha. "Inside the World of Mormon Porn." Fusion.net, July 17, 2015. https://web .archive.org/web/20160118063126/http://fusion.net/story/166513/mormon -lds-porn-sex/.

Arthur, Linda B. "Introduction: Dress and the Social Control of the Body." In *Religion, Dress and the Body*, edited by Linda B. Arthur, 1–7. Oxford: Berg, 1999.

Asay, Carlos E. "The Temple Garment: 'An Outward Expression of an Inward Commitment.'" *Ensign*, August 1997, 35–41.

Austin, Michael, and Ardis E. Parshall, eds. *Dime Novel Mormons*. Draper: Greg Kofford Books, 2017.

Avance, Rosemary. "Worthy 'Gods' and 'Goddesses': The Meaning of Modesty in the Normalization of Latter-day Saint Gender Roles." *Journal of Religion and Society* 12 (2010): 1–20.

Avishai, Orit. "'Doing Religion' in a Secular World: Women in Conservative Religions and the Question of Agency." *Gender & Society* 22, no. 4 (2008): 409–33.

Bailey, Emily J. "Seventh-day Adventist Dress: An Index to the Heart." In *Religion, Attire, and Adornment in North America*, edited by Marie W. Dallam and Benjamin E. Zeller, 23–39. New York: Columbia University Press, 2023.

Barnes, G. H., and D. L. Dumond, eds. *Letters of Theodore Dwight Weld, Angelina Grimke Weld, and Sarah Grimke, 1822–1844*. Gloucester, UK: Peter Smith, 1965.

Bartkowski, John P., and Jen'nan Ghazal Read. "Veiled Submission: Gender, Power, and Identity among Evangelical and Muslim Women in the United States." *Qualitative Sociology* 26 (2003): 71–92.

Bennett, John C. *The History of the Saints: An Exposé of Joe Smith and Mormonism.* Boston: Leland and Whiting, 1842.

Blakesley, Katie Clark. "'A Style of Our Own': Modesty and Mormon Women, 1951–2008." *Dialogue: A Journal of Mormon Thought* 42, no. 2 (2009): 20–53.

Blythe, Christopher James. "The Sacred, the 'Secret' and the Sinister in the Latter-day Saint Tradition." In *The Routledge Handbook of Religion and Secrecy*, edited by Paul Christopher Johnson and Hugh B. Urban, 228–42. Milton Park, UK: Routledge, 2022.

Book of Mormon: Another Testament of Jesus Christ. Salt Lake City: Church of Jesus Christ of Latter-day Saints, 2013.

Brekus, Catherine. "Mormon Women and the Problem of Agency." In *Women and Mormonism: Historical and Contemporary Perspectives*, edited by Kate Holbrook and Matthew Bowman, 15–41. Salt Lake City: University of Utah Press, 2016.

Brinkerhoff, Merlin B., Jeffrey C. Jacob, and Marlene M. Mackie. "Mormonism and the Moral Majority Make Strange Bedfellows? An Exploratory Critique." *Review of Religious Research* 28, no. 3 (1987): 236–51.

Brooks, Joanna. "Equality Is Not a Feeling." *Religion Dispatches*, October 8, 2013. https://religiondispatches.org/equality-is-not-a-feeling/.

Brooks, Juanita. "A Close-Up of Polygamy." *Harper's* 168 (1934): 299–307.

Brown, Brené, *Daring Greatly: How the Courage to Be Vulnerable Transforms the Way We Live, Love, Parent, and Lead.* New York: Penguin, 2015.

Brown, Natalie. "Why LDS Women Turn to the Media." *By Common Consent* (blog), July 23, 2021. https://bycommonconsent.com/2021/07/23/why-lds-women-turn-to-the-media/.

Bruno, Cheryl, Joe Steve Swick III, and Nicholas Literski. *Method Infinite: Freemasonry and the Mormon Restoration.* Sandy, UT: Greg Kofford Books, 2022.

Buerger, David John. "The Development of the Mormon Temple Endowment Ceremony." *Dialogue: A Journal of Mormon Thought* 20, no. 4 (1987): 33–76.

Buerger, David John. *The Mysteries of Godliness: A History of Mormon Temple Worship.* 2nd ed. Salt Lake City: Signature Books, 2002.

Burke, Kelsy C. "Women's Agency in Gender-Traditional Religions: A Review of Four Approaches." *Sociology Compass* 6, no. 2 (2012): 122–33.

Butler, Shanna. "How to Talk about the Temple." *New Era*, January 2006, 44.

Butterworth, Lisa. "Ann Romney, Gossip and Judgement: It's Time to Admit We Have a Problem Mormon Ladies." *Feminist Mormon Housewives* (blog), September 27, 2012. https://www.feministmormonhousewives.org/2012/09/ann-romney-gossip-and-judgement-its-time-to-admit-we-have-a-problem-mormon-ladies/.

Chadwick, Bruce A., Brent L. Top, and Richard J. McClendon. *Shield of Faith: The Power of Religion in the Lives of LDS Youth and Young Adults.* Provo: Deseret Book, 2010.

Chen, Chiung Hwang, and Ethan Yorgason. "Intersectionality." In *The Routledge Handbook of Mormonism and Gender*, edited by Amy Hoyt and Taylor E. Petry, 38–49. New York: Taylor and Francis, 2020.

Church Educational System. *Eternal Marriage Student Manual*. Salt Lake City: Church of Jesus Christ of Latter-day Saints, 2003.

Clark, J. Reuben. "In These Times." *Improvement Era*, May 1943, 269, 314–15.

Clark, James R., ed. *Messages of the First Presidency of the Church of Jesus Christ of Latter-day Saints*. Salt Lake City: Bookcraft, 1965–75.

Collins, Patricia Hill. *Fighting Words: Black Women and the Search for Justice*. Minneapolis: University of Minnesota Press,1998.

Collins, Patricia Hill. *Intersectionality as Critical Social Theory*. Durham, NC: Duke University Press, 2019.

Craik, Jennifer. *The Face of Fashion*. New York: Routledge, 1994.

Crenshaw, Kimberlé. "Demarginalizing the Intersection of Race and Sex: A Black Feminist Critique of Antidiscrimination Doctrine, Feminist Theory and Antiracist Politics." *University of Chicago Legal Forum* (1989): 139–67.

Cunningham, Patricia A., and Gayle Strege. *Reforming Fashion, 1850–1914: Politics, Health, and Art*. Columbus: Ohio State University Press, 2000.

Cunnington, C. Willett, and Phyllis Cunnington. *The History of Underclothes*. New York: Dover Publications, 1992.

Dark, Stephen. "Mormon-Themed Porn Unites Sex, Faith, and Celluloid." *City Weekly*, July 20, 2015. https://www.cityweekly.net/BuzzBlog/archives/2015/07/20/mormon-themed-porn-unites-sex-faith-and-celluloid.

Davies, Douglas. *The Mormon Culture of Salvation*. Farnham, UK: Ashgate, 2000.

Day, Abby. *Believing in Belonging: Belief and Social Identity in the Modern World*. New York: Oxford University Press, 2011.

Dennis, Annette. "Put Ye on the Lord Jesus Christ." General Conference, April 2024. https://www.churchofjesuschrist.org/study/general-conference/2024/04/14dennis?lang=eng#p14.

DeRogatis, Amy. *Saving Sex: Sexuality and Salvation in American Evangelicalism*. New York: Oxford University Press, 2014.

Duffin, Karen. "The Box." *Moth Radio Hour* (podcast), May 25, 2021. https://the moth.org/stories/the-box.

Duffy, John-Charles. "Concealing the Body, Concealing the Sacred: The Decline of Ritual Nudity in Mormon Temples." *Journal of Ritual Studies* (2007): 1–21.

Duffy, John-Charles. "Elders on the Big Screen." In *Peculiar Portrayals: Mormons on the Page, Stage, and Screen*, edited by Mark T. Decker and Michael Austin, 113–43. Logan: Utah State University Press, 2010.

Durant, Will, and Ariel Durant. *The Lessons of History*. New York: Simon and Schuster, 1968.

ELLEK. "What Church Leaders Don't Understand about the Power Dynamics in Worthiness Interviews." *Exponent* (blog), December 17, 2019. https://www

.the-exponent.com/what-church-leaders-dont-understand-about-the-power
-dynamics-in-worthiness-interviews/.

"The Family: A Proclamation to the World." *Ensign*, November 1995, 102.

Fanon, Frantz. *Black Skin, White Masks*. New York: Grove, 1967.

Feller, Gavin. "Conceal, Enhance, Expose, Perfect: A Mid-Century Mormon Swimsuit Designer's Feminine Bodily Discipline." *Journal of the American Academy of Religion* 89, no. 4 (2021): 1406–33.

Ferguson, John E., III, Benjamin R. Knoll, and Jana Riess. "The Word of Wisdom in Contemporary American Mormonism: Perceptions and Practice." *Dialogue: A Journal of Mormon Thought* 51, no. 1 (2018): 39–78.

Fields, Jill. "Erotic Modesty: (Ad)dressing Female Sexuality and Propriety in Open and Closed Drawers, USA, 1800–1930." *Gender & History* 14, no. 3 (2002): 501–8.

First Presidency. "The Message of the First Presidency to the Church." *Improvement Era*, November 1942, 758.

First Presidency and Quorum of the Twelve Apostles. "Statement on Symposia." *Ensign*, November 1991. https://www.churchofjesuschrist.org/study/ensign/1991/11/news-of-the-church/statement-on-symposia?lang=eng.

For the Strength of Youth. Salt Lake City: Church of Jesus Christ of Latter-day Saints, 1990.

Foster, Craig L. "Victorian Pornographic Imagery in Anti-Mormon Literature." *Journal of Mormon History* 19, no. 1 (1993): 115–32.

Foucault, Michel. *Discipline and Punish: The Birth of the Prison*. Translated by Alan Sheridan. New York: Vintage Books, 1995.

Fredrickson, Barbara L., and Tomi-Ann Roberts. "Objectification Theory: Toward Understanding Women's Lived Experiences and Mental Health Risks." *Psychology of Women Quarterly* 21, no. 2 (1997): 173–206.

General Handbook: Serving in the Church of Jesus Christ of Latter-day Saints. Salt Lake City: Church of Jesus Christ of Latter-day Saints, 2024.

George, Laura. "Austen's Muslin." In *Crossings in Text and Textile*, edited by Daneen Wardrop and Katherine Joslin, 73–102. Lebanon: University of New Hampshire Press, 2015.

Gish, Elizabeth. "'Are You a "Trashable" Styrofoam Cup?': Harm and Damage Rhetoric in the Contemporary American Sexual Purity Movement." *Journal of Feminist Studies in Religion* 34, no. 2 (2018): 5–22.

Goodstein, Laurie. "Mormons Expel Founder of Group Seeking Priesthood for Women." *New York Times*, June 24, 2014.

Gordon, Sarah Barringer. "The Liberty of Self-Degradation: Polygamy, Woman Suffrage, and Consent in Nineteenth-Century America." *Journal of American History* 83, no. 3 (1996): 815–47.

Graham, Ruth. "Among Mormon Women, Frank Talk about Sacred Underclothes." *New York Times*, July 21, 2021. https://www.nytimes.com/2021/07/21/us/mormon-women-underclothes.html.

Gregoire, Sheila Wray, Rebecca Gregoire Lindenbach, and Joanna Sawatsky. *The Great Sex Rescue: The Lies You've Been Taught and How to Recover What God Intended*. Grand Rapids: Baker Books, 2021.

Griffin, Alexandria. "(In)visible Piety: Reading Mormon Garments through Hijab." MA thesis, Claremont Graduate University, 2014.

Griffin, R. Marie. *God's Daughters: Evangelical Women and the Power of Submission*. Oakland: University of California Press, 1997.

Hall, David D., ed. *Lived Religion in America: Toward a History of Practice*. Princeton: Princeton University Press, 1997.

Hamilton, Jean A., and Jana Hawley. "Sacred Dress, Public Worlds: Amish and Mormon Experiences and Commitment." In *Religion, Dress and the Body*, edited by Linda B. Arthur, 31–52. Oxford: Berg, 1999.

Hangen, Tona. "Lived Experience." In *The Oxford Handbook of Mormonism*, edited by Terryl Givens and Philip L. Barlow, 209–23. New York: Oxford University Press, 2015.

Harrell, Charles R. "The Development of the Doctrine of Preexistence, 1830–1844." *Brigham Young University Studies* 28, no. 2 (1988): 75–96.

Harris, Matthew L., and Newell G. Bringhurst, eds. *The Mormon Church and Blacks: A Documentary History*. Urbana: University of Illinois Press, 2015.

Heise, Tammy. "Marking Mormon Difference: How Western Perceptions of Islam Defined the 'Mormon Menace.'" *Journal of Religion and Popular Culture* 25, no. 1 (2013): 82–97.

Hendrix-Komoto, Amanda. *Imperial Zions: Religion, Race, and Family in the American West and the Pacific*. Lincoln: University of Nebraska Press, 2022.

Hinckley, Gordon B. "From My Generation to Yours, with Love." *Improvement Era*, December 1971, 71–73.

Hinckley, Gordon B. "Keeping the Temple Holy." *Ensign*, April 1990, 49.

Hinckley, Gordon B. "Reverence and Morality." General Conference, April 1987. https://www.churchofjesuschrist.org/study/general-conference/1987/04/reverence-and-morality?lang=eng#p56.

Holland, Jeffrey R. "Personal Purity." General Conference, October 1998. https://www.churchofjesuschrist.org/study/general-conference/1998/10/personal-purity?lang=eng#p5.

Hoyt, Amy. "Beyond the Victim/Empowerment Paradigm: The Gendered Cosmology of Mormon Women." *Feminist Theology* 16, no. 1 (2007): 89–100.

Hoyt, Amy K., and Sara M. Patterson. "Mormon Masculinity: Changing Gender Expectations in the Era of Transition from Polygamy to Monogamy, 1890–1920." *Gender & History* 23, no. 1 (2011): 72–91.

Hughes, Richard T. "Soaring with the Gods: Early Mormons and the Eclipse of Religious Pluralism." In *Mormons and Mormonism: An Introduction to an American World Religion*, edited by Eric Alden Eliason, 23–46. Urbana: University of Illinois Press, 2001.

"Incorporations." *Salt Lake Herald-Republican*, June 15, 1910, 11.

Johnson, Benjamin F. *My Life's Review: The Autobiography of Benjamin F. Johnson*. Provo: Grandin Book, 1997.

Kane, Nazneen. "'Priestesses unto the Most High God': Gender, Agency, and the Politics of LDS Women's Temple Rites." *Sociological Focus* 51, no. 2 (2018): 97–110.

Katzenstein, Mary Fainsod. *Faithful and Fearless: Moving Feminist Protest Inside the Church and Military*. Princeton: Princeton University Press, 1998.

Kearns, Thomas. "Endowment Oaths and Ceremonies." *Salt Lake Tribune*, February 9, 1906.

Kendall, Joan. "The Development of a Distinctive Form of Quaker Dress." *Costume* 19 (1985): 58–74.

Kesselman, Amy. "The 'Freedom Suit': Feminism and Dress Reform in the United States, 1848–1875." *Gender & Society* 5, no. 4 (1991): 496–98.

Kim, Grace Ji-Sun, and Susan Shaw. *Intersectional Theology: An Introductory Guide*. Minneapolis: Fortress, 2018.

Kimball, Edward L. "The History of LDS Temple Admission Standards." *Journal of Mormon History* 24, no. 1 (1998): 135–76.

Klein, Linda Kay. *Pure: Inside the Evangelical Movement that Shamed a Generation of Young Women and How I Broke Free*. New York: Simon and Schuster, 2019.

Kline, Caroline. *Mormon Women at the Crossroads: Global Narratives and the Power of Connectedness*. Urbana: University of Illinois Press, 2022.

L., Katie. "Pastoral Care Basics and Resources for LDS Bishops and Other Leaders." *Feminist Mormon Housewives* (blog), November 9, 2018. https://www.feminist mormonhousewives.org/2018/11/pastoral-care-basics-and-resources-for-lds -bishops-and-other-leaders/.

Leamaster, Reid, and Andres Bautista. "Understanding Compliance in Patriarchal Religions: Mormon Women and the Latter Day Saints Church as a Case Study." *Religions* 9, no. 5 (2018): 143–60.

Leamaster, Reid J., and Rachel L. Einwohner. "'I'm Not Your Stereotypical Mormon Girl': Mormon Women's Gendered Resistance." *Review of Religious Research* 60, no. 2 (2018): 161–81.

Lerner, Gerda. *The Creation of Patriarchy*. New York: Oxford University Press, 1986.

Lindbergh, Jennie. "Buttoning Down Archaeology." *Australasian Historical Archaeology* 17 (1999): 50–57.

Lyman, Edward Leo, ed. *Candid Insights of a Mormon Apostle, 1889–1895*. Salt Lake City: Signature Books, 2010.

Madsen, Carol Cornwall. "Mormon Women and the Temple: Toward a New Understanding." In *Sisters in Spirit: Mormon Women in Historical and Cultural Perspective*, edited by Lavina Anderson and Maureen Ursenbach Beecher, 80–110. Urbana: University of Illinois Press, 1987.

Mahmood, Saba. *Politics of Piety*. Princeton: Princeton University Press, 2005.

Marshall, Evelyn T. "Garments." In *Encyclopedia of Mormonism*, edited by Daniel H. Ludlow, 2:534–35. New York: Macmillan, 1992.

Mask, Clate W. "Standing Spotless before the Lord." *Ensign*, May 2004, 92.

Mason, Patrick Q. "The Prohibition of Interracial Marriage in Utah, 1888–1963." *Utah Historical Quarterly* 76, no. 2 (2008): 108–31.

Mattingly, Carol. *Appropriate[ing] Dress: Women's Rhetorical Style in Nineteenth-Century America*. Carbondale: Southern Illinois University Press, 2002.

Mauss, Armand L. *The Angel and the Beehive: The Mormon Struggle with Assimilation*. Urbana: University of Illinois Press, 1994.

Mauss, Armand L. "Sociological Perspectives on the Mormon Subculture." *Annual Review of Sociology* 10 (1984): 437–60.

Maxwell, Neal A. "Behold the Enemy is Combined." General Conference, April 1993. https://www.churchofjesuschrist.org/study/general-conference/1993/04/behold-the-enemy-is-combined-d-c-38-12?lang=eng#p28.

McDannell, Colleen. *Material Christianity: Religion and Popular Culture in America*. New Haven: Yale University Press, 1995.

McDannell, Colleen. "Mormon Gender in the Mid-Twentieth Century." In *The Routledge Handbook of Mormonism and Gender*, edited by Amy Hoyt and Taylor E. Petrey, 152–54. New York: Taylor and Francis, 2020.

McDannell, Colleen. "Sacred, Secret, and the Non-Mormon." *Sunstone Magazine*, April 1997, 41–45.

McDannell, Colleen. *Sister Saints: Mormon Women since the End of Polygamy*. New York: Oxford University Press, 2018.

McKay, David O. "The Purpose of Temples." *Ensign*, January 1972, 38.

Michael, Kelsey Sherrod. "Wearing Your Heart on Your Sleeve: The Surveillance of Women's Souls in Evangelical Christian Modesty Culture." *Feminist Media Studies* 19, no. 8 (2019): 1129–43.

Miller-Spillman, Kimberly A., and Andrew Reilly. *The Meanings of Dress*. London: Bloomsbury Academic, 2019.

Mitchell, Jon P., and Hildi J. Mitchell. "For Belief: Embodiment and Immanence in Catholicism and Mormonism." *Social Analysis* 52, no. 1 (2008): 79–94.

Morgan, David. *Images at Work: The Material Culture of Enchantment*. New York: Oxford University Press, 2018.

Morgan, David. *The Thing about Religion: An Introduction to the Material Study of Religions*. Chapel Hill: University of North Carolina Press, 2021.

Morgan, William. *Illustrations of Masonry by One of the Fraternity Who Has Devoted Thirty Years to the Subject*. Batavia, NY, 1826.

Moslener, Sara. *Virgin Nation: Sexual Purity and American Adolescence*. New York: Oxford University Press, 2015.

Mueller, Max Perry. "Playing Jane: Re-presenting Black Mormon Memory through Reenacting the Black Mormon Past." *Journal of Africana Religions* 1, no. 4 (2013): 513–61.

Natarajan, Madison, Kerrie G. Wilkins-Yel, Anushka Sista, Aashika Ananthara-man, and Natalie Seils. "Decolonizing Purity Culture: Gendered Racism and White Idealization in Evangelical Christianity." *Psychology of Women Quarterly* 46, no. 3 (2022): 316–36.

Nelson, Russell M. "Closing Remarks." Church of Jesus Christ of Latter-day Saints. Accessed May 13, 2021. https://www.churchofjesuschrist.org/study/liahona/2019/11/57nelson?lang=eng.

Newman, Dai. "Flaying the Second Skin: Mormon Underwear and Intersectionality." *Quotidian: A Curated Blog about Everyday Religion*, August 26, 2016. https://www.quotidian.pub/flaying-the-second-skin-mormon-underwear-and-intersectionality/.

Newsroom Staff. "Church Updates Temple Garment Video." October 22, 2014. https://newsroom.churchofjesuschrist.org/article/church-updates-temple-garment-video.

Newsroom Staff. "Temple Recommends Change from Yearly to Biennial." *Church News*, October 26, 2002. https://www.thechurchnews.com/2002/10/26/23241403/temple-recommends-change-from-yearly-to-biennial.

Nielsen, Michael E., and Daryl White. "Men's Grooming in the Latter-day Saints Church: A Qualitative Study of Norm Violation." *Mental Health, Religion & Culture* 11, no. 8 (2008): 807–25.

Nuttall, John L. *Diaries of L. John Nuttall.* Special Collections, J. Willard Marriott Library, University of Utah.

Orsi, Robert A. "Belief." *Material Religion* 7, no. 1 (2011): 10–16.

Orsi, Robert A. *The Madonna of 115th Street: Faith and Community in Italian Harlem, 1880–1950.* New Haven: Yale University Press, 2010.

Orsi, Robert A. "The Study of Lived Religion." In *Lived Religion in America: Toward a History of Practice*, edited by David D. Hall, 3–21. Princeton: Princeton University Press, 1997.

Packer, Boyd K. "Talk to the All-Church Coordinating Council." May 18, 1993. https://bookofmormonevidence.org/intellectuals-feminist-and-same-sex-issues/.

Patterson, Sara M. *The September Six and the Struggle for the Soul of Mormonism.* Salt Lake City: Signature Books, 2023.

Pearson, Carol Lynn. *The Ghost of Eternal Polygamy: Haunting the Hearts and Heaven of Mormon Women and Men.* Chicago: Pivot Point Books, 2016.

Perry, Luke. *Mitt Romney, Mormonism, and the 2012 Election.* New York: Palgrave Macmillan, 2014.

Peterfeso, Jill. "From Testimony to Seximony, from Script to Scripture: Revealing Mormon Women's Sexuality through the Mormon *Vagina Monologues*." *Journal of Feminist Studies in Religion* 27, no. 2 (2011): 31–49.

Petersen, Roger K., and Carole Reid Burr. "A Genius for Beauty: Swimsuit Designer Rose Marie Reid." In *Mormons and Popular Culture: The Global Influence of an American Phenomenon*, edited by J. Michael Hunt, 213–28. Westport, CT: Praeger, 2013.

Petrey, Taylor G. *Tabernacles of Clay: Sexuality and Gender in Modern Mormonism.* Chapel Hill: University of North Carolina Press, 2020.

Pitts-Taylor, Victoria. "A Feminist Carnal Sociology? Embodiment in Sociology, Feminism, and Naturalized Philosophy." *Qualitative Sociology* 38, no. 1 (2015): 19–25.

Potter, Kelli. "Trans and Mutable Bodies." In *The Routledge Handbook of Mormonism and Gender*, edited by Amy Hoyt and Taylor E. Petrey, 539–52. New York: Taylor and Francis, 2020.

Powell, Adam J. "Covenant Cloaks: Mormon Temple Garments in the Light of Identity Theory." *Material Religion* 12, no. 4 (2016): 457–75.

Priddis, Ronald. "The Development of the Garment." *Seventh East Press*, November 11, 1981, 5.

"Priesthood Garment History," p. 11. Mace K. Church Papers. Accession 1914. Box 1, Folder 2–2. Special Collections, J. Willard Marriott Library, University of Utah.

Prince, Gregory A., Darius A. Gray, and Margaret Blair Young. "'Let the Truth Heal': The Making of Nobody Knows: The Untold Story of Black Mormons." *Dialogue: A Journal of Mormon Thought* 42, no. 3 (2009): 74–99.

Quinn, D. Michael. *The Mormon Hierarchy: Origins of Power.* Salt Lake City: Signature Books, 1994.

Reeve, W. Paul. "A Century of Black Mormons." Digital exhibition, J. Willard Marriott Library, University of Utah. https://exhibits.lib.utah.edu/s/century -of-black-mormons/page/credits.

Reeve, W. Paul. *Religion of a Different Color: Race and the Mormon Struggle for Whiteness.* New York: Oxford University Press, 2015.

Riess, Jana. *The Next Mormons: How Millennials Are Changing the LDS Church.* New York: Oxford University Press, 2019.

Rosetti, Cristina. "'Hysteria Excommunicatus': Loyalty Oaths, Excommunication, and the Forging of a Mormon Identity." *Journal of Mormon History* 47, no. 3 (2021): 22–43.

Ross, Nancy, Jessica Finnigan, Heather K. Olson Beal, Kirsty Money, Amber Whiteley, and Caitlin Carroll. "Finding the Middle Ground: Negotiating Mormonism and Gender." In *Voices for Equality: Ordain Women and Resurgent Mormon Feminism*, edited by Gordon Shepherd, Lavina Fielding Anderson, and Gary Shepherd, 319–35. Draper, UT: Greg Kofford, 2015.

Ryan, Erin Gloria. "Mormon Ladies Click Tongues Disapprovingly at Ann Romney's Lack of Temple Garments." Jezebel, September 27, 2012. https://jezebel .com/mormon-ladies-click-tongues-disapprovingly-at-ann-romne-30775836.

Sawatsky, Joanna, Rebecca Lindenbach, Sheila Wray Gregoire, and Keith Gregoire. "Sanctified Sexism: Effects of Purity Culture Tropes on White Christian Women's Marital and Sexual Satisfaction and Experience of Sexual Pain." *Sociology of Religion* (2024): srae031.

Shaw, Susan. "Susan Shaw: Intersectional Theology Ep. 6." *Madang* (podcast), May 18, 2021.

Scherer, Mark A. *The Journey of a People: The Era of Restoration 1820–1844*. Independence, MO: Community of Christ Seminary Press, 2013.

Shields, Steven L. *Divergent Paths of the Restoration*. Bountiful, UT: Restoration Research, 1982.

Shupe, Anson, and John Heinerman. "Mormonism and the New Christian Right: An Emerging Coalition?" *Review of Religious Research* 27, no. 2 (1985): 146–57.

Smith, Joseph F. "Fashion and the Violation of Covenants and Duty." *Improvement Era*, August 1906, 812–15.

Smith, Joseph F. *Gospel Doctrine*. 5th ed. Salt Lake City: Deseret Book, 1939.

Stack, Peggy Fletcher. "LDS Leaders Alter Temple Recommend Questions to Make It Clear: No Room for Personal Interpretation on Garments." *Salt Lake Tribune*, April 13, 2024. https://www.sltrib.com/religion/2024/04/13/lds-leaders-alter -temple-recommend/.

Stack, Peggy Fletcher. "Sleeveless LDS Garments Are Coming to the U.S. Here's When." *Salt Lake Tribune*, October 17, 2024. https://www.sltrib.com/religion/ 2024/10/17/heres-when-sleeveless-lds-temple/.

Stack, Peggy Fletcher. "What LDS Women Are Saying about New Sleeveless Garments: Yes, You Will Be Able to Wear Tank Tops." *Salt Lake Tribune*, March 29, 2025. https://www.sltrib.com/religion/2025/03/29/new-lds-sleeveless-garments -are/.

Stapes, Robert. "The Myth of Black Sexual Superiority: A Re-examination." *Black Scholar* 9, no. 7 (1978): 16–23.

Stephens, Evan, and Joseph J. Daynes. "True to the Faith." *Hymns of the Church of Jesus Christ of Latter-day Saints*. Salt Lake City: Church of Jesus Christ of Latter-day Saints, 1985.

Stevenson, Ana. "'Symbols of Our Slavery': Fashion and the Rhetoric of Dress Reform in Nineteenth-Century American Print Culture." *Lilith: A Feminist History Journal* 20 (2014): 5–20.

Talbot, Christine. *A Foreign Kingdom: Mormons and Polygamy in American Political Culture, 1852–1890*. Urbana: University of Illinois Press, 2013.

Taysom, Stephen C. *Shakers, Mormons, and Religious Worlds*. Bloomington: Indiana University Press, 2011.

"Temple Garments." *Sunstone Magazine*, January/February 1980, 49.

"Temple Garments Greatly Modified, Church Presidency Gives Permission, Style Change Optional with Wearer." *Salt Lake Tribune*, June 4, 1923.

Tensi, Victoria. "'Taking Every Thought Captive': A Microanalysis of How Control Mechanisms Operate within Evangelical Purity Culture." PhD diss., George Washington University, 2023.

Thuesen, Peter J. *Predestination: The American Career of a Contentious Doctrine*. New York: Oxford University Press, 2009.

Turner, John G. *Brigham Young: Pioneer Prophet*. Cambridge, MA: Harvard University Press, 2012.

Turner, John G. *The Mormon Jesus: A Biography*. Cambridge, MA: Harvard University Press, 2016.

Vandenbosch, Laura, and Steven Eggermont. "Understanding Sexual Objectification: A Comprehensive Approach toward Media Exposure and Girls' Internalization of Beauty Ideals, Self-Objectification, and Body Surveillance." *Journal of Communication* 62, no. 5 (2012): 869–87.

Vice Staff. "Mormon-Themed Porn Is Apparently a Booming Business." *Vice*, December 5, 2014. https://www.vice.com/en/article/kwp97y/mormon-themed -porn-is-apparently-a-booming-business.

Vieira-Baptista, Pedro, Faustino R. Pérez-López, María T. López-Baena, Colleen K. Stockdale, Mario Preti, and Jacob Bornstein. "Risk of Development of Vulvar Cancer in Women with Lichen Sclerosus or Lichen Planus: A Systematic Review." *Journal of Lower Genital Tract Disease* 26, no. 3 (2022): 250–57.

Watt, George D., ed. *Journal of Discourses*. 26 vols. Liverpool: Latter-day Saints' Bookseller's Depot, 1854–86.

Weaver, Sarah Jane. "'Mormon' Is Out: Church Releases Statement on How to Refer to the Organization." Church News, August 16, 2018. https://www.church ofjesuschrist.org/church/news/mormon-is-out-church-releases-statement -on-how-to-refer-to-the-organization?lang=eng.

White, O. Kendall, Jr. "A Review and Commentary on the Prospects of a Mormon New Christian Right Coalition." *Review of Religious Research* 28, no. 2 (1986): 180–88.

INDEX

Nancy Ross is an associate professor of interdisciplinary studies at Utah Tech University. **Jessica Finnigan** and **Larissa Kanno Kindred** are independent scholars.

The University of Illinois Press
is a founding member of the
Association of University Presses.

———————————————————————

Composed in 10.25/14 Chaparral Pro
with DIN display
by Lisa Connery
at the University of Illinois Press
Manufactured by Sheridan Books, Inc.

University of Illinois Press
1325 South Oak Street
Champaign, IL 61820–6903
www.press.uillinois.edu